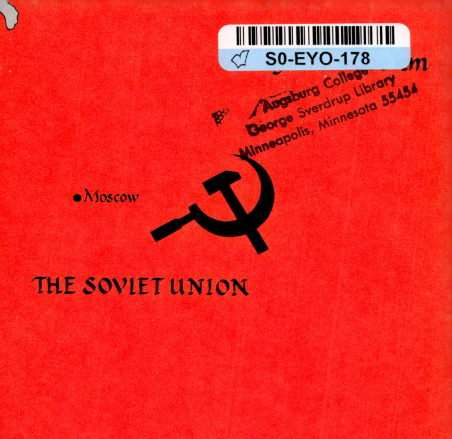

● Moscow

THE SOVIET UNION

NIA

rest

GARIA

Black Sea

TURKEY

The Soviet Union pre 1939

THE KREMLIN'S DILEMMA

*The Struggle for Human Rights
in Eastern Europe*

THE KREMLIN'S DILEMMA

The Struggle for Human Rights in Eastern Europe

TUFTON BEAMISH
and
GUY HADLEY

Presidio Press
San Rafael, California
London, England

Copyright 1979 by Lord Chelwood

ISBN 0 00 262402 8

Published simultaneously with Collins and Harvill Press of London,
England, by Presidio Press of San Rafael, California, and London,
England, with editorial offices at 1114 Irwin Street, San Rafael,
California 94901

Library of Congress Cataloging in Publication Data

BEAMISH, TUFTON VICTOR HAMILTON, SIR 1917 —
    The Kremlin's Dilemma

    Bibliography: P.
    Includes index.
    1. Civil Rights — Europe, Eastern. 2. Self-
Determination, NATIONAL. I. Hadley, Guy,
Joint Author.

JC599.E9284   323.4'094 7   79-10381

ISBN 0-89141-093-7

Printed in Great Britain

CONTENTS

*Endpaper Maps: Central and Eastern
European Boundaries in 1939 and 1979*

FOREWORD

Most people by now have at least a working idea of the Soviet government's attitude towards human rights. This might be described diplomatically as uncomprehendingly negative, but I find it simpler and truer to call it vile. The Helsinki masquerade and its sequel in Belgrade, in so many ways solid gain for Moscow, at least achieved two useful things: they helped to bring home to all but the blindest or the sleepiest in the West certain facts about post-Stalin Russia which should have been common knowledge for years; and they forced the Kremlin to proceed with the calculated extinction of the human rights movement in the Soviet Union in a blaze of undesired publicity with all the world looking on.

But to have some idea of the depths of mental squalor in which the government of Russia remains steeped sixty-odd years after Lenin's proclamation of Utopia is one thing. What is far less well and widely understood is the state of play in the various parts of Europe still ruled by self-styled Communists under Muscovite protection. Some of these captive states and peoples are very much a part of the West in spirit and tradition; nearly all, even after years of Russian exploitation, are far in advance of Mother Russia, who had more to learn from them – and still has, alas – than they from her.

It has been the aim of the authors of this book to examine in some detail the separate records of half a dozen very different states which share nothing at all but the common denominator of Russian overlordship. Lord Chelwood, a soldier turned politician (Sir Tufton Beamish before he was made a life peer in 1974) has

for many years played a very active part in foreign affairs, above all
the affairs of the larger Europe; Guy Hadley, as a distinguished
BBC foreign correspondent, reported widely and in depth over a
long period from many parts of Eastern Europe. I welcome and
warmly recommend their book particularly because, while offering
valuable information about governmental attitudes to human
rights, the four freedoms and basic human decencies, it also serves
as a strong antidote to the common error of lumping together
widely disparate peoples and treating them as though they were
indistinguishable components of an imaginary Communist
monolith.

If politicians, journalists and analysts who compound this error
could only realise that they are playing directly into the hands of
the Soviet leadership, which knows – none better – that Russia and
the satellites are very far from one, we should at least be started on
the way to reclaiming for the West peoples now lost to it who have
played vital parts in its culture. These peoples, and the states to
which they belong, must always be looked at separately and
individually, as they are in this volume. Oddities then begin at once
to emerge. We find, for instance, that the government of Rumania
which has achieved a certain reputation for standing out against
the Kremlin's foreign policy directives, is in fact the most oppres-
sive towards its own people of all the Communist satellite regimes.
We find that Janos Kadar, the man who was installed as Moscow's
puppet after Soviet tanks had blasted their way into Budapest in
1956, has somehow managed to soften the rigours of Hungarian
Communism to a degree which must fill the ageing reactionaries in
the Kremlin with profound unease.

We find other differences as well, which ought to be widely
known. It is important for us to know about them, if only because
they provide opportunities for the West to approach more closely
at least some of the countries under Russian domination. The
governments of these countries, to a greater or lesser degree, are

8

looking to the West for innumerable products, from grain to high technology. This is their main hope of raising living standards in the shadow of Moscow. At the same time, as this volume soberly demonstrates, all of them, to a greater or lesser extent, habitually and sometimes savagely violate human rights in general, and in particular have gone back on solemn undertakings formalised in the Final Act of Helsinki in 1975. It seems to me that the authors of this book are entirely reasonable when they urge that, if these regimes wish to call on the resources of the West, they should at least be required in return to honour specific pledges about human rights voluntarily given as part of what was supposed to be a wide-ranging and binding agreement on East-West relations.

EDWARD CRANKSHAW

INTRODUCTION

Our purpose in this book is to describe the struggle for human rights and self-determination in the Communist satellite states of Eastern Europe, rather than in the Soviet Union itself. In varying degrees, these formerly independent nations have historical and cultural links with Western Europe and at least an awareness of all that is meant by 'political freedom', even if only Czechoslovakia has been a fully fledged democracy. On the other hand, the Russian concept of human rights has been debased by a long tradition of autocratic rule. Moreover, some of the Communist satellite regimes have become more sensitive to the conflict between their national economic interests and those of the Soviet Union, and so less willing to toe the Soviet line than they were under Stalin and Khrushchev.

Taken together, these elements constitute the Kremlin's dilemma in having to strike a balance between harsh repression in the Soviet empire of Eastern Europe, or tolerating some gradual and limited reforms which might put Russian domination at risk. With some backward glances, we have taken as our criterion the Final Act of the Helsinki Conference on Security and Co-operation in Europe in 1975, which gave a new and surprising impetus to demands for basic human rights in Eastern Europe. We have analysed the nature and sources of these demands, described the aims and motives of human rights campaigners, and examined the methods of repression used against them.

Tyranny and injustice are all too prevalent in many parts of the world, and must be equally condemned wherever they occur, but in this book we are mainly concerned with the denial of human rights by Communist rule in the Soviet empire of Eastern Europe. The dissenters in these countries are not expecting the overthrow of Communist rule, but call for its reform in the treatment of human rights and the fulfilment of guarantees written into the Communist Constitutions, the United Nations Covenants and the Helsinki Final Act. We believe that the Kremlin's denial of human rights in these countries, and the inevitable tensions thus created, pose a serious threat to the peace and stability of Europe. The fear of German reunification was indeed a reason for Stalin's creation of these buffer states, but this cannot justify the 'Brezhnev doctrine' asserting the Soviet right to intervene, by force if necessary, in any of the satellites where dissent makes its appearance. Nor do we believe that they can be permanently subjected to Russian domination.

Protests alone have proved worthless and sometimes more futile than silence. We would like to see Britain and the West as a whole taking a far more robust and realistic view of the common danger and of the need for greater unity in facing it. The alternative was well put by the late President Kennedy as 'being nibbled to death in a state of nuclear stalemate'. Defeat by default could well be the tragic outcome of the present timidity and division in Western diplomacy. The Soviet Union is by no means so invulnerable to peaceful forms of pressure as is generally assumed.

Our thoughts and hearts are with the courageous men and women, known and unknown, who struggle against such great odds for the defence of human dignity and freedom in the captive half of Europe. They need and deserve all the support the West can give them and we hope that this book will contribute to a greater understanding and sympathy for their cause.

TUFTON BEAMISH
GUY HADLEY

CHAPTER 1

HELSINKI
AND HUMAN RIGHTS

There has never been, and probably never will be, a universally accepted definition of human rights. Still less likely is the dawning of a golden age when all governments will respect them. For centuries, going back to the Western seed-beds of Greek and Roman civilisation, the arguments have continued between philosophers, lawyers and politicians over what belongs to Caesar or to the individual. There has been much debate about 'moral rights', 'positive rights', 'natural justice', and the *raison d'Etat*, ranging from the theory, at one extreme, that the state has the right to dispose of its members as it pleases, and at the other the claim that no man-made laws have any validity if they contravene a universal natural law of human rights.

The main schools of thought have been well described by Maurice Cranston in his book *What Are Human Rights?* and there is no need to pursue these academic disputations here. The English-speaking democracies have inherited their moral concept of human rights from Christian teaching and their legal enforcement from *Magna Carta*, the great English Charter of 1215; the Englilsh *Habeas Corpus* Act of 1679; and the American Declaration of Independence. Three of the main clauses in *Magna Carta* ran as follows:

(a) No free man shall be seized or imprisoned, or stripped of his rights or possessions, or outlawed or exiled, or deprived of his standing in any other way, nor will we proceed with force against him, or send others to do so, except by the lawful judgment of his equals or by the law of the land.

(b) To no one will we sell, to no one deny or delay right or justice.

(c) In future it shall be lawful for any man to leave and return to our kingdom unharmed and without fear by land or water, preserving his allegiance to us, except in time of war.

These basic principles of human dignity and freedom were reaffirmed in similar language by the men who drafted the American Declaration of Independence and the United States Constitution. Today they are ignored in many parts of the world, but we are concerned in this book with their violations in the Communist states of Eastern Europe.

The Russian Revolution of 1918, followed by the annexation in 1940 of the independent Baltic states, Estonia, Latvia and Lithuania, and the extension of Communist rule after 1945 to Central and Eastern Europe, injected a Marxist-Leninist concept of human rights fundamentally opposed to the Western model. The Communist ideology rejected any belief in a divine will or human survival after death, thus denying that man had a soul or a spiritual nature. Lenin himself said:

Every religion is madness. God is a monstrous corpse. Faith in God is a prodigious cowardice. (Directives to Communist Party Members)

The Communist interpretation of human rights is based on economic materialism and the treatment of individuals as mere units of mass production. In return for work and bread, coupled with economic and social benefits such as 'full employment' and public services for health and education, the Soviet Russian government demands from all members of its society a total and unquestioning obedience. This is justified on the grounds that the Communist Party is the creator and guardian of the beneficent new order, and that its permanent and infallible monopoly of power serves the highest common interest. There is no need, nor room for bourgeois notions of personal liberty which have now become obsolete and irrelevant.

This recipe for dictatorship has been imposed by a reign of terror which Lenin initiated, contrary to the view sometimes expressed by Western apologists that he favoured milder methods. Here is one quotation out of many from his own words:

If we do not cause terror by on-the-spot executions, we shall achieve nothing. It is better to wipe out a hundred innocent people than to miss one guilty one. (Declaration of Lenin to representatives of revictualling organisations, 24 January 1918)

After Lenin, Stalin was responsible for the deaths of at least twenty million people in his wholesale purges and the slaughter of Russian peasants who opposed his forcible land collectivisation. The day came in 1956 when a new Soviet leader and former colleague of Stalin, Nikita Khrushchev, denounced his master's excesses at the Twentieth Party Congress. Lenin's crimes are forgotten, however, and in 1970 the United Nations declared a month of centenary celebrations to mark the birth of 'that great humanitarian', Vladimir Ilyich Lenin.

When Lenin transplanted his version of the Marxist doctrine to Russia, it fell on fertile soil. Inured as they are to centuries of autocratic government, the Russians are among the most naturally conservative of peoples and the easiest to rule. Their submission to Communist despotism is fortified by national pride in seeing Russia become a nuclear superpower, and by a masochistic feeling that forceful measures, however brutal, are the hallmark of virile government. Nor has the Christian faith, which has so powerfully influenced Western thinking on human rights, worked to the same effect in Russia. The Russian Orthodox

15

Church went through periods of sharp conflict with the Tsars when it was harshly treated. It has suffered far worse under their Soviet successors, but it still maintains the Byzantine tradition of identifying the Church with the State. It renders obedience to Caesar in the Kremlin and publicly supports Soviet policies, both at home and abroad, as the price for survival. In August 1968, for example, after the Soviet invasion of Czechoslovakia, the Russian Orthodox Patriarch Alexey sent a letter to the British Council of Churches in which he said:

We regard the events of 21 August as an expression, though extra-ordinary in form, of the solidarity of the brotherly nations and do not see any grounds for its dramatisation. The purpose of this step was certainly not the 'occupation' of Czechoslovakia, as Western and anti-Communist propaganda insists, but the prevention of a ripening crisis.

Because of their national history, and centuries of isolation from Western Europe, most Russians find it hard to understand the Western concept of individual human rights and personal freedom. The main sources of discontent with their Communist rulers are the sacrifices in consumer goods and living standards imposed on them to maintain the Soviet Union as an aggressive world power, and the suppression of demands by national minorities for self-determination.

An early attempt to bridge the gap between Communist and Western views on human rights was made in the UN Charter adopted in October 1945. *Article 55* calls on all states to 'promote respect for, and observance of, human rights and fundamental freedoms', but made no attempt to define them in concrete terms. That task was allotted to a Commission for Human Rights which was instructed to submit proposals to the General Assembly for an 'International Bill of Rights'. The United Kingdom, supported by India and Australia, submitted a draft in the form of a binding agreement which not only specified human rights in detail, but also called for an international enforcement agency to deal with violations. The Soviet Union flatly refused to consider such a provision and maintained that it would be an unwarranted interference with the domestic jurisdiction and national sovereignty of states.

After long and sterile debates, the Human Rights Commission reached a compromise whereby, as the first stage, it would prepare a 'declaration' spelling out the rights and freedoms mentioned in the Charter; and this would be followed by a 'covenant' of a more binding nature. The first stage was accomplished in December 1948, when the General Assembly approved the Universal Declaration of Human Rights. It is written in terms designed to combine both Western and Soviet views. The Preamble states that 'recognition of the inherent dignity and the inalienable rights of all members of the human family is the foundation of freedom, justice, and peace in the world'. The first twenty Articles present a comprehensive list of human rights according to Western definitions. They include the prohibition of torture or arbitrary arrest, detention, and exile; the presumption of innocence, when charged with a penal offence, until proved guilty; the right to legal protection against invasions of privacy in the home, the family, and correspondence; freedom of residence and movement within national borders, and the right of every individual to leave any country, including his own, and return to it; freedom of thought, conscience, and religion, with the right to manifest beliefs in teaching, practice and worship; freedom of opinion and expression, and the right to seek, receive and impart information and ideas through any media and regardless of frontiers; and the right to freedom of peaceful assembly and association.

In later Articles the UN Declaration sets out a list of the social and economic rights stressed on the Communist side, most of which are implemented in Western countries on a much more generous scale than in the Soviet Union. They include the right to work and free choice of employment; social security benefits; equal pay for equal work; the limitation of working hours and the right to leisure, including holidays with pay; and free education, with the significant proviso that parents have a 'prior right' to choose the kind of education to be given to their children. But these rights cannot be put on an equal footing with the Western concept of human rights, since they are not governed by the same universal standards. Their fulfilment depends on national revenues and resources which vary greatly in different countries, whereas the rules of personal freedom are not so restricted and can be honoured or broken by any government at its own choice.

Communist governments claim credit for providing full employment and condemn unemployment in Western countries, but they deny their own workers the right to strike or to set up free trade unions. They also make extensive use of forced labour in prison camps under harsh conditions. Under Communist law it is an offence *not* to work, and critics of the regime are sometimes charged as 'parasites' after being dismissed from their jobs and speaking too freely.

At the same time, when condemning Soviet labour restrictions we should also ask whether the 'closed shop' in Britain, which prevents men and women from working in their trade if they refuse to join a union or to take part in a strike, is consistent with the 'right to work' and 'free choice of employment' laid down in the United Nations Declaration on Human Rights.

The difficulty of defining human rights in terms of reality is further illustrated by *Article 28* of the UN Declaration, which stipulates that 'everyone is entitled to a social and international order in which the rights and freedoms set forth in this Declaration can be fully realised'. And this is a statement as remote from the hard facts of life as saying that 'everyone' is entitled to a merry Christmas and a happy New Year. There is a great divide between 'moral rights' which may be claimed in theory, but could only be universally enjoyed in practice in a Utopian world; and 'positive rights' which civilised governments can and should provide.

The UN Declaration was nothing more than a statement of principles which should govern human rights, and it imposed no obligation on the member states to observe them. The task of turning principles into practice remained with the Commission on Human Rights, where the deadlock continued as the years of cold war rolled on. The Soviet bloc maintained its refusal to accept any measures of enforcement or verification and gained support from non-aligned states which ignored violations of human rights in the Soviet bloc and were blind to their own impending dangers from Soviet intervention overseas.

It was not until 1966, eighteen years after the UN Declaration of Human Rights, that a compromise was reached which combined Western and Soviet views. Instead of a comprehensive 'Bill of Rights', as first planned, the Human Rights Commission submitted two separate Covenants which were adopted by the General Assembly. One of them set out the economic, social, and cultural rights favoured by the Communist side, and the other specified the civil and political rights upheld by the Western countries. In addition, an optional Protocol was attached to the latter Covenant which allowed the right of appeal to a newly-formed UN Human Rights Committee by individuals as well as states.

The two Covenants were equally binding under international law, but they provided no means of enforcement. The Soviet Union refused to accept the creation of any international agency or court for this purpose, or even the appointment of a UN Commissioner for Human Rights. The Human Rights Committee was limited to the purely negative function of receiving annual reports from national governments on their measures to implement the Covenants, in which the Soviet bloc states naturally painted themselves as white as the lilies of the field. The Committee passed these reports to the UN Secretariat, where they gathered dust over the years.

The Covenants were closely modelled on the lines of the UN Declaration, but made two important additions to it. First, under *Article 2* of the Covenant on Civil and Political Rights, the signatories undertook to adopt such legislative or other measures as might be necessary to give effect to the rights recognised in the Covenant. The only Communist states which have observed this commitment are Czechoslovakia and Poland, as noted in later chapters. Secondly, both Covenants stipulated under Part I, *Article 1* that:

All peoples have the right of self-determination. By virtue of that right, they freely determine their political status and freely pursue their economic, social, and cultural development.

In the same Article of both Covenants, it was specified that 'all peoples may, for their own ends, dispose of their natural wealth and resources without prejudice to any obligation arising out of international economic co-operation'. The member states also undertook to promote and respect the realisation of the right of self-determination, including those states responsible for the administration of non-self-governing and trust territories.

This last proviso was clearly designed to prevent states which had obtained post-war mandates to administer such territories from treating them as colonies, but it also held far-reaching implications for the Soviet Union. It could be quoted in support of demands for the former Baltic states to recover their independence, or claims for self-determination by the Soviet satellite states, or indeed by national minorities such as the Ukrainians, Georgians and Armenians. In fact, the Soviet Constitution promulgated by Stalin in 1936 stipulated in *Article 17* that: 'Every union republic shall retain the right freely to secede from the USSR.' *Articles 18A* and *19B* also gave them the right to establish direct relations, and conclude direct agreements, with foreign states; and to organise their own military forces. All these rights are confirmed in the new Soviet Constitution initiated by Khrushchev in 1961, but only completed in 1977. However, as is the case with the other lavish promises of human rights in the Soviet Constitution, there are escape clauses which can be invoked if necessary, such as *Article 74* in the new edition which states that Soviet territory is 'integral' and comprises the territories of the Union Republics; and adds that 'the sovereignty of the USSR shall prevail throughout its territory'.

There was another long delay before the two UN Covenants came into effect. They required ratification or accession by at least thirty-five countries which was not achieved until 1976. Even so, some Western states, including the USA, have not yet ratified either Covenant and France has not even signed them. The optional Protocol became effective in March 1976.

In the UN Commission on Human Rights, the Soviet violations of human rights have been ignored and attention has been focused on other countries, notably South Africa and Chile. A recent example is that of the mass atrocities committed by General Amin in Uganda. These have not been condemned by the Commission, despite new evidence submitted to it in February 1977 by the International Commission of Jurists, which estimated that about 100,000 men, women and children had been massacred in Uganda since Amin seized power in 1971.

In 1969, yielding to pressure from the Soviet Union, the UN Secretariat instructed all its Information Centres abroad not to transmit petitions on human rights to UN headquarters. The UN Information Centre in Moscow had already refused to forward petitions from the Soviet Union.

21

Until Mr Carter was elected President of the USA, no Western government was on record as having made a direct and official protest to the Soviet Union about its abuse of human rights in Russia, although one or two of them made pleas to Moscow for mercy in a few individual cases. The Soviet leadership was therefore justified in reckoning that it had nothing to fear from foreign reactions, and it simply ignored the UN Covenants. Men like Brezhnev and his colleagues, who rose to power as willing accomplices in Stalin's crimes, are no more prepared than he was to tolerate opposition. They cannot afford to revert to a Stalinist reign of terror, because times have changed, even in the Soviet Union. The horror of those tragic years is too deeply burned into Russian memories to risk creating new fears and tensions of that kind. Russian standards of living have also improved, as compared with the Stalinist period, and provide sufficient compensations to make most people accept the role of Stalin's successors as the lesser evil. For that very reason, they hold aloof from the small minority of active dissenters, regarding them at best with indifference or, at worst, as busybodies and mischiefmakers whose activities may end by getting everybody into trouble.

The isolated position of the Russian dissenters has been well described by Dr Valentin Turchin, one of their chief spokesmen, who worked for Amnesty International in Moscow until he was forced to emigrate in October 1977 after he had been repeatedly arrested and threatened with charges of 'subversion'. Dr Turchin said:

Many people want to live decently, but most have no courage to do so. For some people, however, the desire to live decently is stronger than the fear of possible consequences. The dissidents exist as a subculture within the dominant culture. They think otherwise, act otherwise, do otherwise and so defy totalitarianism. You will always find some people to represent the sub-culture.

There are probably many people in Russia who view their Communist rulers either with fatalistic apathy or cynical detachment, but we are concerned here with the small number of human rights campaigners who dare to voice their thoughts. They come from many different sections of Soviet society. Some belong to national minorities, Ukrainian and others, which claim that their constitutional right of racial equality and local autonomy are being denied by a Soviet policy of 'Russification'. Many are religious believers, mostly Baptists but including Orthodox Christians and Jews, protesting against restrictions on their freedom of worship and religious association, or claiming their right to emigrate. A few are practising Communists disillusioned by Soviet perversions of the Marxist-Leninist creed. Among the most active and articulate spokesmen for human rights are the nonconformist writers, scientists, doctors, teachers, who refuse to accept the suppression by the Communist state of independent thought and freedom of expression.

The one thing these men and women have in common is their belief in human freedom and the courage they show in its defence, knowing full well the risks to themselves and their families. Many of them have already paid a heavy price. The indiscriminate reign of terror imposed by Stalin has subsided, but his successors still use the same methods. Some dissenters receive long prison sentences in Siberian labour camps where death is often a merciful release. Many others suffer daily persecution which makes their lives almost unbearable. They lose their jobs and their children are excluded from higher education. They are closely watched by the KGB (the security police), their homes are searched, their telephones cut off, and their letters intercepted.

A particular refinement of cruelty is the confinement of dissenters in psychiatric hospitals. After his arrest, the prisoner is examined by an obedient psychiatric commission which certifies him as 'mentally ill' and therefore unfit to stand trial. The court

23

then orders his detention in a psychiatric hospital or mental institution for an indefinite period. There is no known case where a Soviet court has refused to accept a certificate alleging mental illness. Nor has a Soviet court ever been known to return a verdict of 'not guilty' in trials of political prisoners. Nor is there any case on record in which a Soviet appeal court has annulled a verdict of 'guilty' passed on such prisoners.

Once committed to a psychiatric hospital, the victim is sealed off from the outside world in a kind of medical Bastille. Political offenders are usually held in 'special' hospitals controlled by the KGB where they are denied even the minimal rights prescribed for ordinary prisoners under the Soviet penal code. They are allowed to write letters only to their close relatives, and then only by permission of the hospital staff. These letters are strictly censored and no reference is allowed to the medical treatment and the conditions of detention.

The psychiatric treatment consists of intensive pressure to force the dissenter to renounce his views. If he refuses to submit, as many do, he is injected with dangerous drugs which may make him unable to read or write and sometimes cause a serious heart condition. A cruder form of torture is to wrap the prisoner tightly from head to foot in a roll of wet canvas which is then left to dry and inflicts agonising pain. Factual evidence of these methods has been given by Vladimir Bukovsky and other dissenters who experienced them and survived.

The real motives for this bestial prostitution of medical ethics are revealed quite openly by the Soviet psychiatrists who administer the treatment. For example, when Victor Fainberg was confined in the Arsenalnaya special psychiatric hospital in Leningrad in 1977¹, a doctor told him:

Your discharge depends on your conduct. By your conduct, we mean your precise opinions on political questions. Your disease is dissent.

As soon as you renounce your opinions and adopt the correct point of view, we'll let you out.

Your disease is dissent! Those four words sum up concisely the attitude of the Communist state to those who defend freedom and the way in which Soviet psychiatry is used to crush them. Dissent itself is the crime and the form it takes makes no difference. In 1971 five people were arrested in Siberia on charges of organising a Buddhist sect and their leader, Bidya Dandaron, was sent to a labour camp, where he later died. The other four were certified as mentally ill and detained in a psychiatric hospital. Also in 1971 seven Communists charged with preaching false Marxist opinions in Leningrad were all condemned to psychiatric detention. A veteran Communist non-conformist with a fine war record, General Pyotr Grigorenko, was arrested and examined in 1969 by a psychiatric commission in Tashkent, which declared him to be in full possession of his senses. His case was then referred to the Serbsky Institute of Forensic Psychiatry in Moscow, which recommended his confinement in a 'special' psychiatric hospital.

The Soviet authorities found many willing helpers among Soviet psychiatrists and doctors, some of whom have attended annual meetings of the World Psychiatric Association and for many years succeeded in preventing complaints of Soviet abuses from being heard. In 1971, when Vladimir Bukovsky presented factual evidence to the WPA congress, it was excluded from the discussions. In 1973 a leading Moscow psychiatrist, Professor Snezhnevsky, who worked in the Serbsky Institute, coolly declared that he knew of no case where a healthy patient had been put into a psychiatric hospital in all his 50 years of experience. He led the Soviet delegation at the WPA general assembly that year.

In 1977, however, after mounting pressures from Western

publicity and criticisms, the WPA general assembly which met in Honolulu in September of that year passed a resolution condemning abuses of psychiatry for political purposes and specifically referring to the Soviet Union. Even so, it was passed only by a narrow majority based on a block-voting system allowing delegates one vote for every 100 members of their national associations, a method which gave the Western bodies a numerical advantage, and but for this it would have failed. In a second resolution, the WPA meeting unanimously approved an international code of ethics, after the Soviet delegation withdrew its objections. A third resolution condemned the abuse of psychiatry to suppress dissent, and approved the formation of a committee to examine such allegations. These resolutions may have some influence on the Soviet authorities, who attach considerable importance to Soviet membership of international organisations and might prefer to make some minor changes in their psychiatric practices rather than walk out of the WPA.

A few Soviet psychiatrists have protested openly against these abuses of their profession and have been punished by prison or exile. One of the best known is Dr Marina Voikhanskaya, a Leningrad psychiatrist, who was expelled from the Soviet Union in 1975. Her young son has been kept in Moscow as a hostage, and in August 1977 the Soviet Embassy in London refused to accept a petition for the boy's reunion with his mother. That same month, a Georgian psychiatrist, Dr Avtandil Papiashvili, defected from the Soviet Union to Austria while on holiday with his wife, and at a press conference in London he gave full details of psychiatric maltreatment in the Soviet Union and called on the WPA to condemn it.

All these repressive measures were flagrant violations of Soviet undertakings in the UN Covenants, but they also contradicted guarantees of civil and political rights written into the Soviet constitution, promulgated by Stalin in 1936. These guarantees were fully in accordance with the Western definitions, so much so that they revealed a Communist desire to exploit their popular attractions. Similarly the new Soviet constitution adopted by Brezhnev in October 1977 reaffirms freedom of speech, press and assembly (*Article 50*); freedom of conscience and the right to profess, or not to profess, any religion (*Ariticle 52*); inviolability of the person and protection against arbitrary arrest (*Article 54*); privacy of the home, forbidding entry without lawful grounds and against the will of the occupier (*Article 55*); privacy of correspondence, telephone conversations and telegraphic messages (*Article 56*); respect by all state organs and officials for individual rights and freedoms, and the right of citizens to make complaints against them for illegal actions, and to claim compensation (*Articles 57, 58*).

Under *Article 49* all Soviet citizens have the right to submit proposals to state organs and public organisations 'for improving their work'. This Article also states that 'persecution for criticisms shall be prohibited'. Under *Article 40* the right to work is guaranteed for all Soviet citizens, including the right to choose their own profession or occupation. But these Articles are ignored in the repressive measures used against Soviet dissenters. The Soviet government relies on other Articles which can be invoked to overrule all the rest. For example, *Article 39* of the new constitution says that 'the exercise of rights and freedoms must not injure the interests of society and the state, and the rights of other citizens'. Under *Article 50* the freedoms of speech, press, and assembly must be exercised 'in conformity with the interests of the working people and for the purpose of strengthening the socialist system'. Under *Article 59* 'the exercise of rights and freedoms shall be inseparable from the performance by citizens of their duties'. And *Article 62* states that 'the citizen of the USSR shall be obliged to safeguard the interests of the Soviet state, to contribute to the strengthening of its might and prestige'.

In short, it is the Communist leadership which interprets the law to suit its own purposes and acts as sole judge, jury, and executioner.

The contempt shown by the Soviet rulers for their pledges on human rights simply advertises the fact that it is they who are repudiating legal obligations and punishing the dissenters who call for their fulfilment. But it is also a confession of failure and proof that the Soviet system is politically bankrupt. Marxist teaching assumed that the Communist monopoly of power would be limited to a transitional period, in which the necessary conditions for a socialist Utopia would be established. Under Lenin and his successors, however, Communist dictatorship has reduced Russia to a state of economic and social paralysis. The ideological element of the Bolshevik Revolution has given way to a determination by the Soviet rulers to preserve their own power and privileges, with the support of Communist Party officials and an army of bureaucrats entirely dependent on Soviet state patronage for their careers and promotions.

They must have felt sure of their ability to sterilise the virus of dissent and prevent it from spreading, but they did not foresee the stimulating effects on the human rights campaigners of the Helsinki Conference on European Security and Co-operation (CSCE) which ran from July 1973 to July 1975, with the main sessions being transferred to Geneva. Its purpose was to seek agreement on measures which would reduce tensions in Europe and foster the tender plant of what is called 'detente' in East-West relations. There were thirty-five states represented, among them being the Soviet Union and satellite members of the Warsaw Pact alliance, the NATO partners, and a number of neutral or non-aligned states, including Austria, Finland, Malta, Spain, Sweden, Switzerland, the Vatican and Yugoslavia.

The Soviet Union had long taken the lead in proposing and urging the holding of the conference, hoping to gain substantial benefits from it. The main one would be full Western acceptance of the post-war frontiers in Central and Eastern Europe and hence Soviet domination in that region, not only as an accomplished fact, but given international recognition. The Soviet leaders were also anxious to obtain renewed assurances of Western aid in advanced technology, industrial equipment and trade credits. This aid not only helps to make good the defects in their own backward economy but also contributes indirectly to the Soviet military potential, thus easing the strain on the Soviet budget of its vast expenditure on military forces and support for guerrilla warfare overseas. In addition, the Soviet negotiators probably saw an opportunity of creating and exploiting differences between the NATO allies, and particularly between the European members and the USA, of the kind which coalitions have always suffered when faced with a single and powerful opponent.

The Western governments were understandably reluctant to embark on a new round of talks which might only provoke a fresh outburst of mutual recriminations reminiscent of the 'cold war' in which the West had much to lose and little to gain. The inclusion of human rights in the Helsinki agenda, under the innocuous title of 'Co-operation in Humanitarian and Other Fields', seems to have been an afterthought, aimed at redressing to some small extent the military bargaining power held by the Soviet Union. And indeed, the Soviet side may well have been surprised and annoyed by this injection of an issue which the Western governments had studiously avoided for many years. The fact that it was accepted in Moscow, however grudgingly, gave an indication of the importance which the Kremlin attached to gaining its own objectives.

The British government took a leading part in opening the way for human rights to figure in the Helsinki discussions under the modified formula of 'humanitarian' proposals and in persuading the Western allies, notably the United States, to accept this inclusion. The Foreign Office may later have been as surprised as the Soviet government by the effects this had on stimulating dissent in the Soviet satellites, but it deserves more credit than it has yet received for exposing this weakness in the Soviet armour.

When the Helsinki agreements were announced in the Final Act of the conference, it was commonly assumed that the West had made valuable concessions to Moscow and got little or nothing in return, thus proving yet again the truth of the Soviet formula for negotiations, namely: 'What's ours is ours. What's yours is negotiable.' It can now be seen, with hindsight, that this belief was mistaken. Certainly, on the face of it, the Soviet negotiators appeared to have gained their chief objectives. The Helsinki agreements were embodied in a 'Declaration of Principles', ten in all, followed by proposals for their implementation set out under three headings, or 'baskets', dealing with measures to promote military security and disarmament; co-operation in trade, industry, science, and technology; and co-operation in humanitarian and other fields. The Final Act was not a binding treaty, but the participating states undertook to respect these principles and take steps to apply them in practice.

Under *Principle III*, the signatories agreed to regard as 'inviolable' each other's frontiers and those of all states in Europe, and to refrain now and in future from assaulting these frontiers. They also agreed to refrain from any demand for, or act of, seizure and usurpation of part or all of the territory of any participating state.

Under *Principle IV*, they undertook to respect the territorial integrity of each state and to take no action involving a threat or use of force against their unity or political independence.

Under *Principle VI*, the participating states agreed to refrain from any intervention in the internal or external affairs of another participating state, regardless of their mutual relations; and to refrain from any form of armed intervention, or threat of it, against such states. They also agreed to refrain from direct or indirect assistance to terrorist activities, or to subversive or other activities directed towards the violent overthrow of the regime of another participating state; and to refrain from any act of military, political, economic or other 'coercion' designed to subordinate the sovereign rights of another state to their own interest.

These Principles satisfied the Soviet demand for Western legal recognition of the post-war status quo in Eastern Europe and the frontiers of the Communist satellites in the Soviet buffer zone, but they were qualified by other provisions which had equal standing. Thus, under *Principle I*, it was agreed that the frontiers could be changed in accordance with international law, by peaceful means, and by agreement. The commitment to renounce the use of military force or occupation against other states was an empty phrase. The Western powers had already shown, when Khrushchev crushed Hungary in 1956 and Brezhnev invaded Czechoslovakia in 1968, that they had no intention of intervening. After 1968 the 'Brezhnev doctrine' asserted the Soviet right to use force anywhere in Eastern Europe when 'socialism' was in danger and this was accepted by all the Communist satellites apart from Rumania's hollow protest. In effect, the Soviet rulers have retained a free hand to do as they please in Eastern Europe, if they are prepared to face the consequences of another military intervention.

The Helsinki proposals relating to security and disarmament consisted of 'confidence-building' measures, including prior notification of major military manoeuvres, mutual acceptance of observers on these occasions, and advance notice of major military movements (*Basket I*). Under *Basket II*, dealing with economic and technological co-operation, there were proposals for business contacts, exchanges of economic and commercial information, and mutual assistance for industrial projects and trade promotion. These offered considerable advantages to the Soviet bloc and reinforced its demands for Western industrial, technological, and financial aid. But they also gave some encouragement to direct contacts between the Communist satellites and Western countries and thus might weaken the Soviet economic grip on Eastern Europe exerted through the Communist Council for Mutual Economic Assistance (CMEA, normally called COMECON).

But in *Basket III*, dealing with 'humanitarian co-operation', there were provisions on human rights which, though of a modest kind, subjected the Soviet rulers to critical scrutiny at their most vulnerable point. The Western countries wisely avoided moral exhortations on human rights which would be wasted on the Soviet Union. Instead, they were able to obtain agreement on some limited, but practical, proposals for developing human contacts and exchanges of information. The Soviet government agreed, like the other states, to facilitate meetings between family members living in different countries by easing and simplifying the conditions for travel. They undertook to deal 'in a positive and humanitarian spirit' with applications for the reunification of families, and for marriage between citizens of different states. They confirmed that religious faiths, institutions, and organisations recognised by state constitutions could have contacts and meetings between themselves and exchange information. They also agreed to make travel for personal or professional reasons easier by improving procedures for exit and entry and lowering, where necessary, the fees for visas and official travel documents. Similar encouragement was to be given to tourism, meetings between young people, and in the field of sport.

Under the heading of information, the Helsinki participants expressed their intention to facilitate the freer and wider dissemination of information of all kinds; to encourage co-operation for that purpose; and to improve the conditions of work for journalists posted from one state to another. No journalist working legitimately would be liable to expulsion, nor otherwise penalised. Under this declaration of intent, they would take steps to increase the quantity and variety of newspapers and publications imported from the other states, and help to improve access by the public to them by increasing the number of places where these publications were on sale, developing the possibilities for taking out subscriptions, and providing better opportunities for them to be read and borrowed in large public libraries and reading rooms. Proposals for improving cultural relations and exchanges were also agreed in *Basket III*. Little progress has been made so far in implementing these agreements on either the Soviet or the Western side, mainly because of their fundamental differences. In the Soviet state, where all the information media are strictly censored to conform with official directives, there is a hunger for Western news, publications and films which the authorities dare not satisfy. In the Western societies, where people have a free choice, there is nothing to interest them in the drab uniformity of Communist propaganda and most of them have no knowledge of the language.

If these had been the only provisions for human rights in the Helsinki Accord, they might rightly have been assumed to count for very little by comparison with Western recognition of the Soviet bloc frontiers in Eastern Europe and of Moscow's need for Western economic aid. There were, however, other clauses in the Final Act which held more serious implications for the Kremlin. Under *Principle VII* the Soviet government gave a clear undertaking to 'respect human rights and fundamental freedoms, including the freedom of thought, conscience, religion, or belief, for all without distinction as to race, sex, language or religion'. It also agreed to recognise and respect 'the freedom of the individual to profess and practise, alone or in community with others, religion or belief acting in accordance with the dictates of his own conscience'; and, in the case of national minorities, their right to equality before the law and 'full opportunity for the actual enjoyment of human rights and fundamental freedoms'.

Also under *Principle VII*, the Soviet Union joined with the other states in confirming 'the right of the individual to know and act upon his rights and duties in this field'. And it undertook to fulfil Soviet obligations to respect human rights as set forth in the international declarations and agreements on this issue, including the two UN Covenants on Human Rights. Furthermore, under *Principle VIII*, the Soviet leadership agreed to respect 'the equal rights of peoples and their right to self-determination', acting in conformity with the UN Charter and international law; and their right 'in full freedom, to determine, when and as they wish, their internal and external political status, without external interference; and to pursue as they wish their political, economic, social and cultural development'.

Now it may be thought that these commitments cost nothing to the Soviet Union and its satellites, since they already openly ignored them and would continue to invoke powers reserved by their penal codes as justification. That cannot be doubted, but the Helsinki Final Act also made provision for a 'follow-up' to the conference by stipulating that each participating state would publish the text, distribute it, and make it known as widely as possible to its own people. It was further agreed that the multilateral process initiated at Helsinki would be continued at a meeting in Belgrade in 1977, starting in June that year. These clauses inhibited to some extent the Soviet freedom of action on human rights, since they served notice that this issue would not be shelved and forgotten. In fact, the undertaking to publish and disseminate the Helsinki agreement was carried out more fully in the Soviet Union and its satellites than in Western countries, including Britain.

The Soviet authorities claim that the clauses on human rights in the Helsinki Accord are of minor significance compared with military security and economic co-operation, and that Western insistence on them is a diversion which works against detente in Europe. As Western lawyers have pointed out, however, all the Helsinki Principles are equal and interdependent, based on reciprocal action by the signatory states. If they all fulfil the agreements, no question of interference by one state in the internal affairs of another can arise, but if a state fails to do so, then other states are entitled to point this out. Indeed, were it not so, international agreements would have no meaning or purpose at all.

Whatever different meanings are attached to the Helsinki Accord, its effects on the Soviet Union and its puppets in Eastern Europe were immediate and electric. The official publication and circulation of these agreements in the Communist states reinforced the claims of the dissenters that they were not engaged in any criminal or politically subversive activities, but had legitimate grounds for condemning violations of human rights which their own Communist authorities had acknowledged under the UN Covenants and confirmed at Helsinki. This also gave the campaigners for human rights a common platform for voicing their protests, instead of remaining isolated and solitary as individuals.

A group to 'Promote Observance of the Helsinki Accords' was set up in Moscow and similar groups were formed in the Ukraine, Georgia, Armenia, and Lithuania. By early 1977 the Russian groups had issued nineteen reports dealing with Soviet violations of human rights, including religious persecution, the separation of families, and the denial of constitutional rights to national minorities. This information was passed on to Western journalists in Moscow at meetings with dissenters in their homes.

To avoid giving the Soviet authorities any valid pretexts for charging the monitoring groups with conspiracy against the state, their activities were openly conducted. Their formation, purposes and membership were notified to the Ministry of the Interior which also received copies of their reports. It was an interesting sign of change working beneath the hard crust of Communist rule that such groups could appear at all, and this could not have happened under Stalin. But the dissenters are well aware that his successors will be equally determined to crush all forms of protest. They accept the risks they run as a price well worth paying if their cause gains publicity and support in Western countries.

Even more than death or captivity, there is a greater fear among the human rights campaigners that their fate will remain unknown or disregarded in the free world. They believe that Western interest can have an effect on the Soviet rulers by bringing into the full light of day abuses of power which they would like to keep hidden. As a leading Russian dissenter, Anatoly Shcharansky, said before his arrest in March 1977: 'World opinion is what keeps us going, what keeps us alive.'

In the satellite countries of Eastern Europe, the greatest danger for Moscow is a combination of demands for human rights and hatred of Soviet domination. Inside Russia, where any relaxation in Communist government is bound to be a much longer and more difficult process, the Soviet rulers have no need to make concessions to the human rights campaigners, but demands for 'self-determination' by national minorities present the Kremlin with a much more serious problem. When these demands are limited to questions of racial discrimination and tolerance of separate minority languages and culture, they can be treated as matters of local government which, though potentially divisive in the Russian multi-racial state, remain firmly under control from Moscow. But a very different situation arises when Ukrainians, Georgians or Armenians start to revive memories of former independence, or when Estonians, Latvians and Lithuanians call for the restoration of the free Baltic states forcibly annexed by the Soviet Union in 1940.

In June 1975 Estonian and Latvian Democrats in exile made

an appeal to the governments at the Helsinki Conference for the implementation of human rights in the former Baltic states. The appeal stated:

Among all human rights, the right to self-determination . . . is of the utmost importance for the Baltic nations. The restoration of Estonia and Latvia as independent and sovereign members of the European Community would be their only chance for the preservation and free development of their nationhood, culture, and frame of mind.

In September 1975 six dissident groups in Estonia, Latvia, and Lithuania sent a letter to the Baltic World Conference, an assembly of *émigré* organisations, regretting the failure of the democratic nations at the Helsinki Conference to take a firm and united stand against the Soviet annexation of the three Baltic states. In December 1976 when the Lithuanian monitoring group for human rights was formed, its leader, Viktoras Petkus, talked to Western journalists in Moscow and called on the states which had signed the Helsinki Final Act to remember the fate of his country.

The moral justice of these nationalist claims is undeniable and indeed Britain still recognises *de jure* the Baltic states. But the Soviet government can only regard such claims as a potential threat to the territorial integrity of the Soviet Union. The Western governments, for their part, cannot support claims for the restoration of the Baltic states without giving Moscow plausible grounds for complaint that they are intervening in Soviet internal affairs. The Helsinki agreements, in recognising the post-war European frontiers after 1945 and committing Western powers to renounce any attempt to change them *by force*, were only a public endorsement of a situation which had already existed in practice for many years.

In their efforts to crush the human rights campaigners after the Helsinki Conference, the Soviet authorities decided to apply their measures of repression on more flexible and selective lines. The most active spokesmen for human rights were singled out for the harshest treatment, and many were sentenced to long terms of imprisonment or confined in psychiatric hospitals. Their trials were held in courts far from their place of residence and behind closed doors, so as to exclude relatives, friends and Western reporters. A typical example was the case of Sergei Kovalev, a Moscow biologist, who was charged with preparing and circulating the *samizdat*, or underground publication, called *Chronicle of Current Events*. In December 1975 he was tried in the Lithuanian city of Vilnius and sentenced to seven years of hard labour, followed by three years of internal exile, although suffering from cancer.

Those dissidents who remained nominally free were subjected to intensive persecution by methods already mentioned in this chapter, and eloquently described by Hedrick Smith in his remarkable book *The Russians*. They were also denounced in Soviet newspapers and broadcasts as criminals working for Western intelligence agencies. But in some cases, where the authorities wanted to get rid of troublesome dissenters without attracting attention by a trial, they simply informed them that they had been granted an exit visa and must leave Russia forthwith. Among those expelled were the writer Andrei Amalrik, in 1976 and the psychiatrist Dr Marina Voikhanskaya, in 1975. Another dissident, Vladimir Bukovsky, whose case had received much publicity in Western countries, was exchanged in 1976 for the Chilean Communist leader, Luis Corvalan. In making such releases, the Soviet rulers must have carefully weighed the cost of allowing these victims to describe their experiences to the outside world, tacitly acknowledging the part played by Western protests, against the soothing effects which this relatively 'lenient' treatment might produce. It is unlikely that the KGB has failed to exploit this channel as a means of infiltrating their own agents among the genuine dissenters.

Mr Carter's election as the American President in January 1977, and his firm stand on the importance of human rights in all countries, surprised and angered the Soviet leaders. Western governments had previously taken little notice of the abuses of human rights in the Soviet bloc, but here was a new American President who was not only prepared to condemn the savage cruelties inflicted on dissenters in the Soviet Union, but who publicly declared that the treatment of human rights by governments would be a major factor in determining American foreign policy. The fact that President Carter found in this issue a means of restoring American self-respect and confidence after Vietnam and Watergate, and reviving the moral impulse which has always influenced American foreign policy for better or worse, did nothing to soften the impact in Moscow.

The Soviet authorities reacted sharply to this new development. Early in February 1977 they arrested Alexander Ginzburg, a member of the Helsinki monitoring group in Moscow and administrator of a fund set up in 1974 by Solzhenitsyn to help needy dissenters and financed by royalties from his book, *The Gulag Archipelago*. A few hours later, a Russian-speaking American journalist, George Krimsky, who had closely followed and reported dissident activities for the Associated Press agency, was expelled from the Soviet Union. When the US State Department retaliated by deporting a Soviet Tass agency correspondent, the Soviet government brazenly protested that this was a breach of the Helsinki agreements. The police interrogated a friend of Ginzburg, Dr Valentin Turchin, who had set up a branch of Amnesty International in Moscow, but he was released after refusing to answer any questions about Ginzburg.

These actions were quickly followed by the arrests of Dr Yuri Orlov, a physicist who led the Moscow monitoring group, and another of its members, Anatoly Shcharansky, also a physicist.

39

The leader of the Ukrainian monitoring group in Kiev, Mikola Rudenko, was also arrested, together with another member, Oleksa Tikhy, a teacher. The founder of the Georgian group, Zviad Gamsakhurdia, and another of its members, Mirab Kostava, both philologists, suffered the same fate. But a member of the Moscow group, Mrs Lyudmilla Alexeyeva, was given an exit permit after threats that she would be charged, like Orlov and Ginzburg, with working for anti-Soviet *émigré* organisations in the West.

These arrests were probably designed to test President Carter's firmness of purpose by showing him that his support for the defenders of human rights only made their sufferings worse. If that was the aim, it did not succeed. After receiving a letter from Dr Sakharov, the best-known Russian dissident, appealing for continued American support, the President sent a reply in which he stated that 'our government will continue our firm commitment to promote respect for human rights, not only in our own country, but also abroad'. The Soviet authorities were reluctant to arrest Sakharov himself, because of his international reputation as a scientist, and the President's reply may have given him some further insurance.

At the Belgrade Conference on Security and Co-operation in Europe which met in 1977-78 to review developments since Helsinki, the Soviet rulers rejected Western concern over violations of human rights in Russia as an unwarranted interference in their internal affairs and refused to discuss Western proposals for improvement. This hard line is well suited to conditions in the Soviet Union, but it involves much greater difficulties for the Communist satellite regimes in Eastern Europe which have to contend not only with demands for human rights in their countries, but also with deeply rooted desires for freedom from the Soviet yoke and the recovery of national independence.

In these captive countries, unlike Russia, Western influence is gaining ground through trade and cultural agreements, joint industrial projects, more personal contacts and more freedom for people to travel abroad for holidays or to visit relations. The improvement in East-West contacts varies to a great extent between one satellite and another, but the time is past when the 'iron curtain' sealed off Eastern Europe from Western influence. The military barriers remain, but they cannot halt the rising infiltration of Western ideas into the Communist buffer states of the Russian empire.

In short, the demand for human rights in the Soviet Union is still a relatively innocuous germ which can easily be rendered harmless, but in the satellites it is an infectious disease which is active and spreading. This is the crux of the Kremlin's dilemma which will be illustrated in the following chapters.

CHAPTER 2

POLES APART

Stalin created a Soviet empire in Europe far larger than anything the Russian Tsars ever achieved or even attempted. Since public memories are short and so many years have passed since the defeat of Nazi Germany in 1945, it may be useful to preface this chapter with a brief note on the conditions which enabled Soviet power to be imposed on Eastern Europe. How was it that the heroic Soviet ally against Hitler, the idol of many gullible admirers in Britain and other Western countries, became almost overnight the butcher of freedom in the countries which it claimed to 'liberate'?

The process began in August 1939 when Stalin signed his pact with Hitler. This cleared the way for the invasion of Poland by German armies which followed a week later. In return, Hitler agreed to a partition of Poland between Germany and the Soviet Union, the latest in a tragic sequence of partitions in Polish history, and he also gave Stalin a free hand to occupy the independent Baltic states of Estonia, Latvia and Lithuania when the time was ripe. Less than a fortnight after the German invasion of Poland, when the Polish army was still putting up a heroic resistance, the Red Army moved in and seized a large slice of territory in East Poland including the cities of Vilnius and Lvov and 80% of Polish oil resources. At least one and a half million Poles were despatched to Russian prisons and labour camps and the occupied provinces were incorporated into the Soviet Union after faked elections. In 1940 the three Baltic states were forcibly annexed by Stalin; Soviet forces seized Bessarabia and Northern Bukovina from Rumania; and Finland was forced to cede territory to Russia after a brave fight against long odds. Since 1939, with the addition of further territories acquired at the end of the Second World War, the USSR has taken possession of an area larger than France, Belgium and the Netherlands combined. This is graphically shown on the endpaper maps.

When Hitler's disastrous invasion of Russia in June 1941 made Stalin an ally of Britain and the USA, he succeeded in reaching agreements with them which tacitly recognised Eastern Europe as a Soviet sphere of interest, but stipulated that those countries should be free to choose their own governments after the war by free elections, should be restored as sovereign and independent nations, and should enjoy freedom of expression and religion and the other basic human rights. But Stalin ignored these pledges, as might have been expected by his Western allies who could do nothing about it. While they were busy demobilising their forces, he had Soviet troops and tanks on the ground to enforce his commands. He proceeded to install Communist puppet regimes in East Germany, Poland, Czechoslovakia, Hungary, Rumania and Bulgaria which were directed from Moscow, and despatched Soviet agents to enforce a reign of terror in the captive countries.

The people thus enslaved by Stalin were not primitive tribal societies, but nations which in past centuries played an active part in making European history and in more recent times fought to win freedom from Turkish, Russian or Austrian conquest. They differed in their economic and social stages of development, but they had a common heritage of pride in their national traditions and they all hoped to recover their places as free nations in Europe when Nazi Germany was defeated. The Soviet yoke imposed by Stalin did not destroy those memories of the past

43

and hopes for the future, but drove them underground where they burn more fiercely. Moreover, Tito's successful post-war revolt against Moscow in Yugoslavia, followed by the abortive Hungarian rising in 1956 and the crushing of the Czechoslovak outbreak in 1968, showed that even Communist leaders could associate themselves with demands for national freedom.

Because of their differences in racial character and historical development, each of the six Soviet satellites we are discussing must be treated as a special case. Poland suffered worst of all from Nazi German occupation and equally savage Soviet Russian treatment, but the Polish capacity for survival is a miracle of history which has withstood even the frequent efforts of the Poles to destroy themselves. In the fifteenth century, when England was being devastated by the Wars of the Roses, Poland was a leading European power and a bulwark of Christendom against Turkish invasion. But internal feuds and rivalries undermined the Polish kingdom and a long period of decay ended in the three partitions of Poland in the eighteenth century by Prussia, Austria, and Russia. The Poles did not regain national independence until its restoration in 1919 by the Versailles peace treaties, and then only kept it for twenty years before the new partition of Poland by Hitler and Stalin.

This chequered story of tragedy and heroism has fostered a spirit of ardent patriotism and national solidarity among the Poles which is reinforced by racial and religious ties. Before the Nazi German occupation in 1939, there were some three million Jews in Poland and smaller Ukrainian, German and Byelorussian minorities. The Nazi massacre of the Jews and the Soviet annexation of Polish territory reduced these minority groups to fewer than 700,000 people in 1970 out of a total of over 34 million, according to figures given in May of that year by the Communist paper *Zycie Warszawy*. Most Poles today are at least nominally attached to the Roman Catholic faith and the Roman Catholic

44

Church remains, as it has been through all the joys and sorrows of Polish history, the heart and soul of Polish national survival.

The wartime Primate, Cardinal Hlond, showed great courage in resisting Nazi German atrocities and trying to save Jewish lives. His successor, Cardinal Sapieha, a leader of equally strong character, bravely resisted the suppression of religious and civic rights in the early post-war years by the Communist regime under Boleslaw Bierut. Since January 1949 the office of Primate has been held by Cardinal Stefan Wyszynski up to the time of writing, an even more remarkable leader whose success in drawing a clear line between the roles of the Church and the Communist state, without compromise on basic matters of principle, has brought his Church through a long period of harsh persecution to a position in 1978 where its influence is recognised by the Polish Communist rulers. Cardinal Wyszynski was himself arrested with other Catholic clergy late in 1953 and detained in a monastery, but he was released in 1956 when Gomulka was reinstated as Communist Party leader.

The Cardinal and his bishops play a leading and active part in the defence of human rights in Poland and this alone would distinguish the Polish situation from that of the other Soviet satellites. But there are other elements in the Polish Communist state which preserve the existence of a 'plural' society containing diverse interests and thus prevent that reduction to a drab proletarian uniformity which Communist ideology seeks to achieve. One such group, and the most articulate, consists of writers, scientists, university professors, lawyers and others with high intellectual standards who rebel against Communist censorship and its suppression of independent thought. Polish arts and sciences have long been a part of Western civilisation and their isolation under Communist rule inflicts losses on literature, music, painting and the theatre which are deeply felt.

A second group is formed by Polish students who protest against Communist interference with higher education and the mediocre quality of teaching which this produces. It is a significant fact that a number of students have gone on from the universities to become active human rights campaigners.

A third group is found among Polish Communist Party members, some of whom have held responsible posts, but who have become disillusioned by abuses of power which they regard as breaches of the pure Marxist doctrine. And a fourth group, much larger in numbers though lacking the means for organised protest, consists of the independent Polish farmers. The collectivisation of land carried out by the Communist regime after the war collapsed in 1956 and about 80% of Polish agricultural land is now in private hands. The private farmers have suffered from the small and uneconomic size of the average holding and from Communist policies which make it hard for them to earn a living, but they still provide most of the food supplies and are thus a force to be reckoned with by the government.

But the first major outbreak of discontent in Poland did not come from any of these sources. In 1956 the workers in the Cegielski locomotive plant in Poznan demanded wage increases and sent a delegation to Warsaw to press their claims without success. The locomotive workers then marched through the streets of Poznan in what started as a peaceful demonstration but soon turned into a public riot. The crowd broke into the Communist Party offices, threw its files into the street and made a bonfire of them. The security police opened fire, killing at least fifty people and wounding many others, but order was not fully restored until the Army sent in a few tanks whose presence was sufficient to calm things down without further shooting.

It was the events in Poznan which started the national ferment known as the 'Polish October' of 1956, when all the suppressed hostility to Communist rule and Soviet domination burst into open view. At the trials of Poznan rioters, in September 1956, the defence lawyers spoke out with a freedom unknown before or since in a Communist court and their flats were piled high with flowers from their admirers. In Warsaw and many other Polish cities there was a mounting tide of openly expressed demands for redress of grievances which the Communist regime, led by Edward Ochab, seemed unable to resist. In Moscow, Khrushchev finally decided that the situation called for drastic Soviet action. Troops and tanks from the Soviet forces stationed in Poland moved in towards Warsaw and Khrushchev himself flew there to deliver an ultimatum to the Polish Communist regime.

After a heated all-night meeting in the Belvedere Palace, Ochab and his colleagues managed to convince Khrushchev that the Poles would fight if attacked and they would be joined by the Army and even by the Communist auxiliary units. In fact, Khrushchev would have provoked war on a scale far exceeding the cost to the Soviet Union of crushing the Hungarian revolt which shortly followed. Fortunately for Poland, and also for Khrushchev, he realised that the Poles were not bluffing and ordered the withdrawal of Soviet forces. He agreed that the former Polish Communist leader, Wladyslaw Gomulka, who still had some public support because of his enforced retirement, should be recalled and given the task of reconciling the Poles to their place in the Soviet camp.

Gomulka succeeded in restoring order, but Polish hopes that he would relax the Communist grip were short-lived. He was a dogmatic Communist of the old school, too set in the old mould to question the dictates of Moscow, or to make any fundamental changes. As time passed, his authority declined, and early in 1968 he was faced with another outburst of protest. The immediate cause was a Communist veto on the performance of a popular nineteenth-century play by Adam Mickiewicz called *Forefathers Eve* (*Dziady*). It depicted Polish sufferings under Tsarist

47

Russian rule in terms very similar to Polish sufferings under the Soviet yoke, and was received with an enthusiasm which finally led to its prohibition.

The officially sponsored Polish Writers' Union immediately passed a resolution, despite Communist opposition, calling for a removal of the ban, the restriction of censorship generally, and freedom for writers to participate in shaping cultural policy. The students supported the writers and, on 8 March 1968, 5,000 of them joined in a demonstration in Warsaw University. They were attacked by the police, who invaded the precincts and used their truncheons. Many students were injured and a number were arrested. Next day, a further student demonstration in the main streets of Warsaw was again attacked by the police and further arrests were made, among them that of Karol Modzelewski, a well-known Communist dissenter who had already spent some years in prison. On 11 March the demonstrations were renewed on an even larger scale when 10,000 young people gathered outside the University to express their support for the students. Some of them broke into the Communist Party headquarters and the Ministry of Culture, where they smashed furniture and used it as weapons against police attack. Others sought refuge in the Church of the Holy Cross and were evicted by the police.

According to reports in the Polish Communist press, fifty-eight people were injured and a number of students were arrested as ringleaders, but the agitation quickly spread to three other university cities. Cracow, Poznan and Lublin. The Cracow students carried banners inscribed: 'Warsaw is not alone. We want justice.' The authorities tried to put the blame on 'Zionist propaganda' and on the activities of students whose fathers held privileged positions in the Communist state, including the chief editor of a newspaper, the director-general of a Ministry, and a senior censor in the chief Press Control Office. This latter claim was, of course, double-edged, since it admitted that children brought up in this select Communist circle were some of the most active organisers of student protest. The sins of the sons were visited on four fathers, all Jewish government officials, by dismissal from their posts.

Gomulka took a tough line on these disturbances. Addressing a meeting of senior Communist officials on 19 March, he accused dissident writers and intellectuals of provoking student unrest. He agreed that the clashes between the students and police had started when Communist militiamen, police auxiliaries, had invaded the University precincts, but made no apologies or excuses. He said that over 1,200 people had been arrested, of whom nearly 700 had been released and 207 punished by the courts. The rest were presumably still being held in custody.

Gomulka claimed that the writers and scholars had conspired to mobilise the students against the government by passing their protest resolution in the Writers' Union. He read it out and quoted a remark by the Catholic writer, Stefan Kisielewski, at the Union meeting:

What kind of history is being taught to children at school? It is a lot of nonsense . . . Affairs are in the hands of blockheads with absolute power.

A number of professors and lecturers were dismissed and there were reports that Kisielewski had been beaten up by hired thugs acting for the police.

Later, in March 1968, a pastoral letter was issued by Cardinal Wyszynski and the Polish bishops and read out in Catholic churches all over the country. It condemned the use of force by the authorities against the students as a false answer to social tensions and an insult to human dignity which only served to reopen painful wounds. The letter also revealed that the Polish Episcopate had protested to the government against police brutality in suppressing the student demonstrations. Even before this letter appeared, the small group of independent Catholic deputies in the *Sejm*, or Polish National Assembly, had already appealed to the Prime Minister, Cyrankiewicz, for humane treatment of the students and some recognition of their grievances.

In the 1976 elections the Polish United Workers (Communist) Party obtained 261 seats in the *Sejm*; the United Peasant Party received 113; the Democratic party, 37; non-Party candidates, 36; and the Catholic group, ZNAK, retained 13 seats. The United Peasant and Democratic Parties are Communist allies in the National Unity Front and a massive Communist majority is thus assured, but the very fact that an independent Catholic group is allowed to exist in the National Assembly bears witness to the influence of the Roman Catholic Church in Polish national affairs.

The clashes in 1968, and their savage repression, produced the one thing that the authorities should have been most anxious to avoid, namely a coalition between the Catholic Church, the writers and intellectuals, and the students, but this lesson was wasted on Gomulka. In December 1970 a new and more dangerous challenge appeared, or rather reappeared, in a revolt by the favourite sons of Marxist doctrine, the Polish workers. Shipyard workers in the Baltic port of Gdansk rioted in protest against sudden and drastic rises in the prices of food, clothing, and household fuel. Similar riots quickly followed in other towns. The trouble was basically due to economic mismanagement by the government. After the storm in Poznan in 1956, Gomulka's regime raised the level of wages and kept food prices down by large subsidies. But at the same time the government harassed the private farmers who produced most of the food supply and reduced the amount available on the open market to which most Polish families had to turn for subsistence. The result was a combination of higher wages chasing a shrinking amount of food for sale.

To make matters worse, the government imposed the price increases at one fell swoop, instead of doing it by stages. Meat prices rose overnight by 18%, flour by 16%, jam by 37% and imitation coffee by 92%. Linen fabrics went up by 54%, overcoats by 69%, shirts and pyjamas by 10%, and coke by 20%. The prices of some manufactured goods, such as refrigerators and television sets, were reduced but this was small compensation for Polish housewives who were already spending about 40% of the family earnings on food. An added grievance was the fact that the workers in some shipyards had increased their output by 25% in the previous three years, but their pay had remained unchanged.

Armed security police, militiamen and even troops were called in to crush these Baltic riots. This time, the cost in blood was 45 killed and over 1,100 wounded; of the latter, about half were civilians and the other half were losses on the government side. According to unofficial reports, Gomulka was so badly shaken that he appealed to Moscow for Soviet military intervention, but was curtly refused. However, this final proof of his inability to control the situation in Poland was the last straw for the Kremlin. Gomulka was dismissed from the leadership and replaced by Edward Gierek, an ex-miner from Silesia. The Prime Minister, Cyrankiewicz, a renegade socialist and an expert political acrobat who had kept his balance all through the post-war years, also took the hint and resigned.

Gierek, unlike his predecessors, at first showed a willingness to see for himself and an awareness of public opinion which indicated a softer touch on the Communist keyboard. He publicly admitted that the Polish Communist Party had failed to establish a close link with the working class and the people as a whole. He also frankly acknowledged the gravity of the economic situation and spoke of 'a sickness of incompetence' which the new government must eradicate. He did not withdraw the price increases, but tried to reduce their impact by freezing all food prices for two years and increasing the wages of the lower-paid workers, as well as their family allowances and pensions.

The new regime also sought to improve relations between the state and the Catholic Church. In his first speech to the *Sejm*, Gierek promised 'a full normalisation' of these relations. He gave instructions for legal documents and title-deeds to be prepared which would confer on the Church the ownership of ecclesiastical property in Silesia, which the Polish Church had only been allowed to lease since the war at high rents.

This policy of conciliation brought some easing of the tension, but it did not last long. Since 1970 the situation in Poland has shown a widening gulf between appearances and realities, between an outward semblance of relaxation and the maintenance of Communist repression in all its familiar forms. The Poles have gained a freedom of speech which is the envy of other satellite peoples. They can travel abroad, even to Western countries, with a relative ease which is only comparable with Hungary. There is a large audience for BBC and other Western broadcasts in Polish and listeners incur no penalty, although Radio Free Europe is still sometimes jammed. It is probably easier to buy copies of leading Western newspapers such as *The Times* or *Le Monde* in Warsaw than it is to buy French, German, or Italian papers in many British cities.

On the other hand, Gierek's regime has made no concessions to the mounting Polish demands for human and civic rights, demands which were given a new impetus by the Helsinki agreements of 1975. But it has learned enough from past experience to avoid direct confrontation, if possible, and this in itself is a sign of growing uncertainty in the Communist leadership as to the best methods of containing the human rights campaigners.

Communist nerves were again tested in November 1975, when Gierek proposed amendments to the Polish Constitution for approval by the *Sejm*. These stressed the commanding role of the Communist Party, the 'unbreakable ties' with the Soviet Union, and the dependence of civic rights on the performance of civic duties. Their main purpose seemed to be to reinforce Communist powers to deal with dissenters, and to take out added insurance against a repetition of the crisis in Czechoslovakia in 1968 caused by Dubcek's efforts to reform the Communist system.

Popular feelings again erupted in furious protests. The deputies in the *Sejm*, when considering the amendments, received a flood of angry letters from people all over the country. On 5 December 1975 a group of 59 distinguished Polish writers, intellectuals and scientists sent a long and carefully prepared letter of protest to the Speaker of the *Sejm*. Similar letters were signed by 300 professors and students, and by a group of 11 legal experts. The Polish Episcopate issued a statement in March 1976 reporting that the Church had submitted proposals to the Communist authorities in January that year setting out 'the basic demands of the Catholic community for maintaining harmony, peace and co-existence in our common Fatherland'. Protests also came from Marxist critics of the regime such as Professor Leszek Kolakowski, who has since been given a post at Oxford after being dismissed from Warsaw University and expelled from the Polish Communist Party; and from one of his most able students, Jacek Kuron, a young Communist who had already served a prison sentence of three years.

The influence of the Helsinki Accord was clearly seen in these protests. Both the intellectual 'group of 59' and the Polish bishops referred in their statements to the United Nations pledges of human rights which the Communist states had confirmed at Helsinki, and demanded their fulfilment in Poland. The intellectuals called for an equal right of appointment to state offices for all citizens, regardless of religion, philosophy or party affiliation; the acceptance of the right to strike; the abolition of censorship; freedom for workers' unions, societies of creative artists, religious groups and others, to publish their own literature; and the restoration of self-government in universities and scientific institutes. The Catholic Episcopate insisted that 'indispensable civil rights must not depend on the fulfilment of duties'. It demanded an independent judicial system and civil service, free trade unions, and a parliament formed by free elections. The bishops also urged the need to grant civic rights to the agricultural workers, and especially to the private peasant farmers.

The authors of these protests were certainly well aware that no Communist regime could be expected to accept them without signing its own death warrant, but the sheer weight and unanimity of the outcry persuaded the Communist leadership to make some minor changes in the proposed constitutional amendments. Thus, the declaration that the Polish socialist state was based on the same 'class revolutionary principles' as those of the Soviet Union was discarded. The description of the Polish Communist Party as exercising 'the leading role in society' was altered to read 'the leading force in society in the construction of socialism'. The proclamation of 'an unshakable fraternal bond between Poland and the Soviet Union' was reduced to a statement that 'Poland will strengthen its friendship with the Soviet Union and other socialist states'. The clause making civil rights dependent on duties was replaced by a passage simply requiring all citizens to 'fulfil their obligations to the Fatherland'. And more significantly, two clauses providing for legal measures against dissenters were dropped.

Trivial as some of these concessions may seem, the mere fact that Gierek and his colleagues felt compelled to make them was proof of their growing sensitivity to the pressures of dissent in Poland. It revealed all the more plainly their uneasy posture between force and persuasion under the watchful eyes of the big brother in Moscow. Unhappily for the regime, however, the balance remained in a state of perpetual motion.

In March 1976 the government reopened the explosive issue of increases in food prices. The Prime Minister, Piotr Jaroszewicz, announced in the *Sejm* that they would have to be altered 'to correspond with the economic possibilities'. He said that the increase in meat production over the previous five years had been based on imports of grain and fodder which were becoming more difficult, more costly and sometimes impossible. The government therefore intended to change the pattern of consumption by putting more emphasis on the supply of other consumer goods, such as industrial products, houses, cars, services and tourism. It hoped that this change would help shift the 'excessive demand' for food to other markets.

There was some truth in Communist arguments that food supplies had been hit by several bad harvests, and that food prices had to be raised to catch up with an inflationary rise in wages and incomes. But the fact was that the Communist government in Poland had been living on borrowed time and money, in the shape of Western food supplies and trade credits on highly favourable terms, and the burden of foreign debts had become almost too heavy to bear.

In the four-year period from 1971-74 Poland imported more than 12 million tons of wheat, barley and maize, half of which came from the USA and other Western countries. In an effort to relieve its desperate shortage of hard currency, the Polish Communist regime made a deal in November 1975, with the Federal German government in Bonn, whereby Poland agreed to allow from 120,000 to 125,000 Germans still living in Poland to emigrate to West Germany. In return, Bonn agreed to pay a lump sum of DM 1,300 million (about £370 million at 1977 exchange rates) and granted Poland a long-term credit of DM 1,000 million at a very low rate of interest.

The increases on food prices decreed by the government in 1976 were severe and Polish reactions were equally violent. The food shops were besieged by frantic buyers who cleared the shelves in a few hours. Angry demonstrations again broke out in many industrial towns. Workers in the Ursus motor plant in Warsaw went on strike and tore up part of the main railway line, blocking rail traffic. In Radom, street barricades were put up and several houses set on fire, including the new building of the regional Communist Party Committee. The same sort of trouble erupted in other industrial towns. The number of people killed and injured in the suppression of these riots was not officially confirmed, but eyewitness accounts spoke of 17 civilians killed and 75 policemen wounded.

Thus faced with another national crisis, Gierek's regime reverted to a mixture of fear and force. The Prime Minister immediately announced on television and radio that the food price increases were only proposals subject to public discussion. As a result of 'the valuable amendments and suggestions made by the working class', he added, the government had decided to withdraw the increases. No action would be taken against workers who had gone on strike because they were 'misled' and did not understand what the government was trying to do. But those who had committed criminal offences would be punished.

This was followed by an official statement that 53 people, mostly workers, had received prison sentences of up to ten years for their part in these outbreaks. Hundreds of workers were dismissed from their jobs and blacklisted for re-employment. These harsh reprisals only added fuel to the flames of dissent. A group of Polish intellectuals issued an 'open letter' to the authorities which not only condemned the police action against the workers, but called for 'an authentic dialogue' between the Communist Party and the people, and a 'broadening of democratic liberties'. Jacek Kuron, a leading Communist dissenter already mentioned, wrote to the Italian Communist leader, Enrico Berlinguer, denouncing the imprisonment and dismissal of workers, and asking him to support the appeal for a general amnesty. In reply, the Italian Communist Party urged the Polish leadership to show moderation and clemency and gave an early example of 'Euro-Communist' protest.

The Polish Episcopate also protested strongly to the government and called for an amnesty, but at first in private, hoping that this would carry more weight. Finding, however, that its views were ignored, the Cardinal and Bishops issued a public statement in September 1976 asking the government to show full respect for civil rights, to conduct a 'true dialogue' with the people, and to grant the amnesty. Maintaining its role as mediator, the Episcopate also called on the people to observe peace and order in the national interest. The Communist press published this conciliatory part of the statement, but omitted the rest.

The most important new development took place in that same month. A 'Committee for Defence of the Workers' (KOR) was set up by fourteen intellectuals to raise funds for providing legal, financial and medical aid to the workers who had been imprisoned or dismissed, and their families. The results clearly showed the extent to which the campaigners for human rights had succeeded in winning popular support. Contributions were collected openly in the streets by university students and some parish priests, and received from thousands of people all over Poland. The Communist press denounced the Workers' Defence Committee as an illegal organisation, and Communist officials gave some of its members a warning to that effect. In reply, the Committee pointed out that it operated quite openly and legally, even to the extent of sending copies of its reports to the Ministry of the Interior. It was only demanding the fulfilment of human rights guaranteed in the Polish Constitution, and it was the Communist government which acted illegally by denying them. The Committee also declared its readiness to disband if the authorities stopped harassing its members, granted an amnesty to the workers in prison, reinstated all who had lost their jobs, ordered a public enquiry into charges of police brutality, and punished those found guilty.

The extent to which the human rights movement attracted even Communist dissenters formerly in high office is shown by an 'open letter' written in October 1976 by Wladislaw Bienkowski, Minister of Education under Gomulka from 1956-59, which was widely circulated. It was a blistering attack on police brutality and its deeper social consequences. Referring to the suppression of the food riots in June 1976, Bienkowski commented:

There is ever-increasing evidence that the policeman's club becomes the usual platform for contacts between a citizen and the representatives of law and order; and that beatings, physical and moral tortures, are applied as a 'prophylactic' even to innocent people, even to people not suspected of any crime.

He denounced the corruption spread by police officers and local officials who accepted bribes for their favours, and the perversion of justice by courts which were willing tools of the police apparatus. By violating moral and legal standards, Bienkowski added, the state authorities were promoting anarchy in Poland and destroying the foundations of civil discipline.

The government reacted sharply. At first, they seemed reluctant to provoke another outbreak by putting the dissenters on trial, but members and supporters of the WDC were closely watched and sometimes summoned for police questioning. Two of them were dismissed from their jobs, Antoni Macierewicz, a lecturer at Warsaw University, and Miroslaw Chojecki, on the staff of the Nuclear Research Institute. Nevertheless, the membership of the Committee rose from fourteen to eighteen.

On 3 November 1976 the police searched the premises of two

WDC members – the historian, Jacek Kuron, and Jan Jozef Lipski, literary critic – and seized some documents. Another member, biochemist Pyotr Naimski, was detained on 12 November but quickly released. On 14 November six senior members of the Polish Scouts' Union were arrested on suspicion of helping the Workers' Defence Committee, but freed without being charged. The following day twelve students were arrested on the same grounds, but were also released.

On 23 November the police arrested fourteen WDC members who attended a meeting that evening in the flat occupied by Wojciech Ziembinski, a graphic artist. The four absent members were Professor Edward Lipinski, Jerzy Andrzejewski, a writer, Halina Mikolajska, a well-known actress, and Stanislaw Baranczak, a poet. Most of the arrested members were released within a few hours, but three of them – Jacek Kuron, Jan Jozef Lipski and Ziembinski – were held until early the next morning.

Despite these storm signals, the volume and variety of protests continued to grow. Early in December, some sixty-five Polish workers imprisoned after the food riots in June drew up charges of brutality by police and prison warders, and petitioned the government for an enquiry. On 6 December Cardinal Wyszynski preached a sermon in St John's Cathedral, Warsaw, in which he too accused the police of brutality and quoted evidence from letters sent to him by eyewitnesses and victims. A further appeal for an investigation was sent to the *Sejm* by 28 leading professors, but on 5 January 1977 the Prosecutor-General announced that his office saw no grounds for it. This brought an immediate response from 172 intellectuals who signed a demand for the *Sejm* to investigate 'the abuses and tortures the whole country is talking about'.

This renewed wave of dissent clearly made its mark on Gierek, who announced early in January that he had advised the Council of State to consider pardons for imprisoned workers who repented and could be expected not to commit further breaches of the law. Gierek also told the chairman of the Polish Writers' Union, Jaroslaw Iwaszkiewicz, that no action would be taken against writers who had supported demands for an enquiry into police brutality. On 25 March, the Workers' Defence Committee issued a report stating that 32 people sentenced for their part in the food riots of June 1976 had been released, but at least 23 were still in prison, and those dismissed from their jobs were still finding it hard to get work suited to their qualifications.

Five days later, the High Court in Warsaw upheld prison sentences on two Ursus factory workers who had been found guilty of damaging the railway line outside their plant. The WDC reported that, in Radom, the sentences imposed on two other workers had been suspended, and a third case sent for re-trial, but added that twenty people were still in prison in Radom and the police were 'harassing' workers there and in other towns.

A brief lull then followed which probably indicated a conflict of views in the Communist ruling circle over the merits of using force or moderation against the human rights dissenters. It was again the familiar Communist crunch in Poland between the two extremes, only more acute. If the regime made concessions, it only whetted the Polish appetite for more and made it harder to maintain Communist authority, perhaps with contagious effects in other satellite states. Conversely, recourse to strong-arm methods was equally likely to provoke a fresh eruption and increase the risk of Soviet military intervention, which Gierek and his more cautious colleagues wanted to avoid.

Up to this point, the human rights movement in Poland had shown a firmly united front and an impressive capacity for integrating dissenters of many different kinds. In March 1977, however, a new 'Movement for the Defence of Human and Civil Rights (ROPCO) was formed by eighteen dissidents and announced by their spokesman Leszek Moczulski, a journalist and historian, at an unofficial press conference in Warsaw. The new group included four members of the Workers' Defence Committee: Father Jan Zieja, a Catholic priest; Stefan Kaczorowski, a lawyer and former Christian Democrat; Antoni Padjak, another lawyer and former Socialist; and Wojciech Ziembinski. But shortly afterwards Zieja and Padjak left ROPCO.

Early in May 1977 the Workers' Defence Committee announced that its own activities would be expanded to cover all violations of human rights in Poland. In reply, the ROPCO spokesman, Moczulski, told Western correspondents that it had about 1,000 supporters, but did not consider itself in competition with the WDC. However, on 8 June a representative of the Workers' Defence Committee, Halina Mikolajska, stated that it would not co-operate with ROPCO. She said that the WDC did not know enough about the work of ROPCO to assess its value, but the real reason for the split seems to have been differences in personal and political backgrounds. Most of the WDC members were fervent Marxists who wanted to reform the Communist system, and some were former Communist Party members. The ROPCO founders, on the other hand, contained a high proportion of non-Communist members and some with records of service both in the Polish wartime resistance and in the Polish forces which rallied to Britain and the United States.

Possibly encouraged by these signs of dissent among the dissenters, the hardliners in the Communist leadership regained the initiative. Addressing a meeting of the Party Central Committee on 14 April 1977, Gierek said: 'We cannot accept infringement of the law, and the abuse of socialist democracy and civil liberties, or the activity stemming from alien class positions and directed against our socialist state. Such activity must be unmasked and will be opposed by all possible means.'

In late April and early May, the security police arrested eleven members and supporters of the Workers' Defence Committee, among them Jacek Kuron, Adam Michnik (who made frequent visits to Western countries quite openly and freely as a WDC envoy), Antoni Macierewicz, and Pyotr Naimski. The Public Prosecutor told Kuron's wife that they were being held under an article in the penal code relating to contacts with anti-Polish organisations abroad. He also issued a special warrant allowing the police to detain these prisoners for up to three months while awaiting charges, instead of only forty-eight hours as prescribed by the penal code. This was a new and sinister development. The WDC had often been attacked in Communist newspapers and broadcasts, but without naming individuals or taking legal action against them. They were now threatened with charges which could result in prison sentences of up to eight years.

These arrests coincided with a fresh outburst by the university students of Cracow, following the death of a student, Stanislaw Pyjas, in circumstances which strongly suggested police involvement. Pyjas had been an active organiser of student protests and a supporter of the Workers' Defence Committee. In fact, several of the WDC prisoners were arrested when visiting Cracow, or trying to get there, to attend requiem masses for Pyjas and a procession of mourning through the streets.

The Cracow students broke away from the official Socialist Union of Polish Students and set up their own Students' Solidarity Committee, which demanded a public explanation by the authorities and the punishment of those responsible for the death of Pyjas, whatever their positions. The Solidarity Committee also declared its support for the Workers' Defence Committee. The WDC called for the immediate release of its arrested members and associates and appealed to 'the community' to support this demand. It also announced its intention of appointing an 'Intervention Bureau' to collect and publish information on violations of human rights by state officials, and a 'Social Self-Defence

Fund' to help people deprived of their jobs for supporting the WDC.

On 19 May 1977 Cardinal Wyszynski condemned the repressive measures against students in a sermon at a Warsaw confirmation service. Young people, he said, knew their rights and should not be blamed if they spoke out for them. He called for a change 'in the whole system of rule over man'. The Archbishop of Cracow, Cardinal Wojtyla, a fearless critic of government excesses, also gave a sermon on 9 June in which he accused the Communist press of distorting the truth about student demonstrations in Cracow after the death of Pyjas.

A strong protest against the arrests of WDC members came from a group of seventeen intellectuals that included a violinist, Wanda Wilkomirska, a painter, Anna Trojanowska, and a film director, Bohdan Kosinski. Appeals for the release of the WDC dissidents were also made by the chairman of the Polish Writers' Union, and by the senior member of the Workers' Defence Committee, the octogenarian Professor Lipinski, who wrote to the French, Italian, and Spanish Communist Party leaders asking for their support. A group of eleven Poles, including the wife and sister of a worker still in prison, went on hunger-strike in a Warsaw church.

It must have been obvious even to the Communist hardliners that police repression had only succeeded in reinforcing the strength and cohesion of the human rights campaign. The police did not pursue the hunger-strikers into the church. Nor did they interfere with the celebrations attended by 50,000 people to mark the opening of the first Catholic church at Nowa Huta, the giant iron and steel combine near Cracow. Cardinal Wyszynski again exerted his great influence on the side of moderation in an address to a crowd of some 20,000 people who gathered for the Corpus Christi procession through Warsaw on 5 June. The

Church, he said, prayed for 'social peace for our nation, for our domestic life', and added: 'We have stressed so often that this social peace depends on respect for basic human and civil rights . . We fear anything that might be a violation of rights today, since this might give birth to a new unrest tomorrow.'

In June 1977 the authorities released the WDC member, Jan Josef Lipski, and a supporter, Hanna Ostrowska, both on grounds of ill-health. In July the other members and associates of the Workers' Defence Committee under arrest were also released by virtue of an amnesty in honour of Poland's national holiday. The Communist press maintained that they had only been set free on condition of their future good behaviour, but this they strongly denied. At a press conference in Warsaw, Jacek Kuron thanked all those at home and abroad who had helped the WDC prisoners to obtain their freedom and paid a special tribute to the important part played by the Catholic Church. He described the releases as 'the first step in creating conditions for a real dialogue between the authorities and society', and hoped that others would follow. He also made it clear that the Workers' Defence Committee had no intention of dissolving. It renewed its demand for an enquiry by the *Sejm* into police brutality and announced that its membership had risen to twenty-five. However, one founder-member, Ziembinski, later resigned because of his participation in the new dissident group, ROPCO.

The July releases gave the Polish Communist leadership a new chance to adopt a policy of conciliation which would not be merely a temporary shift in tactics, but a genuine process of consultation and co-operation with the nation. Yet it was still very unlikely that the regime would take this chance, or indeed could afford to do so without undermining its whole position. Gierek probably viewed the release of dissenters as a sop to Polish opinion and Western concern over human rights, which would again find expression at the Belgrade Conference in

October 1977 to review developments since Helsinki. In a speech to the *Sejm* shortly before the WDC releases, he firmly set his face against any radical reforms in the Communist exercise of power. Using language very similar to that of Moscow, he claimed that the Polish Constitution fully guaranteed all civil rights. He stressed the primary importance of economic and social 'liberation', without which 'all declarations about equality and freedom are empty words'. That, he said, was why the government 'must categorically defend the social foundations of our state and the inviolability of its institutions'. He added that civil rights were an internal affair for all states, and that only Communist citizens had a right to decide the issue.

Gierek's regime thus fell back into its well-worn groove between compromise and coercion, with no sign of an exit. Two recent examples of this ambivalent Communist position may serve to illustrate their dilemma. In March 1977 the Communist authorities gave permission for the public performance in Warsaw and some other cities of a new film called *The Marble Man*, made by a leading film director, Andrzej Wajda. It was a satire on the cult of the 'Stakhanovite' movement, or 'heroes of socialist labour', during the Stalinist period in Poland. A Polish bricklayer decides to become a shock worker and lay a record number of bricks in a single shift while helping to build the Nowa Huta steelworks. This feat is exploited by Communist propaganda film producers who feed the bricklayer with vast quantities of meat and show brass bands marching past to spur him on with the job. In a typically Polish touch, Wajda even satirises himself by including allusions to his own past contribution to Communist propaganda.

Unhappily for the bricklayer, his herculean efforts and their publicity arouse the hostility of his fellow-workers, and he ends up by becoming the victim of a 'show trial'. He vanishes behind prison walls, while the marble busts and statues erected to his fame lie derelict in a museum basement closed to the public.

K.D.   65   E

Many years later, a young girl student, an amateur maker of films, decides to find out what became of the bricklayer and produce a film about him, but all she can find is a nameless grave in the Baltic port of Gdansk, suggesting that he might have been killed there during the 1970 riots by workers protesting against increases in food prices.

Wajda's film created a national sensation. Nothing like it had ever been seen in Communist Poland, let alone the Soviet Union and the other satellites. The cinemas showing *The Marble Man* were packed for months on end, and tickets changed hands at exorbitant black-market prices. The audiences burst into laughter and applause during the performances, and after the first showing in Wroclaw there was a standing ovation, followed by the singing of the national anthem.

How or why the Communist film censorship came to pass this film for public showing is still much of a mystery. It was widely thought that the decision must have been made by Gierek himself as the Party leader, but it is possible that some official 'dove' lower down spread his wings. The first Deputy Minister of Culture and the Arts, Mieczyslaw Wojtczak, was 'transferred to other tasks', and he may have been a scapegoat to appease the angry 'hawks'. Wajda himself, though attacked in the Communist press, has so far suffered no penalty, but the authorities refused permission for his film to be distributed abroad. Wajda retorted that they were depriving the Polish film industry of the chance to win a prize at Cannes or some other international film festival.

In the autumn of 1977 light of a very different kind was shed on Polish film censorship by the disclosure of highly secret instructions issued by the chief Communist censors between 1974 and 1976, which were smuggled out to the West. The documents are clearly genuine and provide a mass of detailed information on the workings of the censorship system in all its aspects. The methods used by this bureaucratic machine in its uphill struggle against disaffected writers, journalists and publishers are fully revealed, but the most remarkable feature is the fact that these well-educated and well-paid cohorts of censors obviously do not themselves believe in the game they are playing. To mention only a few examples of their double thinking:

There should be no disclosure about the increasing pollution of rivers flowing from Czechoslovakia.

Information on the annual consumption of coffee in Poland should not be revealed, in order to prevent the disclosure of the scale of our coffee re-exportation.

No permission should be given for publication in the mass media of global figures illustrating the rise of alcoholism in the country.

You are not allowed to let through any attempt to put the blame for the death of Polish officers in the Katyn woods on the Soviet Union . . . When the date of death is given, only dates later than July 1941 are allowed.

In other words, the rivers flowing from Communist Czechoslovakia *are* polluted. The scarcity of coffee in Poland *is* largely due to its re-exportation. More and more people *are* taking to drink to drown their sorrows. And the mass killings of 15,000 Polish officers *were* the work of the Soviet Union, because the German attack on Russia began in June 1941, whereas the massacres took place in the spring of 1940. As *The Times* commented on the work of these Polish censors: 'They are peddling an ideology which has no hold over their own minds. They are salesmen who do not believe in their own products.'

In December 1976 the Paris paper *Le Monde* published an article by Adam Michnik, one of the bravest of the brave among dissenters, in which he suggested that there was a 'convergence of interests' between the Soviet rulers, the Polish Communist leadership, and the democratic opposition in avoiding a Russian military intervention in Poland. He pointed to four main areas in which the situation could be improved.

The trade unions, he wrote, should become independent representatives of the workers. Relations between Church and State should be reformed so that religious Poles were no longer treated as second-class citizens. Catholics must have the right to take part in public life and to publish more information on religious subjects. It was unrealistic at present to demand a complete abolition of censorship, but it should be possible to devise 'a reasonable law for the press'. Even the censored mass media should provide simple political information which ordinary citizens could now obtain only by listening to foreign radio stations. Finally, the Party leaders must give up 'their insane hope of eradicating pluralism among the young people'. The students, at least, should have a legal right to form independent academic societies and research groups. By denying it to them, the government was pushing them into illegal acts and must accept full responsibility for them.

Early in October 1977 the WDC announced that it had decided to disband, but would be reconstituted as a Committee for Social Self-Defence. The new Committee would continue to fight against political, religious and racial persecutions and it would give aid to people who suffered from them. It would also support all activities calling for the implementation of human rights. This reorganisation was a logical result of the success which the Workers' Defence Committee had achieved in securing the release of workers and others imprisoned after the food riots of June 1976 and the re-employment of those dismissed from their jobs. But the decision to form the new committee was not unanimous. Three of the former members dropped out because they did not agree with the new programme. They were Stefan Kaczorowski,

Emil Morgiewicz, and Wojciech Ziembinski. Among those who remained were Halina Mikolajska, Jacek Kuron, Professor Edward Lipinski, and Jerzy Andrzejewski. The other movement for human rights, ROPCO, extended its activities all over the country and opened offices in six large Polish cities. It is clearly an effective body of dissent and seems to enjoy considerable public support.

In Poland, far more than in any other Soviet satellite, there are interesting signs of change and movement beneath the hard crust of Communist rule. In October 1977 a group of fourteen senior Communist Party members, including a former Party leader, Edward Ochab, sent a letter to the present leader, Gierek, in which they called for 'a clear-cut programme of political and economic reforms' and a dialogue between the Communist Party and non-Communists.

Also in October 1977, Gierek had his first official meeting with Cardinal Wyszynski, the Polish Primate and it was announced that they had exchanged views 'on the most important questions of the nation and the Church'. The Cardinal visited Rome a fortnight later and Gierek himself had an audience with the Pope early in December, this being the first time a Polish Communist leader had done so. In February 1978 an address by the Cardinal was read out from all the Roman Catholic pulpits in Poland in which he offered the support of the Church for the Communist authorities to overcome the major social problems caused by the spread of alcoholism and corruption and to persuade the people to work harder. The Cardinal pointed out, however, that the Church could only co-operate effectively 'by acquiring a wider sphere of freedom for preaching the Gospel, by having greater possibilities for action with the help of the public media, especially the press, and by more freedom to issue Catholic publications and to develop apostolic associations'.

President Carter visited Warsaw at the end of 1977 and agreed to provide American credits for Poland amounting to $200 million, a modest contribution to the relief of Polish foreign debts totalling over $10 billion but a welcome support for the imports of grain which Poland badly needed to make up for yet another bad harvest. In return, Gierek promised to look into the grant of emigration permits to some 250 Poles who had so far applied in vain for permission to join their families in the USA. The President did not talk to Polish dissenters, but replied in writing to questions put to him by the underground journal *Opinia*, the organ of the ROPCO group for the defence of human and civil rights in Poland. Mrs Carter and the President's Security Adviser, Zbigniew Brzezinski, himself Polish-born, had a two-hour meeting with Cardinal Wyszynski.

In January 1978 the Polish government published the texts of the two United Nations Covenants on Human Rights in the official gazette. Unlike the Final Act of the Helsinki Conference, these were binding international agreements. They had already appeared in unofficial Polish publications, but the human rights campaigners had maintained that the Covenants could have no legal effect in Poland until they were listed in the official gazette and this action helped to strengthen the legal foundations on which the dissidents based their case.

A month later, the Polish Vice-Minister for Culture, Janusz Wilhelmi, admitted that censorship restrictions might be excessive and said that he proposed to set up a joint committee of Polish writers and Ministry officials to consider appeals against censorship. At the same time, it was reported that the Polish Club for Catholic Intellectuals, an officially recognised body, had held a five-day seminar on human rights attended by 400 of its members.

This sequence of events clearly holds out hopes of a more conciliatory attitude by the Polish Communist regime in its treatment of human rights, though further proofs are still needed to confirm it. On the other hand, the Polish authorities have already made long overdue reforms in their economic policies which indicate a new willingness to recognise public grievances and to seek public support in dealing with them. A main source of discontent is the scarcity of meat, largely caused by the priority given to industrial development at the expense of farming, and a shortage of animal foodstuffs due to the lack of foreign currency to pay for their import. The private farmers were often reduced to slaughtering livestock which they could not feed and many small farms were not worked because the Communist state denied them the help they needed.

In 1977 the government introduced new measures to assist the farmers. Industrial investment, which took 40% of the national income in 1975, was reduced by one third for the next four-year period from 1977 to 1981. Pensions for private farmers were increased, thus enabling them to retire earlier, and farmers who previously received no pension if they handed over to one of their family were now allowed to have one. Credit facilities for new farm buildings were granted and the joint ownership of agricultural machinery by small groups of private farmers was financially assisted. The government hoped by these means to keep farm incomes in line with industrial wages and to secure increases in food supplies which would remove the need for drastic rises in food prices and avoid the violent public reactions to them.

Another source of popular grievance is the chronic inefficiency of the state-run shops and the long hours spent in queues to get even the most basic articles, if they are not already sold out beforehand. Shoddy goods and rudeness from badly-paid shop assistants rub salt into these wounds. In November 1977 a government decree was issued allowing private operators to take over state shops in return for a fixed annual payment. This was limited to shops employing not more than four people and did not include the private sale of meat, alcohol, jewellery or foreign goods. There were already 20,000 private shops in Poland leased from the state, but they were heavily taxed and could only buy their stock from private craftsmen and producers. The new order permits them to buy from state enterprise and co-operative farms, while their tax burden is reduced and they can take out longer leases. These better terms produced thousands of applications, many coming from young married couples.

These economic changes and their encouragement of 'petty bourgeois capitalist elements' represent a major departure from Communist doctrine in the past and could have political and social results indirectly affecting the treatment of human rights in Poland. Western visitors to Warsaw are struck by the number of Poles who can afford to eat in expensive restaurants, drive large foreign cars, keep a country cottage outside Warsaw, and enjoy many other luxuries formerly reserved for the Communist ruling class. Compared with the poor living conditions of most Poles, the 'new rich' are only a tiny minority, but the sources of their wealth are not hard to find and much of it actually benefits from Communist rule. All business concerns employing fewer than twenty-five people are privately owned. An efficient private farmer with enough land to be cultivated by modern methods can now earn a substantial income. The speculators in foreign currency make big profits in a black-market which flourishes openly and is officially tolerated. Many Poles freely receive hard currency remittances from relations living abroad, particularly from the United States, which also help to relieve the Polish government from its desperate shortage of foreign exchange. Since 1974 Polish citizens have been allowed to open bank accounts in Western currencies and only a year later, at the end of 1975, there were over 300,000 of these accounts with a total of $141 million; an ironical contrast with the prohibition of private foreign currency holdings in democratic Britain.

The situation in Poland in the spring of 1979 shows an enigmatic mixture of fantasy and reality. The Communist rulers and the Polish people seem to be living in two different worlds which have drifted so far apart that no bridge can be built between them. The Communist masters look like superannuated actors mechanically repeating their lines in an empty theatre while the real life of the country goes on outside without them.

The human rights campaigners are gaining in strength and confidence. The independent writers are defeating the censorship by getting their work printed on underground duplicating machines and widely circulated, usually with the names of authors and editors openly stated. At least eight unofficial periodicals are appearing regularly despite police efforts to stop them by searching premises, seizing copies, and smashing underground presses. One of the clandestine literary journals *ZAPIS* is being published in English in London by *Index on Censorship* and in other Western language editions. Many university students are attending private extra-mural seminars in which some professors also take part.

The Polish Communist leaders and their guardians in Moscow are thus facing some formidable problems and a difficult choice between compromise and coercion. Whether they can solve this equation without incurring worse trouble still remains to be seen, and only one thing is certain. Anything can happen in Poland and it usually does.

But even the Poles could not have foreseen the surprise election in October 1978 of the first Polish Pope in history, Cardinal Karol Wojtyla, Archbishop of Cracow. He had worked closely with Cardinal Wyszynski in defending human rights in Poland, while improving relations between the Roman Catholic Church and the Communist State. His election as Pope not only caused great rejoicing in Poland itself, but holds out new hopes for peace and reconciliation in a troubled world.

CHAPTER 3

THE CHARTER OF
PRAGUE

Unlike the developments in Poland, the human rights movement in Czechoslovakia did not spring from economic protest over wages and prices. Its origins go back to a struggle for power inside the Czechoslovak Communist Party after Stalin's death in 1953, between Stalinist diehards and a group of reformers led by Alexander Dubcek which wanted to abolish the worst abuses of Communist rule. They believed that such concessions would not weaken the Communist hold on the country but strengthen it by attracting public support which had previously been lacking. The Stalinists, on the other hand, viewed these ideas as a challenge to the overlords in Moscow and a threat to their own privileged positions.

The Party leader, Antonin Novotny, who succeeded Gottwald in 1967, was himself a Stalinist at heart. He was forced to make some minor changes but maintained the full rigours of a Communist state. Even after Khrushchev's denunciation of Stalin's crimes in 1956 and the 'rehabilitation' of his victims in Russia, dead and alive, Novotny delayed and obstructed a similar process in Czechoslovakia. Public feelings of anger and frustration were openly voiced by Communist writers and journalists, university professors, students, and economists who demanded changes in the rigid and inefficient system of state planning and management.

74

Dubcek came forward as the champion of reform and his position as First Secretary of the Slovak Communist Party enabled him to speak with authority. He gained support from other leading Communists and became, overnight, a popular hero. In January 1968, after much manoeuvring in the corridors of power, the Czechoslovak Party Central Committee decided to take action 'in accordance with the process of democratisation which has already begun'. Novotny was dismissed from the Party leadership and the functions of First Party Secretary and President of the Republic which he had combined in his own person were separated. Dubcek took his place as Party leader and Novotny lost his post as President in May 1968 when he was expelled from the Central Committee and suspended from Party membership. According to unofficial reports, Novotny telephoned Brezhnev to warn him against Dubcek's programme but the new Soviet leader refused to listen and banged down the receiver.

Dubcek was an experienced and ambitious politician who genuinely believed in reforms and he was well regarded in Moscow. He received a message of congratulations from Brezhnev on his appointment as Party leader and went to Moscow for consultations. An official announcement said that these talks had resulted in 'a full identity of views on all questions discussed'. But despite this promising start, Dubcek soon found himself in an impossible position. If the reforms he advocated could have been introduced a few years earlier and applied in gradual stages, the Soviet rulers might have been able to live with them and maintain full control. But in Czechoslovakia, as in Poland in 1956, the sudden release of pent-up grievances and anti-Soviet feelings swept away all restraint and found expression even in the Communist newspapers and broadcasts.

Dubcek's 'action programme' published in April 1968 promised a wide range of democratic reforms including freedom of speech, removal of press censorship, real powers for the National

Assembly, compensation for all victims of Stalinist injustice, and equal rights for Czechs and Slovaks. But these came too late to stem the tide of popular expectations, and Dubcek's warnings of Soviet reactions went unheeded. The Soviet leaders were kept well informed of events by their agents in Prague who included some old Stalinists still in key positions. These people urged the need for drastic action and their demands were echoed by Communist satellite leaders who feared the effects of unrest in Czechoslovakia on their own safety. The strongest pressure came from the East German leader, Walter Ulbricht, who saw in the Dubcek reforms a possibility of closer relations between Czechoslovakia and West Germany at East German expense, particularly in trade agreements.

The Kremlin delayed its decision for some months, apparently hoping that Dubcek might still drop his reforms and regain control of the situation, but in August 1968 Soviet forces invaded Czechoslovakia with support from the Warsaw Pact allies in East Germany, Poland, Hungary and Bulgaria. The invasion was not only a flagrant breach of international law but also a clear violation of the Warsaw Pact itself signed by the Soviet Union in 1955. Under *Article 8* of that treaty, the signatories agreed 'that they will act in the spirit of friendship and co-operation . . . adhering to the principles of mutual respect for their independence and sovereignty and of non-interference in their internal affairs'. A supplementary clause stated: 'Distribution of the joint armed forces on the territories of states that are parties to the treaty will be carried out in accordance with the requirements of mutual defence in agreement among those states.' The only Communist satellite voice raised against the invasion was that of the Rumanian leader Ceausescu, who publicly condemned it in strong terms and refused to support it with Rumanian troops. Nobody, he said, had the right to declare: *'Le Marxisme, c'est moi.'*

In Tito's Yugoslavia, the government expressed 'extreme concern over the illegal occupation of Czechoslovakia'. There was a spontaneous demonstration outside the Czechoslovak Embassy in Belgrade to express solidarity with the Czechoslovaks and it was addressed by two of Dubcek's Ministers who were on a visit at the time, Professor Ota Sik, a leading economist, and the Foreign Minister, Jiri Hajek. The Western powers made strong verbal protests but had no intention of intervening. The United Nations Security Council passed a resolution condemning the invasion but the Soviet Union killed it by using its veto for the 105th time.

The Kremlin found a willing servant in Gustav Husak, who had supported Dubcek in his reform policy but now deserted him and set up a puppet government obeying orders from Moscow. Dubcek was briefly removed to Turkey as Ambassador and virtually held as a prisoner in his own Embassy before being recalled home and relegated to provincial exile as an office clerk in Bratislava. He is still living there under strict police observation.

Husak had spent ten years in prison under Novotny and some people in Czechoslovakia hoped that he might still be able to salvage something from the wreck of Dubcek's reform programme. The Poles had welcomed Gomulka's return to power in 1956 for the same sort of reason, only to be bitterly disappointed and Husak was the same kind of unrepentant Stalinist. His prison experience merely seemed to have taught him that blind obedience to orders from Moscow was the only way to secure his lease of power and he acted on that assumption. His quisling government welcomed the Soviet invasion and endorsed Brezhnev's new doctrine asserting the right of the Soviet Union to intervene by force in any satellite country where 'socialism' was in danger. He ordered a wholesale purge of Dubcek supporters which was

77

carried out by the Minister of the Interior, Vasil Bilak, who like him had previously supported Dubcek but now also chose the winning side.

Husak's harsh measures created a political breach between 'ins' and 'outs' in Czechoslovakia as represented by the few who had sold out to Moscow and the many cast out in the wilderness. The latter provided a hard core of opposition from men and women who had inside knowledge of how the system worked and had learned the art of survival in a tough Communist school. But the first and most tragic demonstration of protest came from a group of students in Prague who decided to burn themselves alive rather than submit to Soviet dictation. The first to do so was Jan Palach who poured petrol over himself and set fire to it in Wenceslav Square in January 1969, an example followed by others. National emotions again overflowed two months later when Czechoslovakia beat the Soviet Union in the world ice-hockey championship and a wildly excited crowd wrecked the Prague offices of the Soviet airline Aeroflot.

About 75,000 to 80,000 people are believed to have escaped to West Germany or Austria when the Soviet invasion took place and among them were a number of Communists who had supported Dubcek in his plans for reform. Many others who had held responsible posts stayed on in the country hoping to exert a restraining influence on the Husak regime, but were sacked from their jobs or, in the case of writers, had their work banned from publication. An interesting example of the conflict of loyalties among Communists is given by the case of Jiri Pelikan.

An ardent Communist from his early youth, Pelikan was Chairman of the Central Students' Union under the Stalinist Novotny and was appointed Director-General of Czechoslovak television in 1963. In 1968, however, when Dubcek took over as Party leader, Pelikan joined the reformers and became Chairman of the Foreign Affairs Committee of the National Assembly.

Following the Soviet invasion, he helped to organise a secret Party Congress in Prague which opposed the Soviet occupation. In September 1968 he was dismissed from his television post and sent to the Czechoslovak Embassy in Rome as Counsellor for Press and Cultural Affairs, and in January 1969 he lost his position in the National Assembly. In September that year he ignored an order to return to Prague and went to London where he set up the Palach Press, a news agency named after the Czech student who killed himself in Prague, expressing the views of political exiles opposed to the Husak regime.

In an article, which appeared in *The Times* on 1 October 1969, Pelikan said that he had decided to emigrate after the Central Committee of the Czechoslovak Communist Party led by Husak passed resolutions approving of the Soviet invasion. He added that he could not go on serving a new Party leadership which condemned the Dubcek reforms as 'anti-revolutionary and anti-socialist' when he knew that they still had overwhelming support in his country. He refused to work for a regime which was gradually returning to the language and methods of the dogmatic Stalinist period and he called for the withdrawal of Soviet troops and the restoration of Dubcek's reform programme. In the same article, however, he said he had no sympathy with the views of 'anti-Communist and rightist circles at home and abroad which profess hatred of the Soviet Union'.

Shortly after Husak replaced Dubcek as Communist leader in April 1969, dissident writers and intellectuals smuggled out a message to the West which said:

We can be sentenced but we can never be forced to express anything we do not believe. We can be deprived of freedom of expression yet nobody can take from us our freedom of spirit, clarity of thought, and dignity . . .

When the officially sponsored Writers' Union was purged and

79

reorganised in the middle of 1971, only about 100 out of a former membership of 500 submitted their names as candidates. Books, pamphlets and poems by banned writers were produced in typed or roughly duplicated underground editions and passed on by readers from hand to hand. Opposition to the Husak regime continued among university students despite the official dissolution of their Independent Union which had been set up during Dubcek's brief tenure of power.

Husak's reply was a mixture of bribery and force. Writers and journalists who submitted to the new regime were well rewarded and those who refused to do so suffered harsh treatment. In 1972, for example, four Communist dissenters who had strongly supported Dubcek were arrested and brought to trial. These were Dr Milan Huebl, formerly Rector of the Communist Party training college; Jaroslav Sabata, formerly Party Secretary in Brno; Jiri Mueller, a leader of student protest against the Soviet invasion in 1968; and Antonin Rusek, an engineer and a former Party official in Brno. All four were charged with subversive activities. Sabata and Mueller were accused of organising a leaflet campaign against the Husak regime and urging voters to boycott the Communist election held in November 1971. The four men received prison sentences ranging from five to six and a half years.

Another Communist dissenter who suffered was Ludek Pachmann, the Czechoslovak chess grand master and a political journalist who had strongly supported Dubcek's reform programme. In 1968 he was one of the people who signed a liberal pamphlet entitled *Two Thousand Words* written by a dissident Communist author, Ludvik Vaculik. In August 1969 he was arrested after signing a document in which a group of intellectuals and state officials called for the withdrawal of Soviet troops and for passive resistance to the Husak policy of 'restoring order'. While in prison he was expelled from the Communist Party and so badly beaten up that he could not be brought to trial. He was released for hospital treatment pending trial and sentenced in May 1972 to two years' imprisonment, but set free immediately because of his bad health and the time he had already served in gaol. In November 1972, he was allowed to leave the country with his wife and mother-in-law.

The lengths to which the Husak regime was prepared to go to stamp out any kind of deviation from the Party line was shown by its harsh and ham-fisted treatment of 'pop music'. Communist doctrine looks with a jealous and puritanical eye on any form of social enjoyment which it does not control, especially when its origins are Western. During the 1960s, hundreds of rock and pop groups sprang up all over Czechoslovakia, but the Soviet invasion in 1968 injected expressions of protest into their songs and under Husak they were only allowed to perform in public if they accepted the new regime and served its propaganda. Those who did so were rewarded by lucrative contracts with the state radio and television services, but some refused to yield. One of the most talented groups, calling itself 'The Plastic People of the Universe', had its licence withdrawn but still went on performing at private parties, weddings, and birthday celebrations. They also took their songs from poets whose work expressed the frustration of life under Communist rule.

The security police took drastic measures to repress this new form of musical dissent. The worst use of force took place in March 1974 near Ceske Budejovice, when troops and police with dogs invaded a concert in which The Plastic People group was taking part. About 200 people were arrested and several of them were given prison sentences, but the musical 'maquis' continued its work. In March 1976 the police made over a hundred raids and numerous arrests of dissident performers and their supporters. Some of them were sent to prison for up to eighteen months on charges of 'disturbing the peace'.

Since then the authorities have drawn a sharp line between

orthodox jazz which has flourished in Czechoslovakia, and 'hard rock' music of a politically offensive kind. Thus, for example, they have tolerated the existence of a lively black-market in Prague where records by Western pop groups and singers change hands at high prices. But in April 1978 they arrested the leader of The Plastic People group, Ivan Jirous, a signatory of the Charter 77 manifesto, and sentenced him to eight months in prison. He was charged with 'hooliganism' as a result of remarks criticising the regime he was alleged to have made at the private opening of an art exhibition in Prague in 1977.

Husak showed his belief in the effectiveness of repression against dissenters when he claimed at a Communist Party Congress in April 1976 that the reformers were 'politically isolated' and 'absolutely bankrupt'. But he spoke too soon. Like many Western observers, he had not foreseen the dynamic effects of the renewed undertakings to respect human rights given by the Communist states in 1975 in the Helsinki agreements. In September 1975, only a month after the Helsinki Final Act, open letters of protest were issued by two political dissenters, both of them Communists who had been dismissed after holding responsible positions. One of them, Zdenek Mlynar, had been a member of the Communist Presidium, or governing body, under Dubcek and Secretary of the Communist Party Central Committee. The other, Karel Kaplan, had served as a Communist official on the 'rehabilitation' commissions set up by Novotny and Dubcek.

Mlynar's letter was an appeal to Communist and Socialist Parties in the West for their support of the dissenters. He said that the Helsinki Final Act 'should pose the moral obligation for every participating state at least to refrain from persecuting those of its citizens who upheld the principles of the Helsinki document even prior to its signature'. Much of his letter was devoted to giving proofs of his own early conversion to the Dubcek reform proposals and castigating those of his former colleagues who had deserted Dubcek for Husak. In November 1968, after the Soviet invasion, Mlynar resigned from his posts in the Party and government and found work as an entomologist in the Prague National Museum. He was expelled from the Communist Party in 1970.

Kaplan's letter was addressed to Vasil Bilak, Husak's Minister of the Interior and most powerful colleague. Like Mlynar, Kaplan quoted documentary evidence to show that he had been an early advocate of reforms, while Bilak had betrayed them. Kaplan was a Communist historian who served in 1963 on a commission appointed by Novotny to investigate Slovak political trials during the Stalin period, but he was dismissed for supporting an early and complete rehabilitation of the victims. In 1968 he took part in drafting Dubcek's 'action programme' and was Secretary of a new commission charged with speeding up rehabilitation. In 1970 he was dismissed from his post at the Historical Institute of the Czechoslovak Academy of Sciences, and compelled to find work as a stoker.

In November 1975 an open letter was sent to the Federal Assembly by three former members, Frantisek Kriegel, Gertruda Sekaninova-Cakrtova, and Frantisek Vodslon, who had supported the Dubcek plans for reform in 1968. They said that the situation in Czechoslovakia was in open contradiction with the provisions of the Helsinki declaration on human rights and basic liberties. They called on the Assembly to remedy the situation as soon as possible by reviewing all laws, rules and directives that restricted the freedoms of citizens.

These isolated protests did not shake Husak's belief that he was in full command of the situation, and in December 1975 the four dissenters imprisoned in 1972, Milan Huebl, Jiri Mueller, Jaroslav Sabata, and Antonin Rusek, were released on probation. At the Communist Party Congress in April 1976 Husak announced that Party members expelled in the purges after the

Soviet invasion, when about half a million were struck off, could apply for readmission if they truly repented and proved their loyalty to the Party and the Soviet Union.

It must have come as a shock to the regime when, on 1 January 1977, a group of dissenters calling itself *Charter 77* issued a manifesto calling for the implementation of human rights. (Full text in *Appendix II*.) It was signed by 242 people who included intellectuals, writers, journalists, former politicians, professors, technicians, and workers. Three men were delegated as spokesmen for Charter 77: Vaclav Havel, a playwright with an international reputation; Professor Jan Patocka, a distinguished philosopher; and Dr Jiri Hajek, who had been Foreign Minister in 1968 under Dubcek.

The Charter manifesto began by pointing out that the Czechoslovak government had signed the two United Nations Covenants on Human Right in 1968, confirmed them in Helsinki in 1975, and given them legal status by publishing them in the collection of *Laws of Czechoslovakia*, No. 120, on 13 October 1976. It described in detail how these fundamental rights were being denied by suppressing freedom of expression; excluding dissenters from employment; discriminating against their children in education; prohibiting any creative or political activity differing from the official ideology; restricting religious freedom; interfering in private life by tapping telephones, opening letters and searching homes; refusing to allow workers to form independent unions or go on strike, and many other violations.

The signatories declared that they were not an organisation but a loose, informal, and open association of people of various shades of opinion, faiths and professions united by the will to strive individually and collectively for the respecting of civil and human rights in their own country and throughout the world. These rights, they pointed out, were given to all people by the two international covenants mentioned, by the Final Act of the

Helsinki Conference, and by many other international documents opposing war, violence and social or spiritual oppression, and are comprehensively laid down in the UN Universal Declaration of Human Rights.

The Chartists thus made it clear that they were not engaged in subversion or conspiracy but only exercised a legal right to demand from the authorities the fulfilment of their international undertakings to respect human rights. This made their challenge all the more formidable, since it was difficult to find legal grounds for taking action against Chartists even under a Communist penal code.

The Husak regime began by launching a furious attack on the Charter in newspapers and broadcasts which denounced the signatories as traitors and agents of Western imperialism. This was no easy task for the journalists concerned, as they had not been supplied with copies of the Charter. Similarly, resolutions condemning the Charter were obtained from workers in factories and offices whose jobs depended on their obedience, but many people refused to sign and pointed out that, as the Charter had not been published, they could not be expected to denounce it without even knowing the contents. The Charter signatories received many messages of support from all over the country.

More drastic action quickly followed. On 17 January 1977 the police arrested four of the leading members of Charter 77. These were Vaclav Havel, already mentioned as a Charter spokesman, who had been dismissed from his post as a theatrical director in 1968 for his reformist views and had since worked as a brewery labourer; Jiri Lederer, a leader of student protest against the Soviet invasion in 1968 and a journalist expelled from the Communist Party for writing articles about student protests and anti-Semitism in Poland; Frantisek Pavlicek, a theatrical and film director expelled from the Party in 1970 as a supporter of Dubcek; and Ota Ornest, another theatrical director, also expelled from

85

the Party in 1970 for advocating reforms. Ornest was the only one of the four who had not signed the Charter, but it is worth noting that he worked from 1939 to 1945 as an editor in the Czech Service of the BBC in London.

The arrests in Prague unleashed a storm of Western protests, all the more so because unofficial reports said that the prisoners would be charged under sections of the penal code which could result in sentences of up to fifteen years' imprisonment or even death. In Communist Hungary a group of 34 intellectuals sent a message of support for Charter 77 to Pavel Kohout, a well-known writer and Charter signatory. Strong protests and demands for the release of the Charter prisoners were made by Communist Parties in Western Europe. In Paris an international committee of writers and intellectuals was set up to support the Charter principles. The American State Department issued a statement strongly condemning violations of human rights wherever they occurred and protesting against the failure of the Czechoslovak government to respect its pledges on human rights in the Helsinki agreements. The Norwegian government broke off negotiations with the Czechoslovak government for a trade agreement. The Dutch Prime Minister, Joop den Uyl, told a press conference that the authorities in Prague were punishing people who sought nothing more than the implementation of the Helsinki Accord, adding that this was particularly serious in view of the follow-up conference due to be held later in 1977 in Belgrade.

In the neighbouring state of Austria, the Chancellor, Dr Kreisky, also condemned the arrests as a gross breach of the Helsinki agreements and offered asylum in Austria to Charter 77 members if they applied for, and received, Czechoslovakian exit permits. The Austrian branch of Amnesty International announced that it would give all possible help to Charter 77 and launched a campaign for Austrian public support.

On the day the four leading Chartists were arrested, a statement was issued by the two remaining spokesmen, Professor Patocka and Dr Hajek, protesting against the dismissals of Professors Frantisek Jiranek and Radim Palous from the Charles University in Prague because they had signed the Charter. A week later, on 23 January 1977, another Charter document was issued calling for an end to discrimination by the regime in selecting candidates for higher education. It said that the authorities judged applicants by their family background and not on their academic merits. They rejected those from families which were politically suspect, either because they were regarded as 'capitalists'; or because they had fathers or brothers who had joined the Western forces to fight Nazi Germany; or because they had relations who had emigrated to the West after the war; or because the family was religious.

The Husak regime did its utmost to isolate and silence the Chartists by cutting off their contacts with the West and making their lives a misery. They were subjected to constant police searches and interrogations, threats of arrest, dismissal from their jobs, interference with their letters and telephone calls, and anonymous letters threatening them with death. Some of the most active dissenters could not endure the pressures on themselves and their families, and accepted an offer of exit permits which enabled them to seek asylum in Austria.

In January 1977, shortly after the arrests of the four prominent dissenters, a Prague television broadcast accused the British Embassy of 'espionage activities' and implied that they were connected with the imprisoned men. The British Foreign Office flatly rejected these allegations. Early in February, an American television reporter, Leslie Collit, was taken off a train on the Czechoslovakian side of the Austrian frontier while on his way to Vienna, and his notes were confiscated. On 12 February the *New York Times* Balkans correspondent, Paul Hoffman, was also removed from a train while travelling to Vienna. The police confiscated his notes and documents, held him in an unheated room for eleven hours without food, and then made him walk two miles to cross the frontier. The United States protested strongly in both these cases. On 14 February a West German reporter, Walter Kratzer, was detained for an hour at another frontier post, after being interrogated in Prague about his contacts with Charter 77 signatories. The Czechoslovakian Foreign Ministry refused to grant an entry visa to a *Christian Science Monitor* correspondent, Eric Bourne, unless he gave an undertaking not to contact any dissenters. He rejected this condition and withdrew his application.

On 27 January six leading Charter members were summoned to the Passport and Visa Office in Prague, namely Milan Huebl, Jiri Hajek, Frantisek Kriegel, Zdenek Mlynar, Pavel Kohout, and Ludvik Vaculik. Vaculik refused to attend on the grounds that he had not applied for a visa. The other five were told that they could leave for Austria without losing their Czechoslovak nationality but they all rejected the offer. A fortnight later, Huebl tried to visit Dubcek in Bratislava but was stopped at the door by police guards who warned him not to set foot in Bratislava again if he valued his health. The Austrian Chancellor, Dr Kreisky, denounced this attempt to force dissenters into exile.

On 29 January the two remaining Charter spokesmen, Jan Patocka and Jiri Hajek, were called to the Public Prosecutor's office and warned that the Charter was illegal, and so was its distribution abroad and any activities connected with it. They were told that the Charter could not be considered as an application of the right of petition allowed in the Czechoslovak constitution. Civil rights could only be exercised 'in harmony with the interests of the working people' and 'with due regard for the interests of the socialist state', as specified under *Articles 28, 29, and 34*. After this interview, Dr Hajek told Western journalists that it was still too early to judge the government's intentions, but further repressive measures might be taken. Professor Patocka stressed the complete legality of the Charter and denounced the police persecution. Both men referred to the warning as an attempt at intimidation.

On 3 February the Federal German and Austrian television services broadcast interviews with Pavel Kohout in which he welcomed controversy over the Charter, since it made people in Czechoslovakia realise that it contained nothing illegal. He said he wished for a dialogue with the government and hoped that sensible politicians could be found who would understand that human rights were not a matter for the police, but concerned relations between the authorities and the people. Kohout also revealed that he had received letters threatening to kill him which showed signs of being an officially organised campaign. The Zurich weekly *Die Weltwoche* published an interview with Milan Huebl in which he declared that he would not leave Czechoslovakia voluntarily.

The threat of assaults on dissenters was encouraged by Communist Press attacks on Charter 77 and it was no empty warning. Already, in November 1976, Frantisk Kriegel and his wife had narrowly escaped when two masked men broke into their flat and were only driven off by the intervention of neighbours. Kriegel was a Jewish dissenter and a month later a note was pinned to his door signed by '*La Main Noire*', calling itself a Palestinian terrorist group and saying that, if Kriegel went on supporting Israel, he would have to suffer the consequences. The Communist papers frequently accused Charter 77 of getting support from 'Zionist' sources abroad, as well as 'imperialists', and the regime seems to have tried to attribute the attack on Kriegel to Arab terrorists. The police also made frequent raids on the homes of leading Chartists and on 11 January 1977, they broke into Kohout's flat, seized his wife in the street, and took them both off for questioning.

On 4 February a new Charter document, No. 5, was issued in Prague by Patocka and Hajek giving a list of another 208 people who had signed the Charter, bringing the number up to 448. They included intellectuals, workers, and several priests. Their names were revealed at their own request and the document was notified to the authorities. This was to prevent a repetition of official objections that the original Charter manifesto had been first released to Western journalists. On the same day, it was reported from Prague that at least seven Western ambassadors – those of Austria, Britain, the Netherlands, Norway, Portugal, Sweden and the United States – had been summoned by the Deputy Foreign Minister, Dusan Spacil, to receive protests of 'interference by their governments in Czechoslovak internal affairs'.

Another Western news agency report from Prague on 8 February said that Professor Patocka and Dr Hajek had sent a letter to the Federal Assembly rejecting the Public Prosecutor's claim that Charter 77 was illegal and questioning his authority to interpret the Constitution. This authority, the letter said, was vested in the Constitutional Court which had never been set up. The two Charter spokesmen also maintained their contacts with Western countries through newspaper articles, broadcast interviews and letters. On 8 and 10 February the French national radio network broadcast a telephone talk with Dr Hajek, after explaining that it had been interrupted by the disconnection of his telephone in Prague. On 9 February the Swiss journal *Blick* published an interview with Jiri Hajek in which the former Foreign Minister repeated the Chartist demand that the human rights guaranteed in the Constitution should be implemented. The Czechoslovak Constitution, like those of the Soviet Union and all the satellites, does indeed provide formal guarantees for freedom of expression and assembly, inviolability of the person and the home, privacy of postal and other communications, freedom to profess religious beliefs, and the right to petition state organs. But it also contains the usual Communist catch – all clauses stipulating that these rights must be exercised in conformity with 'the interests of the working people and the socialist state' and with respect for the monopoly of power by the Communist Party.

The Paris paper *Le Monde* published on 9 February a letter from Jan Patocka to the International Committee set up in Paris in January to support the Charter. In it he pointed out that once the state put its signature to international agreements on human rights, it assumed the obligation to subordinate politics to law and not the other way round. Western correspondents also reported that the deposed Party leader, Dubcek, had denied allegations made in the Austrian Communist paper *Volksstimme* that he had refused to sign Charter 77. He was quoted as saying that he had no prior knowledge of it because he was under close police supervision, but it contained ideas which he himself had advocated previously and he therefore supported it.

On 14 February Pavel Kohout returned to the charge in three statements published in the West German paper *Frankfurter Allgemeine Zeitung*. The first was an explanation of his refusal to accept the Communist offer of emigration to Austria. The second was a copy of a letter he had sent to the Public Prosecutor asking for the punishment of letter-writers threatening to kill him. The third was an appeal to Czechoslovak journalists not to take part in the propaganda campaign to discredit Charter 77 by false accusations against its aims and contents. On 9 February a petition by Amnesty International for the release of the arrested Charter supporters, signed by over 15,000 Austrians headed by the Chancellor, Dr Kreisky, was handed to the Czechoslovak Ambassador in Vienna who refused to accept it.

The Husak regime had little to show for its efforts to silence the human rights campaigners by intimidation, by trying to cut off their communications with the West, or by forcing them to seek refuge in Austria. Signs of alarm in the Kremlin were manifested by the despatch of a Soviet delegation to Prague led by Ivan Kapitonov, Secretary of the Soviet Party Central Committee and a close colleague of Brezhnev, for talks with the Czechoslovak leaders; and by the presence in Moscow from 8 to 15 February 1977 of a Czechoslovak delegation led by Antonin Kapek, a member of the Czechoslovak Presidium or governing body. Nothing was disclosed about the talks in Prague beyond the conventional announcement that the talks had shown 'unity of views on all questions'. In Moscow, however, Kapek delivered a fierce onslaught on the Charter. In an article published in *Pravda*, he denounced it as 'an anti-state pamphlet backed by a handful of self-appointed individuals and saboteurs supported by Western reaction'. In another newspaper interview he described the Charter signatories as 'counter-revolutionaries and political adventurers from the years 1968-69' and said their aim was to wreck detente and disrupt preparations for the impending Belgrade conference.

Charter 77 responded by issuing another document, No. 6, on 17 February, which called for the release of Havel, Lederer, Pavlicek, and Ornest, still in prison. The document added that, if the authorities refused to release them, they should give their reasons and reveal the charges. It also gave new information about reprisals against the Chartists. Nearly all the original Charter signatories, numbering 242, had been subjected to police interrogation. The police had searched the homes of 41 signatories and confiscated personal letters, other written material and typewriters. Twelve people had been sacked from their jobs for signing the Charter and five expelled from trade unions or 'socialist worker brigades'. Many others had received warnings. Hajek and Patocka were again interrogated on 17 February 1977, at the Ministry of the Interior and told that the Charter was 'strictly a matter for the police and the courts'.

Also on 17 February Frantisek Kriegel spoke out boldly in an interview published by the West German paper *Die Welt*. He was a prominent signatory of Charter 77, having been a member of the Party Presidium and President of the National Front under Dubcek. In his interview Kriegel described Czechoslovakia as a country occupied by the Soviet Union, and said that the situation was worse than it had been under Stalin because far more people were now suffering under the Husak regime. He also made a perceptive analysis of the different forms which the human rights campaigns took in the Soviet bloc, quoting as examples the major role of the Roman Catholic Church in Poland, the importance of freedom to emigrate in East Germany, and the quest for democracy in the Soviet Union where it had never existed. The Czechs, as Kriegel pointed out, had known it even under the Habsburgs.

Support for Charter 77 in a practical form came from an announcement by Amnesty International in London on 18 February that its national groups in ten countries were working on behalf of the four dissenters under arrest. Vaclav Havel had been 'adopted' as a political prisoner by Austria, Switzerland and the Netherlands; Lederer by Federal Germany, France and Austria; Pavlicek by Italy, Denmark and Norway; and Ornest by Denmark, Sweden and Britain.

Faced with the stubborn refusal of the Chartists to cease their activities, the Communist authorities increased their pressures and added new ones. The most active members had their telephones cut off or removed, their driving licences withdrawn, and their cars confiscated on some trivial pretext. A former popular singer, Marta Kubisova, was told that she might be allowed to perform again if she withdrew her signature from the Charter, but she refused to do so. Two Charter supporters in Northern Bohemia, Vladimir Lastuvka, an engineer and physicist, and Ales Machacek, an agronomist, were arrested late in January

1977 and charged with 'incitement to riot'. This was based on allegations that they had distributed copies of the Charter and were in possession of newspapers published by Czechoslovak exiles. They were held in prison to await trial.

A major diplomatic incident occurred in Prague when the Dutch Foreign Minister, Max van der Stoel, paid an official visit at the end of February 1977. He was reported to have told the Czechoslovak Foreign Minister, Bohuslav Chnoupek, that the treatment of human rights defenders by the Husak government conflicted with the letter and spirit of the Helsinki agreements and cast a shadow over the forthcoming Belgrade conference. He asked the government to let him read the main points of the Charter in a Czechoslovak television broadcast and offered equal time on Dutch television for the Czechoslovak authorities to explain their own position. The exchange was refused. The Dutch Foreign Minister also agreed to meet a Charter spokesman, Professor Jan Patocka, in the hotel where he was staying and had a private talk with him.

The Husak regime put on a great show of virtuous indignation which was expressed in a flood of outraged protests in the Communist papers and broadcasts. Two Dutch journalists who accompanied Max van der Stoel to Prague went to visit the other Charter spokesman, Dr Hajek, at his home but were stopped by police stationed outside and only allowed to enter after a long argument. After coming out, they were taken to a police station and interrogated, but were allowed to leave after refusing to answer questions. On 4 March the Dutch Prime Minister, Joop den Uyl, told a press conference that his government fully supported the Foreign Minister's conduct in Prague and that a cabinet meeting had 'emphatically endorsed' his interview with Patocka. At the same time ninety-two Yugoslav intellectuals signed a message of encouragement to the Charter spokesmen and addressed it to the International Committee for the Support of Charter 77 set up in Paris. A similar message of solidarity was signed by about sixty Soviet dissenters, including Dr Sakharov.

Another visitor to Prague at the beginning of March was the Soviet Minister of the Interior, General Nikolai Shchelokov. His arrival coincided with the meeting between the Dutch Foreign Minister and Professor Patocka and it may have played a decisive part in the tragic death of Patocka which followed on 13 March. After his meeting with the Dutch Foreign Minister, he was subjected to intensive police interrogation for ten hours without a break until he collapsed and was taken to hospital. The police pursued him even to his bedside and gave him no rest. He died of a cerebral haemorrhage, but he was the victim of what can only be described as a judicial murder. His last statement, written as he lay dying, is one of the most eloquent and moving chapters in the annals of human rights. The opening paragraph is quoted here:

Many people ask whether Charter 77 will not lead to increased 'vigilance', which in turn will have an adverse effect on all citizens. Let us be frank about this. In the past, no conformity has yet led to any improvement in the situation, only a worsening. The greater the fear and servility, the more brazen the authorities have become. There is no way to make them relax the pressure other than by showing them that injustices and discrimination are not ignored. What is needed is for people to behave at all times with dignity, not to allow themselves to be frightened and intimidated, and to speak the truth – behaviour which is impressive just because it is in such contrast with the way the authorities carry on . . .

Those Western observers who argue that we should not make a fuss about human rights in Eastern Europe for fear of disturbing relations with the Soviet Union, or because it only makes the dissenters suffer worse, have much to learn from Jan Patocka's testament.

His funeral, conducted by two Catholic priests, was attended by over a thousand mourners who were photographed by the security police. The police prevented leading Charter members from leaving their homes for the funeral, including Hajek, Kriegel, Mlynar, and Vaculik. Kohout slipped out of this net by staying away from home on the night before he attended the funeral. Huebl was intercepted on his way there. The Embassies of Federal Germany, the United States and the Netherlands sent representatives, and messages of sympathy came from many foreign sources including a group of twenty Soviet campaigners for human rights and members of the Polish Workers' Defence Committee who said they would fight on for the Charter principles and ideals.

With the death of Patocka and the continued detention of Vaclav Havel, Dr Hajek was the only remaining Charter spokesman and he himself was virtually under house arrest like other leading members. But somehow or other the human rights movement managed to carry on with its work. On 8 March, a few days before Patocka died, it issued Charter document No. 7, dealing with social and labour questions. This admitted that the guaranteed right to work gave greater social security but listed many restrictions on it, among them being the state monopoly of employment, obstacles to a free choice of work, a virtual compulsion to accept work of any kind to avoid being prosecuted as a 'parasite', Communist Party interference and nepotism, and the ban on independent trade unions. This was quickly followed by document No. 8 which claimed that the number of Charter signatories had risen to 619, including 160 workers, nearly 150 members of academic professions, 34 artists, 24 writers, 47 journalists, 1 police officer and 1 army officer.

On 14 March the authorities released Frantisek Pavlicek pending his trial. He had serious heart trouble and this sudden solicitude was probably due to the embarrassment which another death, so soon after that of Patocka, might have caused to his gaolers. The persecution of Charter supporters still continued unabated by repeated interrogations, dismissals from work, and house searches in Prague and elsewhere. It is a criminal offence in Czechoslovakia to possess a duplicating machine without a licence and the security police keep a specimen typeface of the various makes of typewriters. A report issued by Amnesty International on 27 March gave examples of human rights violations in Czechoslovakia and pointed out that the Communist laws made almost any political or public form of dissent liable to prosecution. It estimated that there were between 50 and 100 prisoners of conscience in Czechoslovakia, not counting an unknown number of people sentenced by provincial courts and military tribunals.

In April and May 1977 there were some indications that the measures taken by the regime against Charter communications with the West were having an effect. There was a marked decrease in the number of interviews given to Western journalists in Prague by leading Charter dissenters and reproduced in Western newspapers and broadcasts. Western support for the Charter continued, but on a smaller scale and mostly from unofficial sources. The Vice-Chancellors of sixteen British universities addressed a letter to the Czechoslovak government through its Ambassador in London, pointing out that Czechoslovakia had accepted international covenants to uphold academic freedom but denied basic rights to people working in that field. A petition for the release of Vaclav Havel and his fellow-prisoners was signed by more than 1,200 people working in the British theatre and taken to the Czechoslovak Embassy by a delegation led by Tom Stoppard, who described conditions in the Czechoslovak police state so graphically in his TV play *Professional Foul*, but they were refused entry. The letter was then sent to the Embassy by registered post. The well-known Yugoslav Communist dissenter, Milovan Djilas, in an article published by the Italian Socialist paper *La Repubblica*, described Charter 77 as the most mature and complete programme of human rights to come out of Eastern Europe since the last war.

On 29 April the authorities struck another blow at the Charter by putting three prominent signatories under house arrest to stop them from being visited by Western journalists or talking to West European Communists who were in Prague at the time for a conference with other Communist Parties. The three men were Venek Silhan, an economist who had deputised as Party leader for Dubcek when he was taken to Moscow in 1968 as a prisoner; Milan Huebl, the former Rector of the Party political college, released from prison in December 1976 after being kept there for over four years; and Peter Uhl, a former teacher and Trotskyite sentenced to prison in 1971 and released in 1975.

Western correspondents also reported that at least six other Charter supporters had been put under house arrest at the end of April. These were Jiri Nemec, a psychologist and Vera Jirousova, an art historian, both Charter signatories; Milan Vopalka and a man identified only as 'Mr Auld', who were described as 'unorthodox musicians and artists'; Svatopluk Karasek, a former Protestant minister and pop singer; and Vaclav Benda, a mathematician.

Despite these reverses, Charter 77 issued another document, No. 9, on 29 April which was signed by the Charter spokesman, Jiri Hajek, although he was under house arrest. It called on the government to lift its restrictions on religious freedom and honour its pledges on human rights under the Constitution and in accordance with its commitments undertaken in the UN Covenants, which had been incorporated into Czechoslovakian law in 1976. The document condemned the use of pressure to make people in state employment renounce their religious beliefs. It insisted that participation in public life must not be restricted to Marxist-Leninist adherents, but should be open to all citizens regardless of their beliefs. Parents should not be penalised for sending their children to receive religious instruction, nor should the children be made to suffer for it. The ban on imports of religious literature should be lifted and the Churches should be free to hold conferences and meetings.

The Roman Catholic Church is the largest in Czechoslovakia but its position is very different from that of the Church in Poland. When the Communists seized power in 1948, the number of Catholics was estimated at nine million, including about half a million of the Eastern or Uniate creed. The clergy numbered nearly 7,000, of whom about 1,100 belonged to religious orders. At the end of 1972 the active Catholic clergy were estimated at about 3,500, only half the 1948 figure, and many of them were prevented by the regime from carrying out their duties. This decline was the result of systematic Communist persecution. In the early post-war years, many Catholic bishops and priests were imprisoned, depriving the Church of its active leaders. In 1952 the Communist government broke off relations with the Vatican and this prevented the appointment of new cardinals and bishops to fill the vacancies until January 1978, when the Communist government accepted the Pope's nomination of Cardinal Frantisek Tomasek as Archbishop of Prague. It has also become very difficult to replace parish priests when they die or retire, partly because the authorities abolish the living unless it is filled within three months and partly because they limit the number of students for the priesthood at Church seminaries to a level far below the needs.

All monasteries and convents were dissolved overnight in April 1950, and the treatment of nuns has exceeded even the normal standards of Communist brutality. Thousands of Czechoslovak nuns were driven out of their convents and many of them died in prisons or labour camps. In 1968, during the false dawn of Dubcek's reform proposals, many nuns were allowed to resume parish work in the cities, but in 1972 the Husak regime forcibly removed them and sent them to work in mental hospitals, state farms and factories. Their conditions are described in an eyewitness report by one who suffered:

Our nuns are being physically destroyed by the irregular meals and disturbed rest at night. The first shift leaves for work at four in the morning and returns at three in the afternoon. The second shift works from one in the morning and returns at six. They return pale and exhausted, famished, drenched with dirty water, especially those working in the wool-washing department. For the most part, their health is ruined. Some have grown deaf through the din of the machines. Many are suffering from TB owing to under-nourishment and lack of exercise and fresh air. Others show symptoms of nervous disease. Even the Communist press has admitted that half of them are tubercular. Of course, they do not mention that this is the result of inhuman labour conditions, but blame convent life which, they say, 'is bad for health'. (From *Nuns* by Marcelle Bernstein. Collins, London, 1976)

Priests who correspond with the West are interrogated and threatened by the political police. Any conversation between a priest and a foreign visitor must be reported to the police with a written account of its purpose, duration and contents. Atheist teaching is an integral part of education at all levels. The regime has sponsored an association of submissive Catholic clergy called, ironically, *Pacem in Terris*, which claims to act as spokesman for the Church in its relations with the state and obediently toes the Communist Party line on all subjects. It has joined in the Communist attacks on Charter 77, but there are several independent Catholic theologians and priests among the Charter signatories, the best known being Dr Josef Zverina, who helped many Jews during the Nazi German occupation. So did Cardinal Stepan Trochta, who spent many years in both Nazi and Communist prisons and said shortly before his death: 'They want to liquidate the Church in a cold way.'

There are several different Protestant creeds in Czechoslovakia, the largest being the National or Hussite Church, as it is now called. In 1970 its membership was said to be about 650,000 and its priests included 80 women. There is also a smaller Evangelical Church of Czech Brethern, a Slovak Lutheran Church, a Reformed Church in Slovakia, a Silesian Luthern Church and a Baptist Church which has less than 6,000 professed members but probably attracts twice as many more to its services throughout the country. All these churches have been compelled to submit to Communist orders but there are still individual Christians among them who stand up for human rights. For example, in April 1977, the West German paper *Frankfurter Allgemeine Zeitung* reported that six Bohemian Brethren had signed Charter 77 and had explained their action in a letter circulating in Czechoslovakia. They said that they saw 'a reflection of the saving power of our Lord' whenever people tried to liberate themselves from despotism. They supported the Charter because it matched the historical heritage of the Czech Reformation and the martyrdom of Jan Hus.

On 4 May it was reported from Prague that Charter 77 had sent another document signed by Dr Hajek, No. 10, to the Czechoslovak authorities, reviewing events since the Charter manifesto appeared in January and proposing conditions for 'a meaningful dialogue' on human rights. These conditions were: a stop to the campaign against Charter 77 and the annulment of all illegal steps taken against its signatories; the re-publication on a larger scale of the official gazette containing the two UN Covenants on human rights; respect for the right of petition laid down in the Constitution; the revision of Czechoslovak laws to make them conform to international agreements on human rights; and action against Communist officials, members of the security police, and journalists who made threats of violence against the dissenters.

The Husak regime made renewed efforts to break up the

Charter movement by knocking out its leading members, and with some success. Vaclav Havel, the Charter spokesman arrested in January 1977, was released while awaiting trial. He told Western journalists that he had agreed not to make any public statements of a political kind and said he had withdrawn from his position as a Charter spokesman. He added that he would never revoke his signature of the Charter 77 manifesto and the moral commitment to it, but his withdrawal was a serious loss to the dissenters.

They suffered further losses in May and June 1977 when several other prominent Chartists decided to accept offers of exit permits and leave for Austria. Among them were Zdenek Mlynar, Milan Huebl, Jan Tesar, Jaroslav Krejci, Jan Lestinsky and Ivan Binar, all of whom had been subjected to severe pressures. Tesar, for example, was a historian who had spent four years in prison and was unable to find work after his release in 1976. Huebl, after his four years in prison, was barred from working as a historian. His daughter was refused admission to an institute of higher education although she passed the examination three times, while his son was excluded from a technical college and forced to work as a labourer. Karel Kaplan, another Charter signatory mentioned earlier, also emigrated. In May 1977 he claimed to have smuggled out of Czechoslovakia a dossier of microfilms and copies of secret papers which gave information on Soviet moves since 1948, including a plan prepared by Stalin for a possible invasion of Western Europe.

Undeterred by these setbacks, Charter 77 issued another document in July 1977, No. 12, examining the effects of Communist censorship on literature and culture. It gave the names of 130 writers banned from publication and said that the membership of the Writers' Union had been reduced by successive purges from 400 to 164. It also reported that about 90 writers who left Czechoslovakia after the Soviet invasion had been blacklisted and many books by well-known authors had been withdrawn from public libraries. Many writers were only permitted to work as translators or write books for children.

The authorities reacted sharply to this continued opposition. On 9 July they arrested Jan Princ, a Charter signatory, while he was giving a farewell party at his home in Prague for a Canadian translator, Paul Wilson, who had been ordered to leave the country a few days earlier. Wilson had been living in Prague for ten years and had made friends among the Charter supporters. Princ was sentenced to three months in prison for 'disturbing the peace', apparently because he had invited unauthorised pop music players to perform at his party. Late in September, a court in Northern Bohemia sentenced Ales Machacek and Vladimir Lastuvka to three and a half years in prison after they had been held for nine months awaiting trial.

Charter 77 promptly replied with a statement signed by its one remaining spokesman, Dr Hajek, saying that the movement would increase its efforts to draw attention to cases where human rights were being violated. Dr Hajek announced that the two vacant places of Charter spokesmen caused by the death of Jan Patocka and the withdrawal of Vaclav Havel would be filled by Dr Ladislav Hejdanek, a philosopher, and Marta Kubisova, a popular singer. He also reported that the number of Charter signatories had risen to over 800.

In October 1977 the Husak regime decided to bring to trial the four Chartists arrested in January that year. These were Vaclav Havel, temporarily released pending trial; Frantisek Pavlicek, who had also been let out of prison on grounds of bad health; and Jiri Lederer and Ota Ornest who had remained in custody. They were all charged with 'subversive activities' under *Article 98* of the penal code which the prosecution defined as having illegal contacts with Western agencies and slandering the state in documents secretly sent out of the country. Ornest pleaded guilty and received a prison sentence of three and a half years. Lederer was sentenced to three years. Pavlicek was sentenced to seventeen months, suspended for three years and Havel to fourteen months, also suspended for three years. As in most Communist political trials, the court was closed to the public and Western correspondents were refused admission.

These sentences, though relatively mild by Communist standards, were passed only a fortnight after the opening of the Belgrade Review Conference on European Security and Co-operation. They clearly expressed the belief of the Husak government that it had nothing to fear from Western attempts to raise the issue of human rights in the Belgrade discussions, a belief fully justified by events. But the Charter 77 movement, though battered, still fought on.

In December 1977 it issued a further report protesting against the harsh treatment of nonconformist pop music groups and gave detailed evidence. In January 1978 another report was issued to mark the first anniversary of the Charter 77 movement, signed by Dr Hajek, Professor Hejdanek, and Marta Kubisova as the Charter spokesmen. It called for the release of all political prisoners and appealed to the Husak regime for a 'dialogue' on public grievances. The three leaders also announced that the list of Charter signatories had risen from its original figure of 242 to 932. The text of this statement was telephoned to Vienna and released by Czechoslovak *émigré* dissenters. In February 1978 yet another report appeared, No. 15, which was described as 'Charter 78' and said that the Chartists would direct their efforts to persuading the authorities to remove the contradictions between Czechoslovak law and the international covenants on human rights which the government had signed and ratified.

The situation then resolved itself into a test of endurance between the dissenters and the Husak regime. The Chartists braced themselves to maintain their defence of human rights and the

Husak regime, contrary to its earlier hysterical reactions, settled down to a war of attrition against its opponents. Already in January 1978 Vaclav Havel, the actor Pavel Landovsky, and the musician Jaroslav Kukal were arrested while trying to enter a ball organised by railwaymen in Prague and were temporarily detained. Another prominent Chartist, the distinguished playwright Pavel Kohout, was knocked unconscious by the police.

The Communist leader, Gustav Husak, visited West Germany in April 1978 and signed an agreement to expand scientific, educational, and cultural exchanges. He met with a mixed reception. The former chess grandmaster Ludek Pachmann, one of many Czechoslovak exiles living in West Germany, bluntly described Husak as a quisling at a press conference in Bonn. Cardinal Joseph Hoffner of Cologne, head of the Roman Catholic Church in West Germany, called on the Prague government to change its repressive policies. Husak told Western journalists that there were 'very few' political prisoners in his country and said they has been sentenced for violating specific laws and not for expressing their views.

Charter 77 took a hard knock in April 1978 when its senior spokesman, the former Foreign Minister Dr Jiri Hajek, resigned from this position. Observers in Prague said he was exhausted by police persecution and also by disagreements within the Charter movement. The questions in dispute were not revealed, but they may have arisen from differences between Communist and non-Communist dissenters similar to the appearance of two human rights movements in Poland. Dr Hajek's place was taken by Professor Sabata, former Dean of the Faculty of Philosophy at Brno University, who was himself arrested on 1 October and beaten up by the security police when he tried to meet some Polish dissidents. This led 52 Czechoslovaks, not all of them Chartists, to appeal to Western Socialist leaders to support Dr Sabata, 'a test case for international opinion', by sending observers to his trial and demanding that it be held in public. He received a nine-month prison sentence in January 1979 for 'threatening and slandering an official'.

The two new spokesmen for Charter 77, Marta Kubisova and Ladislav Hejdanek, sent a long open letter to Dr Kurt Waldheim, the UN Secretary General, with copies to all Heads of State who signed the Helsinki Accords. They appealed for more attention to be paid to the harassment and persecution to which anyone active in defending human rights was subjected, claiming that more than 1,000 Charter 77 members had been bullied to such an extent that the whole country was 'living in an atmosphere of fear . . . People are not only afraid to express their opinions but are even afraid to keep company with those who do so'. This moving appeal coincided with the condemnation of the Czechoslovak government by the governing body of the ILO which by a large majority vote accused it of 'hounding' Charter 77 signatories and depriving them of their jobs.

As Professor Patocka wrote in his deathbed statement:

We thus have to report that people are again aware that there are things for which it is worthwhile to suffer: that the things for which one may have to suffer are often those which make life worth living: that without these things, art, literature, culture and so on are mere crafts engaged in to earn one's daily bread. All this we know today and to a large extent this knowledge is due to Charter 77.

That message should be heeded wherever freedom is in danger. The human rights campaigners in Czechoslovakia know that a long and perilous path lies ahead of them and they look for support to Western governments and public opinion. If we value our own liberties, that appeal cannot and must not be ignored.

CHAPTER 4

ANTI-CLIMAX IN
HUNGARY

The Hungarian Communist regime is the only Soviet ally in
Eastern Europe which has succeeded in winning some measure
of respect and co-operation from its own people. Its leader, Janos
Kadar, has done much to heal the deep wounds left by the bloody
suppression of the Hungarian national revolt by Khrushchev in
1956. He has reversed Lenin's maxim that 'he who is not with us
is against us' and declared that 'he who is not against us is with
us'. Kadar has reached a sort of tacit understanding with his subjects. They have learned to live with him and he with them. At
the same time Kadar has managed to retain his position in Soviet
esteem as a loyal servant and trusted adviser.

This is a remarkable achievement by any standards and a strik-
ing contrast with Kadar's own previous record. Like Husak in
Czechoslovakia he took a leading part in the Communist seizure
a power in Hungary after the defeat of Nazi Germany in 1945.
As Minister of the Interior in the early post-war years, he was
directly responsible for enforcing Stalin's reign of terror in
Hungary and carrying out the Party purges in which some of
Kadar's own Communist colleagues were killed. Also like Husak,
Kadar was dismissed and spent some years in prison where he
suffered the brutal treatment which he had inflicted on so many
others.

After his release in 1954 Kadar was given a minor Party post, but in July 1956, when the Stalinist leader, Matyas Rakosi, was forced to resign, Kadar was re-elected to the Political Committee. When the Hungarian revolt broke out in October that year, he was in Belgrade with the new leader, Erno Gero, on an official visit to Yugoslavia. On his return, he succeeded Gero as First Party Secretary and joined the revolutionary government set up by Imre Nagy. He made several speeches supporting Nagy's liberal programme, but deserted him when the Soviet forces marched in and formed a puppet government which welcomed the Soviet invasion.

After the revolt was crushed, Kadar took drastic measures to wipe out all remaining opposition. His former colleague, Nagy, had taken refuge in the Yugoslav Embassy in Budapest but left it after Kadar gave a written undertaking to the Yugoslav government that Nagy and his family would be allowed to return home. Despite this promise, Nagy was handed over to the Russians and shot.

Nearly 200,000 Hungarians got out of the country before the revolt was ended and a great many were deported in cattle trucks to Siberian labour camps. Thousands of 'freedom fighters' were shot by Kadar's firing squads or received long prison sentences. A particular refinement of cruelty was the postponement of death sentences on teenage prisoners until they were eighteen, as stipulated by Communist law. They were then taken out and shot.

This period of savage repression continued until 1961, when Kadar seems to have decided that he had fulfilled Moscow's instructions to 'restore order' and could safely afford milder measures. In 1962, at the eighth congress of the Hungarian Socialist Workers' Party – the name adopted by the Communist Party – Kadar set out new lines of policy designed to show that the Party had renounced its Stalinist past. An amnesty was declared for those who had taken part in the 1956 rising. Kadar had already started to remove Stalinist hardliners from responsible positions and some of them were expelled from the Party. He also began to underline the need to employ non-Party experts in government service, especially in the conduct of economic affairs.

The Hungarian economy, like that of other satellites, was based on the Soviet model which gave priority to industrial development at the expense of agriculture, consumer goods and living standards. It was a system of centralised state control which allocated investment and labour, set fixed production targets, and left the managers of state enterprises no voice in policy decisions. The results were low productivity, frequent bottlenecks and erratic deliveries of shoddy and often unwanted goods.

In May 1966 Kadar introduced major changes in economic policy. The 'new economic mechanism', as it was called, kept long-term planning and use of resources under central control but allowed managers to operate on a new basis of market demand and profit margins. The state levied higher taxes on factories producing goods of inferior quality but allowed the more efficient managers to pay their workers higher wages, a share of the profits, and bonuses in return for higher productivity. A key feature of the new system was the relation of prices to market values. These reforms did not always work smoothly but they succeeded in reducing the number of prices fixed by central planners from about one million in 1968 to roughly one thousand in 1970. They also increased the quantity and quality of consumer goods.

Kadar showed a similar grasp of reality in his policy for agriculture. In the early years of Communist rule, a rapid process of land collectivisation had been carried out and imposed by force. Apart from the resistance which this provoked among the Hungarian peasants, the new co-operative farms were burdened by compulsory deliveries to the state at low prices, heavy taxes, lack of skilled management, and shortages of farm machinery. As a result, the production of bread grain from 1950 to 1954 was less than it was from 1911 to 1915, when the population was only three-quarters of its present size. In Hungary, which has always been self-sufficient in food, the Communist regime was forced to import grain from the West.

Kadar reduced the burden of state demands on the co-operative farms, gave them better equipment, and enabled their members to increase their earnings. He also made it easier for the holders of small plots of land, which account for 10% of the total arable land, to produce more food and supplement their incomes by selling it at high prices on the open market. The success of these measures, and the need for them, is shown by the fact that the small private farmers make the largest contribution to Hungarian food supplies. By giving them encouragement, the Kadar regime also provides inducements for the peasants to stay in the countryside instead of moving into the towns.

These economic changes have led to a steady rise in Hungarian incomes and living standards over the past decade. They have also created a new social background to the discussion of human rights under Communist rule. The new industrial incentives have brought large financial rewards to many managers, technical specialists, commercial agents, and factory workers. Similarly, in agriculture, the rise in earnings from co-operative farm work and private holdings has gone a long way towards abolishing, and even in some respects reversing, the historical yawning gap between the amenities of urban living and primitive existence in the villages. Peasants and factory workers have been able to make savings which they can use to set themselves up in business in a city as private plumbers, motor mechanics, small builders and owners of small cafés and restaurants, all earning good money by supplying personal services which are conspicuously lacking in Communist countries. The professional middle-class has also benefited from a greater demand for its special skills.

The new infusion of wealth is plainly seen on the streets of Budapest, which show more signs of recent prosperity than any other Communist capital, bearing in mind the massive destruction during the Soviet invasion in 1956. The number of private cars, the well-stocked shops, the smart hotels and restaurants, the theatres and cinemas often showing Western productions are all pleasant surprises to the Western visitor and offer far more attractions than drab Moscow. The effect of this rise in Hungarian living standards, and its political dividend for Kadar, is to cool the pressure for civil and political rights and make the Hungarians more thankful for what they have received than disposed to demand freedoms which stand little chance of being granted. The prevailing mood is summed up in the popular phrase 'Don't rock the boat.' Most Hungarians seem to prefer the devil they know, in the shape of Kadar, to a new leader who might put the clock back to far harsher times.

Kadar has also been relatively lenient in his treatment of foreign travel and other contacts with the West. The favourite choice for a holiday abroad is Yugoslavia, which is not only a near neighbour, but a country where the rigours of Communist rule have been greatly relaxed since Tito broke away from Stalin in 1948. Nearly a million Hungarians visited Yugoslavia in 1974 as compared with 143,000 in 1970. It is also easier for Hungarians to visit Western countries than it is in other satellite states, except for Poland. The chief obstacles are the shortage of foreign currency and the high cost of travel permits.

A Hungarian who has lived in England for many years told us that the bell rang at his flat one day and he opened the door to find his mother, who still lived in Budapest, standing there to greet him. Her visit to England had received official approval and she was returning to Hungary after it. She was not a Communist, but she had experienced the far worse years of terror under Rakosi and she gave Kadar credit for making life easier.

She felt that he had to a large extent redeemed his own association with Rakosi in Stalin's time, and she feared what might happen when Kadar left the scene.

Since the Helsinki Conference on European Security and Co-operation in 1975, Kadar's government has made some modest concessions on exchange of information and cultural contacts with Western countries. It has granted more exit permits for the reunion of families. There has been some improvement in working conditions for Western journalists in Budapest. Western news-papers are still not available for public sale, but they can be obtained from under the counter in the expensive hotels frequented by the richer Western visitors. Details of church services are included in the information notices put up in some hotel lobbies. The Hungarian television service has broadcast special programmes on East-West relations in which disarmament, cultural exchanges, and human rights have been discussed with a freedom unknown in other Communist countries. The programmes were for the most part unrehearsed and uncensored. The panel of commentators also included a Western member who was only asked beforehand not to mention the Soviet dissident writer, Solzhenitsyn, clearly regarded as too much of a red rag to the Kremlin.

Foreign travellers would be wise not to congratulate Hungarian Communist officials on this more relaxed atmosphere. Perhaps understandably, they do not like to be singled out as an exception to the other Communist regimes.

The biggest break-through in Hungarian relations with the West is to be found in the commercial field. Like other Communist states, Kadar's government has sought to attract foreign investment to finance industrial development and relieve the strain on its slender stock of hard foreign currency. A decree authorising joint ventures between Hungarian and foreign partners was issued in 1972, mainly for the purpose of modernising Hungarian industrial production and enabling it to supply goods for export of the higher quality required to compete in Western markets. The results, however, were disappointing, and in May 1977 a new law was announced which offered further inducements. The tax on profits from joint ventures was reduced, but the most unusual feature was the authority given to the Hungarian Finance Minister to allow foreign partners who provided finance and services in joint ventures to have majority holdings. This was another bold departure from orthodox Communist doctrine, and Kadar may have had some difficulty in persuading Moscow to accept it.

An even bolder move by Kadar, and equally typical of his pragmatic approach, was reported in an article by Hella Pick in the London *Guardian* on 27 October 1977. Writing from Budapest she said that the Hungarian government had reached an understanding with the United States which recognises the importance of human rights as a factor in American economic policies. Hungary, it seems, is willing to accept this connection in return for the agreement of Congress to lifting the restrictions on trade between the two countries. If this information is correct it marks a new departure in East-West trade relations. The Hungarian side, like other Communist governments, still maintains that it fully respects human rights and has nothing to fear from Western scrutiny on that issue; but by accepting the right of Congress to use it as an element of trade policy, Kadar's government is breaking away from the position taken by the Soviet Union and its other satellites, who flatly reject Western concern over human rights as an unjustified interference with their internal affairs and national sovereignty.

Coming at a time when the Soviet Union and its economic partners in COMECON are being forced into an increasing reliance on Western economic support, this new Hungarian initiative can hardly find favour in Moscow. The Soviet Union itself, as a world power, is not likely to admit the inclusion of human rights in any formula for trade with the United States. The rather clumsy attempt by Congress in 1974 to get the Soviet Union to agree to more exit visas for the Jewish minority in exchange for most-favoured-nation treatment proved this pretty clearly. But some of its satellites might be tempted by the Hungarian example. Poland and Rumania have already been granted most-favoured-nation status in trade with the USA. If a new form of economic 'detente' linked with human rights were to spread further, it might help to remove the barriers which separate Eastern Europe from the West, it would certainly be a legitimate form of European co-operation under the 1975 Helsinki agreements.

Another example of Kadar's economic management is the way in which he handles price increases. In Poland, these were too long delayed and then imposed overnight, thus causing widespread riots which were a serious threat to the Communist government. Kadar, on the other hand, has taken care to give public warnings and explanations in advance and to make price increases by stages which were more easily absorbed and less of a sudden shock. This has not always prevented trouble. In January 1975 price increases were announced on a number of foodstuffs and manufactured consumer goods. Prior warning had been given a month earlier, but there was a stampede of buyers to beat the increases which cleaned out many shops. The Hungarian authorities responded by giving an assurance that the consumer price index would rise by less than 4% in 1975, and they raised the amount of state subsidies to support this limit.

One feature of the Communist society which arouses fierce resentment in Hungary as in other Soviet satellites, and perhaps some envy, is the life of ease and luxury enjoyed by a small privileged minority. This applies not only to high-ranking Party officials, but also to people who have made money from the new opportunities presented by Kadar's economic reforms. In the other Communist countries, this resentment is suppressed and festers in silence, but in Hungary Kadar has allowed it to be publicly expressed in Communist newspapers and broadcasts. They naturally stop short of criticising the Communist leadership, but they denounce in no uncertain terms the 'golden' or 'banana' youth, the children of the privileged 'new class'. For example, in February 1975 Radio Budapest and Radio Kossuth broadcast a review by Erika Szanto of a film about juvenile problems which she used as a peg for some bitter comments:

Why is it so difficult to be an adolescent? We ask ourselves doubt-fully and with some malice while watching a movie about teenagers living in a luxurious suburb of a wealthy city. Their houses are surrounded by lawns that could be the envy of an Englishman, to whom a beautiful lawn is, and has been for centuries, a matter of honour. The interior decoration of these mansions resembles Domus Store designs for some foreign exhibition, not so much for its artistry as for its opulence. Their fathers' liquor cabinets are stocked with the choicest foreign brands. No wonder the tastes of their children lean towards the most expensive French wines. These teenagers do not know the taste of water, nor does anyone else in their circle . . . The spoiled darlings walk out with dogs of exclusive breed and their pockets are full of money. I bet they do not even know the price of a loaf of bread. Seeing the antics of these pampered upper-class brats on the screen fills me with intemperate rage.

The main point of interest here is that Kadar has permitted the open expression of popular resentment over inequalities which are not supposed to exist in a *Communist* society. The same feelings exist in the other Communist states but they are suppressed. Kadar obviously thinks it more sensible to let people blow off steam in a way which does not threaten his own rule and may improve his image both in Hungary and in Western countries.

He has shown the same sort of common sense in his treatment of human rights. He still maintains the familiar props of Communist power; the security police, a host of informers, newspapers and radio stations devoted to Communist propaganda. But the police are kept in the background much more than in the other East European satellites and Kadar tolerates more cultural deviations from the Party line and more freedom of speech than they do. He does not employ an army of official censors issuing directives on everything which might conceivably overstep the permitted limits, but relies on 'self-censorship' by state publishing houses, editors and directors of television and radio, which is almost as effective and looks better. Any tendency for these unofficial censors to turn a blind eye is checked by Party committees which act as watchdogs and hold regular meetings to see how publishers and editors are performing their duties. But this does not prevent the appearance now and again of critical comments.

For example, in November 1975 the Hungarian literary and political weekly journal *Elet és Irodalom* published an article about the treatment of news written by Tibor Dery, born in 1894 and a venerable literary critic. He has since died. His remarks showed that he had lost none of his mental faculties:

Even if we were not perfectly well aware of it, we could guess that to reveal the facts is certainly not the only function of news; indeed, it is often called upon to conceal the truth. Even when it states the facts correctly, it lies inasmuch as it is authorised to tell only half the truth. The part, however, is not the same as the whole, and a partial avowal sometimes achieves a completely opposite effect. The newscaster chooses among these part-truths according to the way he feels about things. We are manipulated, as we all know, from our birth onward.

Dery said that the only programmes he watched regularly on television were the football matches and sometimes the evening newsreel before eating his supper, because 'vexation stimulates the appetite'. What annoyed him, he added, was not so much the dishonesty of the news as the over-optimistic and complacent manner of its presentation. In his view, ordinary gossip was much more 'human' than the information provided by the news media. Gossip was not invented on paper, or on the TV screen, or by the faceless voice on the radio, or by an office or person hidden away in the mystery of an abstract figurehead. Gossip came from a neighbour, said Dery, and even if one had misgivings about the absolute truth of her words, 'I prefer her fibs to anonymous truths.'

These sharp remarks reflected a widespread distrust among Hungarians of the official news served out to them, but other articles appeared at this time which complained about rumours and scares circulating all over the country. An article in *Magyar Nemzet* spoke of a general belief that everything people needed from hospitals, shops and state officials could be obtained with the help of a small bribe. It mentioned another rumour about a government proposal to abolish the privately owned plots of land, which had caused great public concern. This story was strongly denied by Radio Budapest in its programme '168 Hours' and several Communist papers pointed out that such rumours caused sudden setbacks in production by private farmers which had serious effects on the supply of food. For many Hungarians, however, these comments only confirmed tales of corruption among officials and discrimination against small agricultural holdings which they knew from their own experience to be founded on fact.

Public fears of a return to harsher measures were revived by two government decisions in November and December 1975. The first was a joint decision by the Ministries of Education and Labour to specify the social origins of pupils attending kindergarten, primary and secondary schools. This conjured up visions of children being made to suffer for having parents whose social origins might predispose them against the regime. The second shock was a joint decree by the Ministers of Finance and Labour imposing a 'freeze' on the number of clerical and administrative workers. This was very unpopular with industrial enterprises and co-operative farms whose office staffs had been increased as a result of the greater freedom given to managers by Kadar's economic reforms. They also pointed out that the same state officials who wanted them to cut office staffs had for years been demanding more and more written returns of detailed, and often irrelevant, information. For the general public, the 'freeze' carried a threat of unemployment in a Communist system which always boasts of having solved this problem and fears that young people whose education had prepared them for 'white collar' work would not be able to find jobs.

These criticisms were broadcast by Radio Budapest and produced a statement by two officials dealing with labour and education who thanked the radio for conveying public protests. They admitted that the title of the decree on classification of school pupils was misleading and said it had been corrected. They pointed out that information about parental employment had always been required in school records and explained that the new measure was only intended to register social changes in the number of parents who were workers and peasants. They agreed that discrimination against pupils by 'social status' had been forbidden by a Party Congress resolution and claimed that they invariably obeyed such decisions.

The 'freeze' on office staffs, to which Radio Budapest also gave critical attention, was stoutly defended by official spokesmen in radio interviews. They recalled that the enterprises had already been asked to co-operate in this action, which was essential to relieve the shortage of manpower, but they had ignored this appeal. A labour official suggested that it would not be a tragedy if some high school graduates had to spend a few years at the machines before going on to finish their education. The Ministry of Education promised to review the employment situation after a few months and to propose any necessary changes. There was little satisfaction in these answers for public opinion, but the coverage given by Radio Budapest was a rare exception to the usual Communist practice.

By his judicious mixture of pressure and persuasion, Kadar has avoided a major confrontation on human rights. There is no organised body of dissent in Hungary, as there is in Poland and Czechoslovakia, and most members of the Hungarian intelligentsia have outwardly made their peace with the regime and enjoy the rewards of submission. But there are exceptions to this and the case of Andras Hegedus is one of the most remarkable.

Hegedus is a veteran Communist who was a close colleague of Matyas Rakosi, the Party leader who enforced the Stalinist reign of terror in Hungary in the post-war period. Hegedus was Prime Minister in 1955 but fled to Russia with his family when the 1956 uprising took place, together with Rakosi's successor as leader, Erno Gero, and his Minister of the Interior, Laszlo Farkas. After the revolt was crushed, Hegedus stayed on in Moscow where he studied sociology and philosophy, but he returned to Hungary in 1958 and was given several high posts in academic work and journalism. He soon fell foul of the Kadar regime by calling for liberal reforms in the Communist system and in 1965 he was dismissed from an editorial post on the grounds of 'an incorrect bourgeois attitude, oppositional tendencies, and a decadent approach'.

In 1968 he opposed the Soviet invasion of Czechoslovakia and wrote an open letter of protest to the Party Central Committee, an offence which led to his removal from a senior academic post and demotion to a lower rank. His final eclipse came in May 1973, when he was expelled from the Party with two others who shared his views, Mihaly Vajda and Janos Kis.

The official announcement of their expulsion gave the following reasons:

According to the description provided by the Hegedus group it is entirely clear that in their view the socialist countries of Eastern Europe can be regarded as socialist countries only by virtue of the official ideology dominant in them. However, they cannot actually pride themselves on either greater dynamism, or the establishment of more humane social conditions, than the advanced capitalist countries.

In the final analysis they (the Hegedus group) attach their hopes to the same 'development trends' of socialism as do the enemies of socialism; to the reduction of the mass influence of the Communist parties of the socialist countries; to the masses turning away from the programme of socialist development and hardening of conflicts within socialist society; to a trend which will give the bureaucracy a pluralistic orientation; and to the shaping of international relationships in such a way as to favour the development and exploitation of internal conflicts.

The official statement added that Hegedus had been warned several times about his 'political mistakes', and that Vajda had already been 'disciplined' by the Party. These remarks indicate that Kadar had shown considerable patience with these dissenters and had tried in vain to make them mend their ways.

The three men were officially described as members of a group called the 'New Left' which was sometimes known as 'the Budapest School'. Several of its members were former pupils of Gyorgy Lukacs, a philosopher who died in 1971, and were influenced by his ideas. They included Maria Markus and her husband Gyorgy, Ivan Szelenyi, Agnes Heller and Gyorgy Bence, all sociologists; Miklos Haraszti, Gyorgy Konrad, and Tamas Szentjoby, who were writers or poets; and Ferenc Feher, professor of languages and a literary critic.

When Hegedus, Vajda and Kis were expelled from the Party in 1973, four other dissenters came under attack, these being

Gyorgy and Maria Markus, Agnes Heller and Gyorgy Bence. They were accused of producing works which gave 'arbitrary interpretations of basic Marxist concepts' and attempting to revise 'the theory and basic principles of the policy of Marxist-Leninist Parties'. They were not themselves Party members and may have been singled out for that reason. All four were dismissed from their professional employment and temporarily forbidden to publish their work or to travel abroad.

Kadar's treatment of the dissenters was relatively lenient compared with the persecution which went on in Czechoslovakia. Haraszti was arrested in 1973 because of the views expressed in his book *Piece Rate*, an account of his experiences as a factory worker in Budapest. It was rejected by the publisher who commissioned it but was issued in a limited edition of *Szociologia*, the journal of the Hungarian Academy of Sciences. Haraszti was briefly detained and then released. In January 1974 he was given a suspended prison sentence of eight months for 'diffusing unauthorised writings'. Three of his colleagues came forward as witnesses for his defence: Ivan Szelenyi, a former editor of *Szociologia*, Tamas Szentjoby and Gyorgy Konrad. They were themselves arrested in October 1974 on charges of 'subversive activities' but were released after agreeing to leave the country. Szelenyi and Szentjoby received exit permits and emigrated to Britain, but Konrad changed his mind and remained in Hungary.

Konrad is a novelist with an international reputation whose first book *The Case Worker*, published in 1969 after the Soviet invasion of Czechoslovakia in 1968, gave an early indication of his doubts about Communist rule. This critical attitude was maintained in his second novel *The City Founder* which was published in Germany in 1975 and in France in 1976 but did not come out in Hungary because the authorities wanted to make cuts which Konrad would not accept. His decision to stay in Hungary in 1974 was probably influenced by an official promise to publish his book there with some changes but it has not yet appeared. Konrad was kept under police observation but was not arrested. He was allowed to make an extensive tour of the USA and Western Europe in 1977 and was one of the speakers at the Venice Biennale discussions on cultural freedom that year. Like many other dissenters in Eastern Europe, Konrad is a disillusioned Communist faced with a choice between emigrating to the West or defending freedom of speech in his own country, as he has so far preferred to do.

Hegedus has also remained in Hungary and pursued his academic studies without further trouble. In October 1976 he gave an interview to the French paper *Le Quotidien de Paris* in which he maintained that Stalin's death in 1953 had been greeted with immense relief by the Hungarian Communist leader at that time, Rakosi, and his colleagues. According to Hegedus, they were terrified by Stalin's 'murderous anti-Semitism'. When asked whether he had 'de-Stalinised' himself, Hegedus replied that it would be conceited for him to say so but at least he believed he had made a good start.

In January 1975 there was considerable alarm in literary circles when the preliminary guidelines for the Communist Party Congress that year indicated a tougher line by the authorities on cultural uniformity. But when the Congress met in March, Kadar talked to a delegation of non-Communist writers and gave them assurances which calmed their fears.

A highly critical and uninhibited view of life under Communist rule was expressed in an article by Istvan Csurka, published in February 1977 in the monthly journal of the Trans-Danubian group of the Hungarian Writers' Union. He had been imprisoned after the uprising in 1956 and banned from publication, but was released under the amnesty declared by Kadar in 1962. Csurka is a lively extrovert with a love for horse-racing and card games. Some of this spice comes through in his article:

Hungarian social consciousness would probably be different today without a few dozen of our contemporary writers. I believe that their influence is even greater than it seems, or is admitted to be. But then it is another question just how big it would be if there were fewer restrictions and less self-control on the writers' part. After all, democracy is rather sparsely represented in the general Hungarian consciousness. We have no accurate ideas about democracy. The writers know more about it than they indicate at present.

Referring to the social situation of the writers, Csurka said that there were not enough distinctions between them. It was not talent that counted, but membership of the Writers' Union. The fundamental problem was confusion:

Matters have become mixed up. Unparalleled wealth coexists with unparalleled poverty. Humanity has lost its sense of direction. Writers see and write only about symptoms.

He added:

Only one social stratum lives prosperously, while the great majority exist from hand to mouth. Indeed, by the end of the month they subsist on loans or the pawnshop, and our purchases are narrowed down to bread and dripping.

Csurka is a prolific writer of short stories, novels, plays and film scripts. His latest play *Derby Day* opened in Budapest in February 1977 and continued to run after his article quoted above appeared. The play is set on a racecourse and the main characters are 'intellectuals' who are keen racegoers like Csurka himself. He seems to be arguing that such forms of escapism provide no solution to the frustrations of creative thought in a totalitarian state. The writer cannot detach himself from the human problems of ordinary people living under those conditions but must become involved and say what he thinks.

In January 1977 a message signed by thirty-four Hungarian dissenters and expressing their solidarity with the Charter 77 manifesto which had just appeared in Czechoslovakia was sent to Pavel Kohout, one of the leading signatories. The Hungarian sympathisers condemned the repressive measures taken against the Charter movement and added: 'We are convinced that the defence of human and civil rights is a common concern of all Eastern Europe.' The authors of this message included writers who had been in trouble with the regime before, like Miklos Haraszti, and others who were still in good standing and had not previously been counted as dissenters. A large majority of those involved consisted of people from the younger generation which had grown up under Communist rule and indoctrination.

Faced with this open gesture of defiance, Kadar again kept a cool head. The offenders were let off with a friendly warning to behave themselves in future, something like: 'As a good and intelligent Hungarian, you must understand our delicate situation. We simply cannot afford to offend our friends in Moscow and risk the sort of trouble we had before, you know when. We can over-look it this time but you won't be so lucky if it happens again, so please watch your step.'

By taking this common-sense line, so different from the frenzied reactions of other Communist rulers, Kadar not only gained more credit in Western eyes but also voiced the feelings of his own people. More than twenty years had passed since the Soviet invasion of Hungary in 1956, but its tragic memories still live on. The Hungarians are inclined to look upon the dissenters more as incendiaries than saviours. Nor can they be expected to feel very warmly towards Communist reformers who now admit that the Marxist god has failed, a fact of life which has been obvious to the Hungarian man in the street for many years. Looking back on the Stalinist nightmare, most Hungarians regard Kadar as by far the lesser evil.

There is more religious freedom in Hungary today than in any other Communist state, except Poland. The Roman Catholic

Church, though much less strong than it was before the Communists took over in 1948 and far less influential than it is in Poland, is still easily the largest in Hungary. Nearly 70% of the population is at least nominally Catholic. The Protestant minority is divided between the Reformed Church of Hungary, the Evangelical Lutheran Church and a smaller number of Baptists and Methodists. The American evangelist, Billy Graham, visited Hungary in September 1977 and preached to large audiences. The number of Hungarian Jews was reduced by Nazi German exterminations from 725,000 in 1941 to about 80,000 in 1975.

The Kadar government does not interfere with church services and these are well attended by many young people as well as their elders. Catholic education has been cut down to a fraction of its former size before the Communist revolution, but the Church is still allowed to maintain eight secondary schools giving a full Catholic education and run by members of Catholic orders paid by the Communist state. There are also six seminaries for the training of priests. Religious instruction is permitted in Hungarian state schools on a voluntary basis and is given by priests and pastors paid by the government. Copies of the Bible are freely available and are also exported to Yugoslavia, Rumania and Slovakia for the use of Hungarian minorities. The government has provided financial aid for the restoration of Catholic and Protestant churches destroyed in the last war.

All this shows a highly unusual degree of religious tolerance by a Communist regime, but Church activities are strictly controlled by a government Office for Church Affairs. There is a state-sponsored 'Peace Movement' of Catholic priests who support the Communist regime, and in some cases priests have been forced to join it by threats of suspension or dismissal from their parishes. Other priests were imprisoned in the 1960s for their work among young people. Relations between the Communist government and the Catholic Church were disrupted by the imprisonment of the pre-war Primate, Cardinal Mindszenty and many of his clergy for their refusal to accept Communist dictation. Mindszenty was released by the 1956 uprising and found shelter in the American Legation in Budapest for fifteen years before being allowed to leave for Rome. But he refused to resign his office as Primate until 1974, when he was compelled to do so by Pope Paul. His death shortly afterwards made it easier for the Vatican and the Kadar regime to come to some agreement.

Kadar had already been working for that end with his distinctive blend of self-interest and opportunism. In 1964, after a visit to Budapest by a Vatican delegation, the two sides agreed on a basis for 'regular and reciprocal relations'. Though limited in scope, it was the first such agreement between the Vatican and a Communist state. It allowed Rome to nominate bishops of its own choice in Hungary, subject to approval by the Kadar government and an oath of allegiance to the Communist state. Kadar's guiding principle, which he had already publicly declared, was that Hungarians could be good Catholics and accept the Communist order at one and the same time without conflict between their duties to the Church and the state. The Vatican accepted this compromise.

Under the 1964 agreement, the government had promised that discrimination against Catholic children who received religious instruction would cease, and that restrictions on parish priests in the exercise of their ministry would be eased. It was also agreed on both sides that the case of Cardinal Mindszenty was now closed. But on some subjects they still disagreed and these were deferred for further consideration. The matters of most concern to the Church were the free exercise of episcopal jurisdiction in each diocese; the freedom of priests to carry out their mission; and Church work among young people. These still remain unsettled.

In the autumn of 1972, the Hungarian Catholic journal,

Teologia, was allowed to publish an article by Dr Tamas Nyiri, a professor in the Budapest Theological Academy, in which he spoke about the crisis facing the Catholic Church and its clergy. He said:

Half the priests of Hungary live in isolation without any personal contacts. They are tired and broken, and cannot express themselves as men, let alone as Christians or messengers of the Gospel.

The article pointed out that two-thirds of the clergy were over the age of fifty, and there were not enough new priests coming forward to replace them. Many priests were living in poverty, without confidence in their theological training or in the leadership of their bishops.

In November 1975 Kadar's Prime Minister, Gyorgy Lazar, had an audience with the Pope during a state visit to Italy. He told reporters that the Hungarian government saw no obstacles in principle to the appointment of a new Primate to replace Cardinal Mindszenty. He also held out hopes that Hungary would eventually establish diplomatic relations with the Vatican. Soon after, in February, the Vatican appointed Laszlo Lekai as Archbishop of Esztergom and Primate of Hungary and made him a Cardinal. He took the oath of loyalty to the Communist state.

In June 1977 Kadar himeslf met the Pope during a visit to Italy. This was interpreted as a further step towards diplomatic relations, but the results of the meeting were not made public. Judging by an interview which Cardinal Lekai gave to Lady Listowel, published in *The Times* of 8 September 1977, the Catholic Church is still facing a hard struggle. The new Primate summed up his main task as one of adapting the Church to meet the new conditions of life under Communist rule, while carrying the essence of the Catholic faith into the future. The Church needed priests with a different training, teachers who 'carry the Bible in one hand, and the day's paper in the other'. They must be able to hold the interest of children living in a materialist world and to inspire them with a higher and more spiritual view. The Hungarian Primate hoped for a renewal of the great medieval reforms in religion which were born in the French abbey of Cluny. 'Cluny arose to defeat the materialism of the twelfth century,' said the Cardinal. 'I believe that we shall have another Cluny. I pray for it. I am certain it will come.'

Hungarian national feelings were deeply stirred when Kadar accepted in January 1978 an offer by the United States to return the Crown of St Stephen, which has been the symbol of Hungarian independence for over a thousand years. It was smuggled out of Hungary near the end of the Second World War to Austria to save it falling into Nazi German hands and delivered to the American forces in Austria by whom it was sent to the United States for safe custody. Possession of the Crown and its regalia has always been regarded as the essential title to the legal exercise of power in Hungary and no doubt Kadar welcomed its return for that reason. But the Crown is also an ancient symbol of Hungarian monarchy and Christianity, a fact which may have made Kadar hesitate before accepting its return. On the American side, this was not only a token of goodwill to the Hungarian nation but also a tribute to Kadar's relaxations in Communist rule.

One of his biggest unsolved problems is the fate of over one and a half million Hungarians living in Transylvania on the other side of the frontier with Rumania. Transylvania was for many centuries part of Hungary, but it was lost to Rumania after the war of 1914-18 and remained there under the peace treaties which followed the Nazi German defeat in 1945. The Rumanian Communist leader, Ceausescu, has adopted a policy of suppressing the language and culture of the Hungarians in Transylvania and assimilating them into the Rumanian population. This has been a source of mounting friction in relations between the two Communist states which was prevented for many years from finding open expression.

In the summer of 1977 the two Communist leaders had two private meetings to discuss this problem, but they apparently failed to reach agreement. Signs appeared of growing concern in Hungary and this was voiced by the Communist press. An article in the Budapest daily paper *Magyar Nemzet* blamed the Western powers for the post-war settlement in 1947, while carefully avoiding any mention of the Soviet Union, but it gave a warning that Hungary could not remain indifferent to the treatment of its kinsmen in Transylvania. In a further article the paper said that Hungary

cannot accept the imposition [on the Hungarian minority] of a single language and a process by which the tongue of the state-organising nation first eclipses, and then forcibly dissipates and finally ousts the old mother tongue of the indigenous people. It is the duty of the mother nation to protect speakers of the mother tongue wherever they may be living . . . While the Basques of France and Spain have no mother nation, the Transylvanian Hungarians do have one.

Kadar has been in power since 1957, a longer period than any Communist leader since Stalin. From being a hidebound Stalinist in his earlier years he has developed into a more liberal ruler than any of his fellows in Eastern Europe. At the same time he has remained on good terms with his masters in Moscow. He has served them well as a mediator in the quarrel between the 'Euro-Communist' Parties in Western Europe and the Kremlin by a typically skilful defence of independence for every Party combined with the leading role of the Soviet Union.

He is now sixty-six and there is some talk of his retirement. A Party shuffle took place in April 1978 which promoted Karoly Nemeth, now regarded as a moderate and a reformer, who had been in charge of economic affairs, to the key post of

Secretary for Party administration and suggested that he might in due time succeed Kadar. He replaced a leading hardliner, Bela Biszku, still only fifty-seven. The Hungarians devoutly hope that Kadar will stay at the helm as long as possible. They do not know whether his moderate policies will survive him and they fear a return to the bad old days. That in itself is the biggest tribute to the old Stalinist leopard who has changed his spots and made life more tolerable for his people.

CHAPTER 5

DEEP FREEZE IN
RUMANIA

While Kadar in Hungary has eased the daily burdens of life for
his people and shown some tolerance in his treatment of human
rights, the Rumanians suffer the worst of both worlds, economic
and ideological. The Communist boss, Nicolae Ceausescu, has
undertaken a vast and ambitious programme of industrial development which demands heavy sacrifices in terms of inadequate supplies of food and other consumer goods, long hours of toil for
little pay, and much personal hardship. He drives his people to
the limits of endurance and beyond, with promises of a golden
age which will dawn in the year 2000, and his rule is the harshest
of any satellite regime. Yet in his foreign policy, Ceausescu has
broken loose from Soviet dictation and follows an independent
line which has caused many headaches in Moscow.

He was the only satellite leader who roundly condemned the
Soviet invasion of Czechoslovakia in 1968 and refused to send
troops to support it. He further declared that the Rumanian
frontiers would be defended against attack from any quarter, a
piece of bombast which stood no chance of success in action against
Soviet military might, but which must have seemed grossly im-
pertinent to the Kremlin. And Ceausescu has continued to play
his part as the *enfant terrible* of Eastern Europe. He has held
aloof from the quarrel between the Soviet Union and Communist

China and established cordial relations with Peking, reinforced by a state visit there in 1971. Alone among the Soviet puppet states, Rumania maintains full diplomatic relations with Israel, the chief object of Soviet hostility in the Middle East, and warmly welcomed the Israeli Prime Minister, Menachem Begin, when he visited Bucharest in 1977 before his peace talks with President Sadat in Egypt.

Ceausescu has worked hard to secure new friends for Rumania outside the Soviet circle, especially among the 'third world' or non-aligned states seeking an independent role between the American and Russian giants. He is on terms of warm friendship, almost amounting to alliance, with Tito in Yugoslavia. The Rumanian leader has taken a close personal interest in expanding and diversifying Rumanian foreign trade, with a keen eye to the benefits of Western technology and finance for his industrial programme. He is the most widely travelled of all the satellite rulers and has flown all over the globe in his personal jet aircraft to countries as far apart in distance and forms of government as Brazil, Japan, Turkey, France and Portugal. He has made three visits to the United States, the first time in 1970 when he met American businessmen and negotiated a contract for delivery of an American aluminium sheet-rolling plant to Rumania; the second in 1973 when he secured an agreement for economic, industrial and technological co-operation between Rumania and the USA; and the third in April 1978. In 1975 President Ford visited Bucharest and signed a trade agreement granting Rumania most-favoured-nation status in trade with the USA and also credits from the American Import-Export Bank.

Another important departure by the Rumanian Communist government from the strict Marxist-Leninist line laid down by the Kremlin was seen in Ceausescu's recognition of a link between his trade relations with the West and his treatment of human rights in his own country. This was tacitly admitted in an agreement

132

between Rumania and the Federal German Republic in January 1978 whereby the Rumanian government undertook to allow 11,000 members of the ethnic German minority in Rumania to emigrate to West Germany in return for an increase of DM 300 million in bank credits for Rumania from the Federal German Export Guarantee Fund. These credits, which are used by Rumania to buy West German goods and services, were raised from DM 700 million to DM 1,000 million. The East German Communist regime had already adopted this practice of bartering 'bodies for cash', and a similar agreement with the Federal German Republic was signed by the Polish Communist government in 1975. Rumania is the only member of the Soviet bloc that is negotiating a general trade agreement with the European Economic Community. This would cover about 85% of their external trade. Yet the EEC is not recognised by the Soviet Union which has no trading relations with it. A further strain is thereby imposed on relations between the Kremlin and Ceausescu.

There was a time not so long ago when either Stalin or Khrushchev would have quickly put a stop to this display of independence, but times have changed even in Russia. The 'collective leadership' headed by Brezhnev has nothing to gain, and much to lose, from a military intervention in Rumania, following the invasion of Hungary and Czechoslovakia. Ceausescu has relieved them of any anxiety on that score by ruling at home with a rod of iron and ensuring that no Rumanian Dubcek emerges inside the Communist regime to sponsor a programme of reform. The ideological virginity of orthodox doctrine remains intact, and so long as this continues, Moscow can afford to tolerate Ceausescu's independent line abroad.

The Rumanian leader has taken care to consolidate his power base at home by uniting all the key posts in his own person. He is not only the Secretary-General and master of the Rumanian Communist Party, but also President of the Republic, Chairman of the State Council, Commander-in-Chief of the Armed Forces, Chairman of the Supreme Council for Economic and Social Development, and head of the Commission which presides over ideological and political propaganda. He has brought his wife, Elena, into the Politbureau, where she is second only to her husband. As a Doctor of Chemical Engineering, she sits on the Executive Bureau of the National Council for Scientific Research. Several other members of the family have been installed in high positions in government and Party. There is a popular joke in Rumania which says that the difference between the Hohenzollern dynasty which formerly reigned there and the Communist successors is that 'the Hohenzollerns ruled in succession, while the Ceausescus all rule simultaneously'. The Rumanian leader has created a 'personality cult' in his own image, like that of Stalin in Russia, with an inner circle of admiring courtiers and a chorus of adulation from newspapers, radio, and writers.

Ceausescu himself has described his ambivalent relationship with the Soviet Union quite clearly. Speaking in the Grand National Assembly, the Communist caricature of a parliament, on 19 December 1975, he called for a new kind of unity between Communist Parties, based on the right of each of them 'to work out its political line in complete freedom'. It was no longer possible, he said, to have a 'centre', meaning Moscow, from which their work could be conducted. There must be 'co-operation based on fully equal rights and excluding any interference in their internal affairs'. In August 1977 he invited the Spanish Communist Party leader, Santiago Carrillo, to meet him at his holiday home on the Black Sea. Carrillo is one of the most outspoken critics of Soviet claims to dominate other Communist Parties. The two men issued a joint statement upholding the right of every Communist Party to decide its own policy.

At a trade union congress, in April 1976, Ceausescu spoke of an attack from two sides on 'the free and independent develop-

ment of peoples'. On one hand, there were 'reactionary imperialist forces' which argued that national independence was obsolete
since mankind had entered the era of supra-national organisations.
These, said Ceausescu, were merely 'a new form of political
domination and oppression'. On the other hand, there were
philosophers and theorists who tried to prove that the historic
role of the nation was finished, and that the defence of national
independence was 'a nationalist deviation from Marxism-Leninism and a sliding towards bourgeois nationalism'. Ceausescu maintained that the defence of freedom and independence was 'the
real touchstone of proletarian internationalism', and he added:
'He who does not defend this right deserves to be a slave, despised
by his own nation and by other peoples.'

But he has also given Moscow assurances that the 'freedom
and independence' which he claims for his own Communist
Party are not going to be extended to the Rumanian people. For
example, at a congress of local councils in February 1976, he
said that the Rumanian Communist Party firmly adhered to the
Marxist thesis of the revolutionary dictatorship of the proletariat
during the transition from capitalism to communism. He added
that even the most democratic bourgeois state was 'nothing else
but rule by the capitalist class'. He said it was unthinkable to
make revolutionary changes without the uniform and planned
direction of society, since otherwise the building of a new society
would only be 'sabotaged' by reactionary forces. One might add
that there are still Western socialists who think in much the
same terms.

In the other Soviet satellites, and indeed in the Soviet Union
itself, the deeply rooted desire of formerly independent nations to
regain their freedom, and the suppressed demands by national
minorities for their civil rights, are the main source of danger to
Communist dictatorship. But in Rumania Ceausescu has harnessed
nationalism to the Communist yoke and exploited it, with some

success, to prevent any serious outbreak of popular discontent. Put in another way, he has trumped the nationalist ace and made it serve his own purpose.

The modern Rumanians have inherited a potent strain of patriotic feelings. They claim descent from a Roman colony established in Dacia by the Emperor Trajan, and the Rumanian language still contains a majority of words with Latin derivations. For many centuries, the Rumanians have regarded themselves as an island of Latin culture in a sea of Slavs, closely linked with the civilisation of Western Europe. Ceausescu has revived these memories and turned them to political advantage. In October 1974, for example, the Grand National Assembly approved a law 'for preserving the national cultural heritage' which illustrates his political technique of reconciling national pride with Communist dogma. It was based on the assumption that the 'national cultural patrimony' was the property of the people. A special committee was set up to examine artistic relics and treasures and list them in a national catalogue. Private owners were allowed to keep these possessions, but were ordered, as a 'patriotic duty', to report them to the Ministry of the Interior within two months. Failure to comply was made a criminal offence and detailed regulations were issued to enforce the new law. It thus combined a laudable desire to preserve the Rumanian cultural heritage with a considerable extension of Communist intervention in private life. The private owners have since been ordered to hand over their collections to state museums.

Also in October 1974 the Rumanian State Council issued a decree changing the name of the old city of Cluj to Cluj-Napoca. This was to celebrate the 1,850th anniversary of the date when the Dacian settlement of Napoca was raised to a township. It was intended 'to immortalise the name of this ancient settlement as evidence of the long-term establishment and continuity of the Rumanian people in these parts'. But the change of name also had a political purpose. Cluj, which is situated in southern Transylvania, was annexed by Rumania fifty years ago. Some Hungarian scholars still dispute the Rumanian claim of continuous ethnic occupation. The change of name was meant to support the Rumanian title to possession. In November 1977 the Grand National Assembly adopted a new national anthem with words and music taken from a nineteenth-century patriotic song, previously banned by the Communist government. Two new verses were added in praise of the glorious achievements of Communist rule.

It is this highly eccentric and personal style of Communist leadership which provides the setting for the treatment of human rights in Rumania. Ceausescu's blowing of the national trumpet helps to divert the attention of Rumanians from the harsh discipline and sufferings which he imposes on them in pursuit of industrial expansion. The worldwide publicity given to his differences with Moscow, and his foreign expeditions to promote Rumanian interests help to build up his image as a patriotic leader dedicated to the service of his country. In domestic affairs, however, he enforces a strict conformity with Communist Party doctrine and directives in all walks of life. Unlike Kadar in Hungary, he does not accept a passive attitude to Communist rule as a tolerable form of social conduct, but his methods of repression are subject to changes of mood and tactics.

When Ceausescu took over the Party leadership in 1965, all visible signs of opposition had long since disappeared. Under his predecessor, Gheorghiu-Dej, the regime had felt strong enough to ease its restrictions on the work of writers and intellectuals, to the extent of allowing a few young writers and literary critics to publish work which expressed some dissatisfaction with the subordination of art and literature to Communist ideology. The Rumanian Churches, after a period of savage persecution when Communist rule was established in 1948, had been placed under the orders of a Department of Religious Cults which controlled their appointments and administration with the help of church leaders who collaborated with the Communist regime.

The Rumanian Orthodox Church is by far the largest with a membership of thirteen or fourteen million out of a total population of nearly twenty million. Its Patriarch, Justinian, who led his Church for twenty-nine years from 1948 till his death in 1977, was a willing servant of the Communist government. He interpreted his Bible reading as a call for radical social reform and felt some sympathy for the revolutionary changes in the Communist programme. In keeping with a long tradition of collaboration by the Eastern Orthodox Church with the state, dating back to the Byzantine Empire, the Rumanian Patriarch set his clergy the task of serving the workers in a Communist society, believing that this was the best, and indeed the only, way in which to ensure survival.

The Roman Catholic Church, with a much smaller membership estimated at one and a quarter million, mainly drawn from the Hungarian and German minorities in Transylvania, suffered brutal punishment. A reign of terror began as soon as the Communist Party, few in numbers but backed by the Soviet Union, seized power in 1948 by means of faked elections and set about crushing all opposition. Maniu, the popular 76-year-old Peasant Party leader, had already been sent to prison where he soon died.

The Communist authorities revoked the Rumanian Concordat with the Vatican and dissolved the Uniate or Greek-rite wing of the Roman Catholic Church, forcing it to accept reunion with the Orthodox Church. This action was warmly welcomed and supported by Patriarch Justinian, whose Church was the main beneficiary. Strong protests by the Catholic prelates led to the arrest of six Catholic bishops, four of whom died in prison.

The Protestant creeds are represented by the Hungarian Reformed Church, still under that name, the Lutheran Church, and also a Rumanian Baptist Church founded in the nineteenth century which has shown remarkable growth since 1900, despite some harsh treatment by pre-war and wartime governments. In 1955 the Baptist community had risen to 65,000, but in 1973 it was estimated at 120,000 with over 1,000 churches. Some independent Protestant sects have also gained ground in recent years, including Pentecostalists, Seventh Day Adventists, and Jehovah's Witnesses.

For Ceausescu, with his political emphasis on national independence, the Orthodox Church is a natural ally, and Patriarch Justinian constantly stressed its traditional patriotism and its loyalty to the Communist state. When Ceausescu's father died in 1972, his village funeral was conducted by an Orthodox bishop with full religious ceremony, and it was shown on the Communist television service, a startling breach of normal Communist behaviour. But the Dubcek plan of reform in Czechoslovakia, and its destruction by Soviet invasion, seems to have been taken by Ceausescu as a warning to tighten up his own rule and prevent any disturbance of the same kind from arising in Rumania.

He told his Party colleagues that religion would remain a force to be reckoned with for a long time, and imposed new Communist restrictions on the Churches. He spoke of creating a 'new man' in the Rumanian social system who would be cleansed from the infection of religious belief and other 'bourgeois' influences. In July 1971 he personally took charge of a new 'programme for political and ideological education', with special attention to reinforcing atheist propaganda. In an address to students at the opening of the school year 1972-73 he criticised members of the Communist Youth Union for attending church services and saying prayers. But the Old Adam in Rumanians showed a stubborn reluctance to be re-born as the 'new man', and progress in his education moved slowly. So much so that Ceausescu, in June 1976, called a congress on 'political education and socialist culture' and gave orders for more intensive propaganda work in these fields. It was decided to start the indoctrination of youth at the age of four through a new organisation called 'Falcons of the Fatherland'. Another measure was the formation of 'special educational brigades' moving from one place to another and giving instruction to young workers and students who migrated from the countryside to the towns, or who spent the day working in towns and then returned to their villages.

The writers and intellectuals, who had been breathing more easily for several years, were now required to make their contribution to the cultural revolution by preaching it in their own work. Most of them toed the line, but there were a few exceptions. One of them was Dumitru Tepeneag, a leading member of the so-called 'oneiricist' group of younger Rumanian writers. He had been allowed in previous years to make several long visits to Paris, where he had friends in French literary circles, and he had published some of his work there. He was in Paris in 1971 when Ceausescu started his drive for political and ideological conformity, and he made a public protest against it. He went back to Bucharest in 1972 to take part in the Writers' Union congress that year, but was not nominated as a delegate. In April 1975 he was expelled from the Union but still permitted to go back to Paris, where he has since lived in exile. His wife joined him later, but had to leave their child in Rumania.

Ceausescu's relatively mild treatment of Tepeneag may have been due to the fact that he was dealing with an isolated case of dissent which might spread to other writers if the authorities magnified it. Ceausescu evidently felt strong enough, at that point, to view such incidents as minor matters, and his confidence was again demonstrated a year later, in July 1976, when the Rumanian government granted an amnesty to people who had illegally left the country and settled abroad, and pardons for those sentenced in their absence for this offence. The Communist penal code provides for prison sentences of from six months to three years in such cases, and sentences of from one to seven years for people who have had access to 'secret' information and refuse to return to Rumania from an 'approved tourist trip' out of the country. It is not known whether the amnesty persuaded illegal emigrants to come home, but it seems unlikely that many were tempted to do so. Similar amnesties had been granted before, but with little effect.

Beneath the smooth surface of Communist rule, however, signs of disturbance were beginning to appear. In May 1976 twenty students at the Baptist seminary in Bucharest staged a 'sit-in' strike for ten days as a protest against their teaching standards and living conditions. They also called for the reinstatement of a popular Baptist teacher, the pastor Josif Ton, who had been dismissed from his post at the seminary in 1974. These demands were rejected by the Baptist Union, the governing body of the Baptist Church, and two of the rebel students were expelled. It might seem, at first sight, that Ceausescu would welcome internal divisions in the Baptist Church as a success for his drive against religion, but this affair had more serious political implications. The Baptist Union was the officially sponsored council which collaborated with the Communist Department of Religious Cults, and it soon became clear that the strike by Baptist students reflected a more widespread sense of outrage among Baptists generally over the failure of their leaders to put up a fight against Communist persecution.

The students were supported by many of the Baptist churches in Bucharest and their feelings were expressed in an anonymous letter dated Christmas Day 1976 which was received by Western friends. The following is an extract:

One of the most important and most effective methods of the Communists in Rumania has been, and still is, to corrupt or win over the leaders of the Christian denominations. The very thing which the authorities failed to do with the apostolic Church, and which the authorities in Poland are failing to achieve with their own Catholic Church leaders, our own atheist Communists have easily succeeded in doing in Rumania. Through certain reactionary, fearful, profit-seeking and vain men – many of them without much education – the atheist authorities have managed to introduce into our Church restrictions and regulations which have particularly affected the religious movement. Who can directly accuse the authorities for these measures when they stem from the actions of our own organisation or Union?

The discontent among Baptists was aggravated by the way in which their leaders in the Baptist Union used delaying tactics to extend their period in office beyond the appointed time. The normal practice was to hold a congress every three years to discuss Church affairs and elect a new council. A congress was due to meet in 1975, but the leadership in the Union contrived to postpone it until February 1977. When it finally met, the election returned a council which still showed a majority in favour of co-operation with the Communist regime, and this was indeed essential for the Church to remain in being. But the dissident viewpoint was plainly stated by a number of speakers, among them Pastor Josif Ton, who had received his university education at Oxford.

In his speech, he said that Baptist groups which had no regular meeting-place authorised by the Department of Cults were harshly treated by the Communist authorities. He pointed out that these groups were forced by the local police to pay heavy fines under a decree issued in 1970 which condemned 'parasitic and anarchist attitudes contrary to the socialist system'. He produced documentary evidence in the shape of a police report about a Baptist group which had been fined for 'singing illegal religious songs', although the songs in question were taken from the officially recognised Baptist hymnbook. He also quoted evidence of discrimination by the Communist authorities against the children of Baptists in schools and universities, and he called for an end to such violations of human rights. Pastor Ton added that he had talked to the official Inspector of Cults, who was present in the hall as an observer, and this official had told him that the authorities were not aware of any infringement of religious rights and would be glad to hear of such incidents.

The appearance of the Charter 77 movement in Czechoslovakia in January 1977, and its manifesto defending human rights, gave a stimulus to the expression of dissent in Rumania. A Rumanian novelist, Paul Goma, wrote a letter to one of the leading Charter signatories, Pavel Kohout, in which he declared his solidarity with the Czechoslovak campaign and said that the Communist government in Rumania was denying its citizens their fundamental rights and ignoring the guarantees written into the Rumanian Constitution. The man who threw down his challenge to Ceausescu was a writer of no great literary reputation, but he has since become, almost overnight, the stormy petrel of intellectual dissent in Rumania. As a young man, Goma had already served a prison sentence for opposing the Soviet invasion of Hungary in 1956. In 1968, however, when Ceausescu condemned the Soviet assault on Czechoslovakia, Goma was so impressed that he joined the Rumanian Communist Party, but he was soon disillusioned by its suppression of freedom. He became an active member of the 'oneiricist' group of younger writers and criticised the regime with a frankness which led to his expulsion from the Party. After the departure of Tepeneag and another dissident writer, Virgil Tanase, for the West, Goma followed them in 1972 but returned to Rumania a year later.

Goma followed up his letter of support for Charter 77 by writing another letter addressed to all the governments which had signed the Helsinki Accord of 1975. In it he protested against violations of human rights in Rumania, saying that they were no more respected in so-called 'independent' Rumania than in 'occupied' Czechoslovakia. He pointed out that human rights guaranteed by the Rumanian Constitution (1965) were suppressed, and quoted the relevant clauses: equal rights for all citizens in economic, political, juridical and social life (*Article 17*); the right to work (*Article 18*); freedom of speech, press and meetings and demonstrations (*Article 28*); freedom of conscience and religious belief (*Article 30*); inviolability of the person and the home (*Articles 31, 32*); and privacy of correspondence and telephone conversations (*Article 33*). The letter also rejected the Communist claim that the Helsinki provision for 'non-interference in the internal affairs of another state' prohibited any foreign protests alleging violation of human rights.

Seven other people added their signatures to this letter. These were: Goma's wife; Erwin Gesswein and his wife Maria, both ethnic Germans and members of the Bucharest Philharmonic Orchestra; Carmen Manoliu and her son Sergei, both artists; Serban Stefanescu, grandson of a pre-war Cabinet Minister; and Adalbert Feher, a Hungarian metal-worker. In a telephone interview with the Swiss paper *Tribune de Genève*, Goma said that he had received many messages of support from people at home and abroad. He added: 'We are without rights, almost slaves, deprived of our freedom of movement. The law recognises this freedom exists, but it is not applied.'

Not content with these activities, and the risks they involved, Goma then proceeded to write a letter to Ceausescu himself, addressing it: 'Mr Ceausescu, Royal Palace, Bucharest.' He appealed to the President to act consistently with his declaration of support for Czechoslovakia in 1968 and to confirm it by expressing his solidarity with the Charter 77 manifesto on human rights. Goma said that the attitude of his compatriots had made him sad. When he had asked people to sign his letter to the

Helsinki signatory governments, some of them had refused from fear of the penal code and the security police. Others had said they would sign, but illegibly. Some had advised him to wait and see 'what the score will be at half-time'. Goma continued:

All our neighbours are beginning to stir and demand the rights due to them; even the Russians are raising a hue and cry that they are not free and their rights are trampled on. Only we Rumanians remain silent. And we are waiting, waiting for all this to be presented to us on a platter. Our Rumanians are thinking only of what they stand to lose when the security police hear about it. But they do not think of what they stand to gain despite the security police.

Goma added that he had been enraged when somebody told him he was behaving like 'a bad Rumanian'. He had replied that Ceausescu was a Rumanian through and through, but he had gone to Prague in August 1968 to assure Dubcek of Rumanian support, and he had strongly condemned the invasion of Czechoslovakia by the Warsaw Pact forces. Goma further remarked, in his own inimitable style:

Mr Ceausescu, I realise that you will not put your lofty signature next to that of a plain citizen, let alone an ungifted writer. And even if this miracle came true, what can one do with only two signatures? True, my wife could sign as well, but this would not alter the situation much. If 30 Hungarians were ready to sign, at least 90 Rumanian signatories would be needed to maintain relative proportions. Or at least 50. Or at least 10. But where should I find them? As I told you before, the Rumanians are afraid of the security police. It follows from this that in Rumania only two people are not afraid of the security police; your esteemed person and myself. But, as I have said before, with only two signatures . . .

It looked as if Goma was positively inviting trouble, but Ceausescu was apparently determined not to make a martyr of him. Goma was not arrested and taken away for police inter-

rogation, as might normally have been expected, but he was confined to his flat and subjected to various other forms of harassment. Security policemen in plain clothes were posted outside to
observe and photograph his visitors. He received anonymous
letters threatening him, and his wife, with death. His telephone
calls were monitored. At the same time, however, several of those
who had signed his letter to the governments represented at
Helsinki were allowed to emigrate, including the Gessweins,
husband and wife, who had been seeking permission to leave for
five years, and Carmen Manoliu and her son.

The Communist authorities then made a sudden and quite unexpected move by inviting Goma to meet a Deputy Prime Minister,
Cornel Burtica, and discuss the situation with him. Such a conciliatory gesture was quite unprecedented and it showed that
Ceausescu was still trying to use persuasion rather than force
to deal with dissent. The meeting took place in February 1977,
and a West German journalist succeeded in telephoning Goma
when he returned home from it. Goma told him that the situation
had not been 'clarified' on either side, but that his talk with
Burtica had been 'promising'. He had been told that the ban
on publication of his work might be lifted, and in fact a poem
he wrote on the Rumanian earthquake in March did appear in
print. When asked how people in Rumania had heard about his
letter to the Helsinki governments, Goma replied that it had been
broadcast by Radio Free Europe, and that this was the only source
available for information of that kind. The members of his group,
he added, had no thoughts of revolt, but only wanted the government to fulfil its commitments on human rights in the Rumanian
Constitution and the Helsinki agreements. Goma said that he
had been told by Burtica that none of his co-signatories had been
arrested, but he, Goma, would be glad to hear that from them
personally. He had complained that he was still being followed,
to which Burtica replied that Goma was 'having hallucinations',

but if it was true, the necessary measures would be taken.

The shock of the earthquake shortly afterwards in March created a wave of national unity in the task of rebuilding and probably helped to prolong the truce between the Communist authorities and the dissenters. Events soon showed, however, that the struggle for human rights was gaining ground and spreading beyond a small group of writers and intellectuals. Despite Goma's pessimistic view of Rumanian support, in his letter to Ceausescu, the number of signatures to his appeal to foreign governments rapidly increased from the original eight to over two hundred. Some of these came from people encouraged by the exit permits granted to a few of the original signatories, and hoping that they, too, would receive 'Goma passports' as they were commonly called. Goma's petition, like his letter to the governments which took part in the Helsinki Conference, was broadcast by Radio Free Europe and thus reached a large audience in Rumania.

In April 1977, quite separately from Goma's action, a petition was issued by six Evangelical leaders entitled 'Appeal for Respect of Human Rights for Evangelical Believers in Rumania'. Its main author was the Baptist Pastor Josif Ton, and the other signatories were Pavel Niculescu, Radu Dumitrescu and Aurel Popescu, all Baptists; Constantin Caraman, a Pentecostalist; and Dr Silviu Ciota, a Seventh Day Adventist. The petition charged the Communist government with violating its undertakings at Helsinki in 1975 to respect religious freedom and other human rights. It protested against persecution under three main headings: interference with religious meetings, loss of employment and discrimination in education.

The petition condemned the imposition of heavy fines on small groups of believers who met to talk or pray without official permission. It said that some people had been punished merely for eating supper together after a church service. One group had been fined for singing Baptist hymns at home, and another for meeting in a room with Bible verses on the wall which were alleged by the police to be 'contrary to the rules of decency'. The petition gave the names of fifty people who had been down-graded or dismissed from their jobs because of their religious activities. Secret instructions had been sent to factory foremen ordering a purge of Evangelical Christians from key positions. Despite the constitutional guarantees of equality in education, there was flagrant discrimination in schools against the children of religious believers. They were systematically excluded from some branches of higher education by means of a rule compelling applicants to produce a certificate from the Communist Youth League.

Amnesty International in its Report for 1976-77 gave further concrete evidence confirming the abuse of human and civic rights in Rumania. It has received numerous reports of prison sentences imposed on members of the Hungarian minority for protesting against discrimination in the treatment of their rights, and the imprisonment of ethnic Germans for trying to cross the frontier without permission after vainly applying for years for exit permits. The Communist authorities, as the Report confirms, have used the law of 1970 against 'parasites and anarchists' to persecute Baptists, Seventh Day Adventists, and members of the Pentecostal sect. Police officials often make them hold Bibles while being photographed, as evidence against them. They have been punished by fines, dismissal from jobs and other forms of harassment.

The Report quotes, among others, the examples of a man called Dobrescu who was fined in 1976 for holding religious meetings, and a Baptist pastor, Olah, also fined for unauthorised preaching of the Gospel. In 1977 fines were imposed on Alexander Monacu and several friends for illegally singing religious hymns. Referring to the petition on human rights issued by Pastor Josif Ton and others, already mentioned here, the Amnesty International Report says that they were arrested in April 1977 and interrogated daily for several weeks. They were badly beaten by the police and Pavel Niculescu was reported to have suffered from broken ribs. They were told that they would be tried for treason because they had sent their petition to 'hostile foreign agents' (probably meant to refer to Radio Free Europe), but they were released without being formally charged. The Report gives an estimate of neo-Protestant sectarians held in Rumanian prisons as numbering from 50 to 200. It also estimates the strength of the neo-Protestant community at 400,000 members, a figure which, if correct, reveals a great increase over the 1973 estimate of 160,000. The severity of Communist repression may well be due to this rapid growth, and in part responsible for it.

Other abuses of human rights in Rumania were quoted in the Amnesty International Report. It said that, in May 1975, the government had issued a decree, supplementing the Press law, which gave the authorities the exclusive control over the import and export of printed matter and made any Rumanian citizen who privately imported religious or other literature liable to prosecution. Reports said that hundreds of Bibles were confiscated in 1974. As the printing of Bibles in Rumania is severely limited, many copies are imported from other countries by believers, but this is treated as an offence punishable by prison sentences of up to seven years.

The Report expressed great concern about the treatment of Rumanian citizens who applied for permission to leave the country. According to internal sources of information, about a hundred members of the German minority, descended from Saxons who settled in the country centuries ago, were dismissed from their jobs after submitting applications for emigration permits. In other cases, the authorities had granted formal permission, but had kept on delaying the issue of passports, during which time the applicants were harassed, threatened, and fired from their jobs. Many of those arrested when trying to cross the frontier illegally said that they were beaten by the police and kept in cells without proper clothing or sanitary facilities for up to six months before being put on trial.

Amnesty International has adopted as 'prisoners of conscience' two ethnic Germans, Rudolf and Aneta Jorgovan, who tried to cross into Yugoslavia without permits in August 1976 after repeated applications for emigration papers, but were caught and sentenced by the district court of Timisoara to prison terms of three years and eighteen months respectively.

We may now resume the story of Paul Goma, whose interview with a Deputy Prime Minister at the end of February 1977 had left him a precarious degree of freedom subject to good behaviour. But he had given no pledge to stop his activities on human rights, and he was getting support from other dissenters who backed his letter to Pavel Kohout, expressing solidarity with Charter 77 in Czechoslovakia, and his appeal to the governments that had signed the Helsinki Final Act. Moreover, the petition drawn up by Josif Ton and his five colleagues showed that the agitation for human rights was growing among the Baptist churches and the neo-Protestant sects. The arrests of Ton and his co-signatories early in April 1977, gave a clear sign of determination by the Communist regime to stop the rot by sterner measures.

Goma was arrested on 5 April together with many of the people who had signed his letter to foreign governments. Later that month, Amnesty International submitted to President Ceausescu a request for a public enquiry into the cases of Paul Goma and other members of the human rights movement who had disappeared under mysterious circumstances. It also launched an 'Urgent Action' appeal calling for public support on behalf of Goma. The Amnesty Report for 1976-77 states that 170 people in Rumania signed this appeal, and that many of them were re-ported to have been detained, interrogated, and sentenced to hard labour. Some were beaten or threatened to make them sign incriminating statements. Among them were prominent Rumanian intellectuals, including the literary critic, Ion Negoitescu, and Professor Vlad Gheorgescu. Another signatory of the Amnesty appeal, Stefan Toia, was reportedly interned in a psychiatric hospital. Nicolae Dascalu, a teacher of English in Bucharest, was reported to have suffered daily interrogations lasting up to eighteen hours, with severe beatings. After his release, he went to the American Embassy to seek political asylum, which was refused, and the police re-arrested him when he left.

Amnesty International also heard from private sources that although some people who had signed human rights appeals were released after weeks of interrogation, others were held in forced-labour camps working on the building of a canal between the Russian Black Sea ports and the Danube, a project of special interest to the Soviet Union. According to a report in the *Observer* on 21 August 1977 seven Rumanians wrote to Amnesty International saying that they had been sentenced to work for a year in the 'Gulag prison camp system on the Danube-Black Sea canal', as they called it, after sending an appeal on human rights to the Swiss paper *Die Weltwoche*. After their arrests on 1 July they had been interrogated for long periods, beaten up, and warned to sever their connection with the international human rights movement. This suggests that they were among the Rumanian signatories of the Amnesty International appeal on be-half of Paul Goma. They said that their trial was held in secret and that they had no defence lawyer. They ended with a promise that on 1 September 1977, wherever they might be, they would go on hunger strike and maintain it 'to the end'. Their names were given as Josif Nita, Ion Marinescu, Radu Negrescu, Raymond Paumescu, Nicolae Vindisch, Vasile Constantinescu and Dragos Neantzu. Their ages ranged from twenty-six to thirty-three.

Support for Goma was particularly strong in Paris, where he had many friends. In a letter to them written before his arrest in April 1977, but not published till 25 April in *Le Matin de Paris*, Goma said that he had never taken part in any conspiracy to overthrow the Rumanian Communist regime. He considered that any attempt to arrest him and put him on trial would be illegal. If that happened, he would refuse to answer questions and would go on a 'hunger and silence' strike. The publication of this letter gave fresh impetus to French support for him. Street marches and demonstrations outside the Rumanian Embassy were organised. The French PEN Club announced that it had made Goma an associate member 'in recognition of his literary work and to demonstrate its solidarity with the writer in his present plight'. The French Committee on Civil Rights in Rumania issued a statement demanding Goma's release and an end to the measures against human rights defenders. This was signed by many French intellectuals, including the Communist poet, Louis Aragon, the existentialist writer, Jean-Paul Sartre, the left-wing novelist, Simone de Beauvoir; and by Soviet exiles, among them Vladimir Bukovsky, Leonid Plyushch and Natalya Gorbanevskaya.

Western protest of this kind must have made little impression on Ceausescu, but his own position was far from easy. He had to take into account the adverse effects which the arrests of Goma and other dissenters might have on the discussion of human rights at the Belgrade follow-up conference on Helsinki, due to start in June that year. Nor could he risk losing the benefits of Western economic aid through trade and advanced technology for his industrialisation programme. These were perhaps the main reasons which led him to tread more softly. Goma was released on 6 May 1977, with many of his supporters. A few of them had already been given exit permits, while others, among them Ion Negoitescu, had disowned their support for Goma and thus been restored to official favour. Two days later, a government decree was published announcing a general amnesty to mark the 100th anniversary of Rumanian independence. It freed prisoners serving terms of up to three years and reduced longer sentences. The total number who benefited was estimated at nearly 29,000 but most of them were ordinary criminals. The number of political prisoners affected was thought to be relatively small.

At the same time, Ceausescu made it clear that the releases and the amnesty in no way implied a more tolerant attitude to human rights campaigners, though he seemed to have somewhat modified his earlier view that 'he who is not with us is against us'. In a speech to a peasant congress on 20 April, shortly before the amnesty decree, he said:

It is true that in our society there still exist elements with backward, noxious concepts and attitudes of mind which they have inherited from the old society; sick elements, so to speak. As you well know, we have adopted a clear-cut position. All citizens, notwithstanding their past, who work side by side with our entire people can find a place in our society and nobody will bother them as long as they mind their own business. They are citizens of our homeland, and we treat them accordingly. We must, however, eliminate the dead wood and the tares. We must endeavour to free our homeland's field forever from anything that might infect healthy plants. Let us never admit such things. Let us take the necessary educational and political measures, and let us also put to work those who believe they can live in Rumania without working, but idle along and jabber right and left.

The Communist government also took a more aggressive line against Western attempts to apply the Helsinki provisions on human rights to Communist states. In an article published in June 1977 the Rumanian Foreign Minister Gheorghe Macovescu, asserted that the insistence of 'certain circles' on the Helsinki clauses dealing with human contacts and exchanges of information had been one of the main obstacles to their implementation. There had been a tendency to make use of these provisions to put political pressure on some governments, with a view to securing the free circulation of 'tendentious information'. Macovescu added:

Anyone who ever feels tempted to teach us democracy or anything else will be well advised to refrain from doing so. It is the exclusive right of every people to decide if it has something to say and when to say it.

In July 1977 Ceausescu gave an interview to American journalists in which he said that the Western approach to human rights problems 'contradicts the spirit of the Helsinki documents and their provision for the observance of non-interference in the domestic affairs of other countries'. He added that there was a difference between Rumania and the capitalist countries in their approach to human rights, but the starting-point at Helsinki was the need 'to observe the right of each people to settle its own problems as it wishes, and to find methods of collaborating among states compatible with the integrity of their social systems'.

In August that year, however, the Communist regime was suddenly faced with a challenge from a most unexpected and highly embarrassing quarter, namely Rumanian workers. Coal miners in the Jiu valley pits, which produce 60% of Rumanian coal, went on strike and demanded improvements in their pay, pensions, food supplies and working conditions. The strike was not reported in the Communist press or broadcasts, but eyewitness accounts eventually reached the West. The miners were angered by a new pensions law which increased the contributions from higher-paid workers, among whom the miners held a lead-

154

ing place, in order to raise pensions for the lower-paid. Food shortages were another major grievance. The miners also protested against having to work overtime in pits with obsolete equipment, as they were being required to do to make up production lost in the earthquake disaster. They stayed down the mines and refused to come up until they received satisfaction. When a Deputy Prime Minister, Ilie Verdets, and a Politbureau member went to talk to them, they were booed and jeered, and one report said they were held as hostages.

Ceausescu immediately broke off his holiday in a Soviet resort on the Black Sea and hurried to the scene of the trouble. Eyewitnesses said he was met by a hostile crowd of miners who refused to let him speak for several hours and shouted complaints at him about their conditions, saying that these had been better under capitalism. Finally, after Ceausescu had promised to meet their grievances, the men went back to work. The new pension law was hastily withdrawn. Lorries arrived with supplies of meat and other foods. The regional Communist Party leadership was purged, and three months later, in December 1977, the Minister of Mining, Constantin Babatu, lost his job. Order was soon restored. The Jiu valley was sealed off and closed to foreign visitors. Several thousand miners were dismissed and sent back to their native villages with their families, where the local authorities ignored their needs. The Communist press, following a familiar technique of Communist rule, published messages of loyalty to the regime which miners in other pits were forced to send.

There are two aspects of this affair which merit special attention. First, the strike was no minor incident. The number of miners said to be involved was 35,000, and they were mainly recruited from former peasants who had no experience of combining to organise a strike of this magnitude. Ceausescu's programme of rapid industrial expansion had produced a result he did not anticipate in the creation of large new groups of industrial workers who, though prohibited from forming independent unions, were developing their own methods of combining together to voice their demands. Secondly, and more ominous for the regime, this strike by Rumanian workers had much in common with the spontaneous outbreaks by industrial workers in Poland, where they have at times forced the Communist government to make major policy changes. This danger to Communist rule is less in Rumania, where the movement for human rights is much smaller, but the miners' strike was proof that it exists, and Ceausescu's hasty concessions showed his awareness of it.

The summer of 1977 passed without further agitation over human rights and Ceausescu's mixture of threats and persuasion seemed to have the situation well under control. Paul Goma, when he was released in May, refused to talk to Western journalists, and this may have been a condition for restoring his freedom. He managed to telephone friends in Paris and told them that he was weakened by going on hunger strike while under arrest and was going to see a doctor. He also said that his address book had been taken from him and he was forced to occupy a room without a telephone, so he must have made the connection elsewhere.

In November 1977 the Communist authorities felt strong enough to allow Goma, with his wife and son, to leave for Paris, a decision which they may since have regretted. Goma gave a press conference on his arrival. He said he had been warned by the Rumanian police before leaving that they had a long arm and he knew what to expect if he failed to keep his mouth shut. His subsequent remarks showed that he had no intention of keeping silent. He said that he planned to return to Rumania, perhaps within a year or even six months, but while abroad he thought he could best serve his countrymen by voicing 'their cries of revolt and despair'.

He then talked about the victims of Communist repression in Rumania. He said that forced-labour camps on the Danube had been reopened, and that the use of internment in psychiatric hospitals against dissenters had been revived. Thousands of people had been taken from their homes and resettled, among them the 4,000 miners and their families sent back to their villages. He intended to make a full list of names and would try to find out what had happened in each case. He said that the Rumanian population was far too accustomed to having only one master. Their repression was carried out with more imagination than in the Soviet Union or Czechoslovakia, where the Communist rulers were lacking in what he called 'Balkan subtleties'. As an example, he quoted his own treatment by a Vice-Minister of the Interior in Bucharest, Piesita, who had first beaten him after his arrest and then, just before his departure for Paris, had clapped him on the shoulder, called him 'Paulika', and wished him *bon voyage*.

Goma said that Ceausescu's statements about 'national independence' and patriotism had deceived many people in Rumania, himself included, but they were only a smokescreen for him to do whatever he wanted, or what Brezhnev wanted. He described Ceausescu's wife, Elena, as 'a real misfortune' for Rumania because she meddled in everything. She had revised the statutes of the Academy of Sciences, suppressed the Institute of Mathematical Researches, and ordered the demolition of an old church in Bucharest which had been restored only a year earlier. She had also caused all books, albums and postcards on monasteries and churches to be withdrawn from sale, because the Mass had not been interrupted when she visited the Agapia monastery in Moldavia.

Referring to the treatment of minorities in Rumania, Goma said that the problem of the German minority was on the way to being settled by large-scale emigration. The position of the Hungarians was far more delicate and serious. As an example of Rumanian assimilation, he recalled that the Hungarian section

157

of the University in Cluj had been closed down after a visit by Ceausescu. Questioned about Rumanian views of 'Euro-Communism' and disagreements between the Soviet Communist Party and those in Western Europe, Goma said that his own people had a hard life under Communist rule and they doubted whether Communism in France or Italy could or would change its basic nature.

In 1939 the Jewish minority in Rumania numbered about 800,000, but 415,000 were living in Bessarabia and Northern Bukovina, territories which were handed over to the Soviet Union in 1940 with a small part going to Hungary and Bulgaria. The Jews remaining in Rumania were saved from Nazi German extermination by King Carol's government after its enforced alliance with Hitler and their wartime losses amounted to 15,000, of whom 3,000 to 4,000 were killed during the brief tenure of power in Rumania by the Fascist Iron Guard regime. When the Second World War ended in 1945 about 280,000 Jews emigrated from Rumania mainly to Israel, leaving a present Jewish community in Rumania estimated at about 90,000. They have found it difficult to get exit visas in more recent years. At the same time, many Jews occupy high positions in the Rumanian Communist Party and the government.

In principle, Ceausescu has always opposed emigration by members of national minorities and insisted that they must make their future in Rumania, although he has allowed a small number to leave on compassionate grounds of family reunion. In practice, the German minority has been given far more latitude in emigration than the Hungarian, probably from fear of making concessions which might tend to encourage protests in the neighbouring Communist state of Hungary for their kinsmen in Transylvania, which was a part of Hungary for over a thousand years. In October 1977, however, articles began to appear in the Hungarian Communist press which for the first time openly expressed deep concern over the fate of the Hungarians in Transylvania. Ceausescu and Kadar, having failed to find an answer to this thorny problem, had only agreed to open a Hungarian consulate in Cluj, the capital of Transylvania, and a Rumanian consulate in Debrecen in Hungary, which has a Rumanian minority of about 20,000. No concrete action was taken, however, and tempers run high on both sides.

In January 1978 a letter protesting against the enforced assimilation of the Hungarian minority was sent to Ceausescu by Karoly Kiraly, a former member of the Rumanian Party's Central Committee and a deputy in the National Assembly, who is himself of Hungarian birth. He accused the Rumanian authorities of trying to abolish teaching in Hungarian in secondary schools and technical colleges and closing down Hungarian language institutions. He also claimed that the best jobs in predominantly Hungarian areas were invariably given to Rumanians who spoke no Hungarian. Following the publication of his appeal in Western newspapers, Kiraly was banished to the small town of Caransebes in Transylvania and accepted this decision in return for guarantees that friends who supported his protest would not suffer reprisals. He has since been kept under close police observation and in virtual isolation.

More than a dozen prominent figures in Rumanian political and cultural circles openly associated themselves with Kiraly's appeal, including Ion-Gheorghe Maurer, a former Prime Minister; Janos Fazekas, then a Deputy Prime Minister and member of the Party's executive bureau; three members of the Central Committee; and several editors of Hungarian-language literary reviews. In April 1978 personal appeals were made to Ceausescu by three leading members of the Hungarian community: Janos Fazekas (already mentioned); Professor Lajos Takacs, a member of the Communist Party's Central Committee and formerly Chancellor of the University of Cluj in Transylvania; and Andreas

THE KREMLIN'S DILEMMA

Sueto, a popular Hungarian writer and deputy chairman of the Rumanian Writers' Association. Professor Takacs complained that out of nearly 35,000 Hungarian pupils in secondary and vocational schools about 16,000 were given instruction only in Rumanian. He also demanded greatly increased powers for the Hungarian Nationality Council set up in 1969, including the right to select the Hungarian minority representatives on local and central bodies and a new statute for minorities.

In May 1978 a vitriolic reply was made by Mihnea Gheorghiu, a Rumanian writer and President of the Academy of Social and Political Sciences as well as being a Central Committee member. His target was Gyula Illyes, the leading poet in Hungary, who had published two articles several months earlier in a Hungarian paper in which he accused the Rumanian authorities of practising 'apartheid and ethnocide' and said he wanted to call the attention of Europe to this matter. In an article in the Rumanian literary review *Luceafarul* attacking Illyes, Gheorghiu said that he had an 'anti-Rumanian obsession' and was spreading 'painted lies'.

These exchanges of literary gunfire were probably approved by Communist leaders on both sides, but Ceausescu in Rumania is in a more difficult position than Kadar in Hungary. Ceausescu has to reckon with the adverse effects which his treatment of the Hungarian minority might have on his valuable trade with the West, especially in the United States with its own large Hungarian community. Nor can he be at all sure of support from the Kremlin where the immediate post-war attitude to the settlement of Transylvania on Rumania was by no means reassuring, and where annoyance with Ceausescu's independent line in external affairs is growing. This comparatively minor issue is a pointer to the problems which demands for self-determination by larger national minorities can cause for Communist governments no less than for the West.

Ceausescu is not the sort of man to lose any sleep worrying

160

about his problems. He has ruled in Rumania since 1965 and his grip on power is stronger than ever. He was sixty in January 1978 when he and his wife, Elena, received semi-royal honours, but he looks much younger and seems to be in the best of health. He is courted and flattered by Western governments. In June 1978, at the invitation of Mr Callaghan's government, he made a state visit to London and stayed at Buckingham Palace, being the first Communist leader to enjoy that distinction. Yet only a month earlier, the Rumanian authorities refused an entry visa to *The Times* correspondent in Belgrade, Dessa Trevisan, who wanted to prepare a special report on Rumania, coinciding with Ceausescu's London visit. Her accurate reports on the coal-miners' strike and the treatment of the Hungarian minority had angered the Communist regime, as well as her interviews with Paul Goma and other dissenters. She had been warned in 1977 to stay away from them if she wanted to return, but the Rumanian reaction was a gross breach of the Helsinki provisions allowing freedom for journalists to carry out their legitimate tasks.

While Ceausescu was welcomed in London, his relations with Moscow soon took another turn for the worse. In November 1978, while attending a Warsaw Pact summit meeting in Moscow, he flatly rejected a Soviet demand for the Communist allies to increase their contributions to the joint military budget. Moreover he announced this publicly on his return to Bucharest, saying that the international situation did not justify this increased military expenditure which would prevent an improvement in Rumanian living standards. The angry response in Moscow showed that the Kremlin was losing patience and gave a sharp reminder of the risks run by Ceausescu in his balancing act between East and West.

CHAPTER 6

EAST GERMANY—
A PEOPLE CAGED

While Ceausescu in Rumania has prospered by turning nationalism to his advantage, the Communist regime in East Germany
has had to contend with a much more difficult situation. Ceausescu
could draw on deeply rooted memories of past struggles and
achievements which provided a strong bond of unity and national
pride among Rumanians. In East Germany there was no such
foundation on which to build. The East German Communist state
is an artificial post-war creation carved out of the greater Germany created by Bismarck. It remains a Soviet zone of military
occupation in the heart of Europe manned by twenty Russian
divisions kept on a war footing. The East German government is
merely a political instrument of Soviet policy in keeping Germany permanently divided.

It has to compete with a West German rival, the Federal
German Republic, which has arisen from the ashes of Nazi
defeat and exerts a dynamic power of magnetism on the East
Germans. Their Communist rulers have carried out a programme
of economic recovery and industrial reconstruction which, though
much less impressive than the West German 'economic miracle',
has still provided higher living standards in East Germany than
those of the other Soviet puppet states, except perhaps in Czechoslovakia. International recognition has been secured by the admis-

sion of the so-called 'German Democratic Republic' (GDR) to the United Nations and by establishing full diplomatic relations with many states of different political systems, notably the Federal German Republic. An East German entity has been created with many formal trappings of sovereignty, but it has totally failed to win the loyalty of its own people. The Berlin Wall and the heavily guarded East German frontiers which prevent East Germans from leaving the country are a shameful and public admission by the Communist regime of that failure.

The first Soviet *Gauleiter* of East Germany, Walter Ulbricht, spent the war in Russia and returned to Berlin in the baggage train of the Red Army. He was a Stalinist of the deepest dye, both by ideological conviction and for reasons of self-interest. The harshness of his rule provoked a revolt in 1953 by East German workers and he called in Russian troops and tanks to crush it. But in the years between 1949 and the building of the Berlin Wall in 1961, nearly three million East Germans 'voted with their feet' by escaping to the West in a massive and overwhelming demonstration of their protest against Communist rule. As those who talked to the refugees in the West Berlin reception centres soon discovered, their main motive was a feeling of frustration and despair which made their lives intolerable.

For example, a farmer drafted into a collective farm would say: 'I got into trouble because I criticised the new system. I asked them how it was possible to run a collective farm efficiently when there were not enough men and machines.' A veterinary surgeon would say: 'I couldn't stand by any longer watching valuable livestock die like flies because of bad conditions which I could do nothing to improve.'

Many doctors were driven to desperation because they could get no supplies of medical drugs and surgical instruments. A teacher said: 'I got tired of having to teach Communist politics in my geography lessons.' An electronics engineer working in

163

Berlin was posted to Dresden, but not allowed to take his family with him because of a housing shortage. A young mechanic said: 'I was fed up with having to do all sorts of "voluntary service" without pay, either for the *Vopos* (the People's Police), or on a building site, or at weekends on the land.' Another young man had lost his job because he refused to 'volunteer' for the East German army. When he appealed to a labour court, he was threatened with a trial for 'slandering the state'. Some young people left because they were not allowed to travel abroad but a few went back to East Germany when their money ran out. So did a handful of professional people, doctors, architects, engineers, who found the competition in West Germany too much for them. But nearly all the refugees settled in the West and made a new life there.

The Communist police and frontier guards did their best to stop this flood of refugees, but with little success. The mass exodus was on such a scale that it imposed a mounting strain on the East German economy from loss of manpower. About half of the refugees were under 25 and over one-third were employed in industry, transport, trade and agriculture, mostly as skilled workers, technicians and specialists of one kind or another. In March 1961 at the annual Congress of the Socialist Unity (or Communist) Party, the Chairman of the State Planning Commission had to admit that there were serious labour shortages. He also announced that the East German aircraft industry, in which large sums had been invested, had been closed down so that its machinery and skilled labour could be switched to other tasks. In August 1961 Ulbricht decided to seal off the escape routes by building a concrete wall twelve miles long between East and West Berlin, and a belt of barbed wire, mines and watch-towers along the 875 miles of frontier with West Germany.

Khrushchev's denunciation of Stalin's crimes in 1956 encouraged hopes in East Germany, as in other satellites, of some relaxation in Communist repression, but Ulbricht would have none of it. In 1962, after the publication in Russia of Solzhenitsyn's devastating book, *One Day in the Life of Ivan Denisovich*, describing conditions in a Soviet labour camp, some East German Communist writers called for its publication in East Germany. The sequel is recalled by William Treharne Jones in an article published in *Survey*, October 1975. Ulbricht summoned the writers to a special meeting and told them bluntly that any liberal innovation of that sort was out of the question.

Some people (he said) are interested in writings on the labour camp atmosphere in Siberia. We do not need such literature here, as we have no labour camps. But we do enjoy good relations with the Soviet Union, and we can organise visits for comrades who want to learn more about the Siberian camp atmosphere . . . There have been demands for the publication of books by an author called . . . (a pause, as if he did not know the name. A voice called out 'Solzhenitsyn'. Ulbricht nodded and went on.) If the comrades in Moscow wish to print anti-Soviet literature, that is their business. But such literature will not be published here in the German Democratic Republic.

In 1968, when the new 'collective leadership' formed in Moscow by Brezhnev and Kosygin were debating what should be done about Dubcek's explosive programme of reforms, it was Ulbricht who led the way in pressing for invasion. But when Brezhnev set his sights on a detente between East and West, Ulbricht became an embarrassment to the Kremlin. In May 1971 he was replaced by Erich Honecker as Party leader and put out to pasture in the honorary post of Chairman of the Party. He died in 1973.

Honecker was himself a die-hard Communist cut in the Stalin pattern. As the Minister for State Security under Ulbricht, he had directed the building of the Berlin Wall, but he began by making some concessions. He had kept in touch with the writers and may have felt that Ulbricht had carried repression to a point where it threatened to destroy all creative talent. This in itself was not likely to cause him much concern, but the writers who might cause trouble were few in number and perhaps Honecker still hoped to win them back. At the 1971 Congress of the Communist Party, Honecker admitted that artistic creation was showing signs of what he called 'superficiality, formality, and boredom'. Six months later, at a meeting of the Party's Central Committee, he caused a sensation by telling his audience: 'There can be no taboos in the fields of art and literature, so long as one's starting point is basically socialist.'

With this encouragement, new signs of life began to appear in the cultural desert. Writers previously banned from publication took up their pens again and new ones appeared in print. The seeds of dissent had already been sown in East Germany by the Soviet invasion of Czechoslovakia in 1968, when there were protest demonstrations in the streets of East Berlin and other cities, and also by students in several universities. A number of people were arrested and sentenced to prison terms of from 15 to 27 months. But although this played its part, the 'new wave' of criticism in art and literature bore little resemblance to the campaigns for human rights in Poland and Czechoslovakia. The East German dissidents were a small and scattered minority, and many writers among them were practising Communists and proud of it. They did not challenge the Communist monopoly of power, but only sought to expose its worst abuses. They chose themes and characters in their books and plays who suffered from these abuses and were instantly recognised by readers and audiences. And they were powerfully reinforced by popular actors, singers, and 'rock' musicians who used satire as their weapon.

One of the first to profit from Honecker's cultural truce was Reiner Kunze, a lyrical poet whose work was much admired in

East Germany, especially among young people. In the earlier post-war years, he was more interested in poetry than politics, and he steered clear of trouble with the regime. But he frequently visited Czechoslovakia, where he made friends with writers, and married a Czech doctor. These influences led him away from conformity to an independent line. He was deeply stirred by the Soviet invasion of Czechoslovakia in 1968 and protested strongly against it, which caused the East German authorities to prohibit publication of his work, even including his translations of Czech and Hungarian poems. His poetry continued to appear in the West, but he was forced to pay heavy fines for 'breaking East German copyright laws', no matter whether a volume of his poems was involved or merely a single poem. After Honecker's cultural thaw, Kunze was allowed to have his work published again and to give public readings of it. In 1976 a book of short stories by him called *The Wonderful Years* came out in East Germany. It described the physical and moral pressures applied to young people who criticised the Communist regime.

Another early beneficiary of the cultural relaxation was Ulrich Plenzdorf, a hitherto obscure writer of film scripts for the Communist state studio, DEFA. He had already written a film scenario called *The New Sufferings* based on his own frustrations and difficulties from bureaucratic repression, but this and other scripts he wrote were rejected on various pretexts. In 1972, however, he re-wrote *The New Sufferings* as a play and sent it to a leading provincial theatre, where it was immediately accepted and performed to crowded audiences in many cities and towns.

Plenzdorf's play made its strongest impression on the younger generation. It tells the story of a young factory worker, Edgar Wibeau, who quits his job after dropping, with malice aforethought, a metal plate on the foot of the foreman. Edgar goes to East Berlin, where he lives in a hut in the suburbs and gives himself up to a gipsy existence, free from the bonds of daily routine, order and discipline. There he indulges his passion for 'rock' music and abstract painting. He falls in love, but the girl rejects him for a soldier, perhaps not surprisingly. Edgar consoles himself by inventing a new machine for spraying paint, but electrocutes himself while testing it. His machine is reassembled by his mates from a building site, where Edgar worked sometimes to keep body and soul together, and of course it proves to be a great success.

This conventional ending was probably intended as a sop to Communist feelings, but this did not soften its impact on the East German younger generation. They saw in Edgar the mirror of their own drab and meaningless existence in a Communist society, and they saluted the hero who had broken away from it. Edgar wore jeans as his badge of independence, and for him they were not just part of the current fashion among youth, but a cult, an act of social defiance, a declaration of independence. Edgar rams this home in crude, but topical, language:

Can anyone imagine life without jeans? Jeans are the classiest pants in the world. For them, I'd give up all those synthetic rags from the Young Fashion shops which always look so straight. In fact, I could give up everything for jeans, except perhaps for the most way-out thing of all. And except for music. And by music, mates, I don't mean some 'Handelsohn Bacholdy' – no, not that, but genuine music . . . I mean, of course, real jeans . . . anyone who wears real jeans knows what I mean. But that doesn't mean that every guy who wears genuine jeans is a genuine jeans-wearer. Most people haven't a clue what they're wearing. It half kills me when I see some 25-year-old git who's squeezed his fat hips into his jeans . . . You know, for me jeans are not so much a kind of trouser as an attitude. I've sometimes thought one shouldn't grow older than 17. Once they reach 18, they're finished. At least, that's how I've found them. You know what I mean?

This language was drawn from life and the message was loud and clear. A whole generation of teenagers born and bred in the

Communist environment, suckled on the milk of Marx and lapped in the love of Lenin, could find no purpose or meaning in their lives.

Plenzdorf followed this up with a film *The Legend of Paul and Paula* which was also a social allegory, but expressed in romantic and erotic terms. Paul is a government official with an eye to the main chance, a married man who has an affair with an unmarried mother, Paula, who is a badly-paid and over-worked assistant in a supermarket. Paul falls in love with her and is prepared to give up his privileges, as well as his wife, to marry Paula. She finally agrees, but she is pregnant by Paul and is told by the doctor that she will die if she has the baby. She decides to take the risk and it proves fatal.

Their love story is told with a mixture of genuine emotion and a generous display of bare flesh, highly offensive to a strait-laced Communist regime. It also contains flashes of satire equally wounding to Communist self-esteem. As a highly-placed government official, Paul lives in the bourgeois comfort of a modern flat, while Paula, on the other side of the street, is miserably lodged in a condemned building. Paul goes to his office every morning in a chauffeur-driven car with other colleagues who wait for him impatiently but, as soon as he gets into the car, they all start playing cards.

Satire was used with much more devastating effect by Stefan Heym, a veteran writer with an established reputation. Born in 1912, Heym left Germany in 1933 as a Jew and a Communist to seek refuge in the United States, where he married. He served with the American forces during the war and was commissioned in the field. He left in 1952 and chose to settle in East Germany, but found it increasingly hard to reconcile his life under Communist rule with the freedom he had known in the USA. He wrote a pamphlet on the 1953 revolt by East German workers, but withdrew it before publication on the advice of Party officials.

He then wrote a novel on the German socialist thinker Lassalle; a short novel on Daniel Defoe, not in his capacity as the author of *Robinson Crusoe*, but based on Defoe's pamphlet in 1702 about the right way to deal with dissenters, for which Defoe was arrested and put in the pillory; and a book called *The King David Report*, which is a biting satire on Stalinist rule, thinly disguised as an official biography of King David commissioned by his son, King Solomon.

These works were banned from publication in East Germany, but Heym wrote English translations which appeared in Britain. In April 1973, after Honecker had taken over as Party leader, the East German veto was lifted, a decision which seems to have taken Heym by surprise. *The King David Report* tells the story of a historian called Ethan who is given the task of producing a biography of King David, but finds himself caught between Solomon's orders for a book which will glorify David and strengthen Solomon's own position and Ethan's discovery that the historical truth about David is very different and could only be told at serious risk to the author. This, of course, was a situation closely resembling Heym's own relations with the Communist regime. He makes Ethan describe his dilemma in these words:

I saw that Solomon had thought of practically everything, and that there was no escaping his favour. I also saw that I might end, as some writers did, with my head cut off and my body nailed to the city wall, but that, on the other hand, I might wax fat and prosperous if I guarded my tongue and used my stylus wisely. With some luck and the aid of our Lord Yahveh, I might even insert in the King David Report a word here and a line there by which later generations would perceive what really came to pass in these years, and what manner of man David ben Jesse was; who served as a whore simultaneously to a king and the king's son and the king's daughter; who fought as a hired soldier against his own blood; who had his own son and his most loyal servants murdered while loudly bewailing their death; and who forged a people out of a motley of miserable peasants and recalcitrant nomads.

Solomon's ministers try to dissuade Ethan by using the same kind of arguments employed by Communist regimes today. Zadok the Priest says to him:

Where would we arrive if everybody doubted everything and went on his own search for the truth? Why, the great resplendent temple we are building would collapse before its construction was finished; the throne which King David erected, and on which his son Solomon sits, would topple!

Solomon's Chancellor, Josephat, also tries to urge the need for discretion:

But contradictions are there to be smoothed over, Ethan, not to be stressed. Contradictions puzzle and embitter the heart; but the Wisest of Kings, Solomon, wishes all of us, and especially the writers of books, to accentuate the more edifying aspects of life. We are to strike a happy medium between what is, and what we want people to believe, and to reflect the greatness of our epoch.

But Ethan persists and he finds that David and Solomon maintained their power by means of secret police, rigged trials, mental homes for dissidents, and concentration camps; in short, by the whole apparatus of terror which Communist rule employs. So Ethan is punished by being outlawed as a 'non-person', the Orwellian fate reserved for writers who sin against the Communist law and are declared enemies of society.

Stefan Heym described his own approach to the problem in a West German interview in 1972:

The repression of criticism represents a fear that, if people begin to think about their own problems, they might be less amenable to being good citizens – which I think is ridiculous. I think the more that people are made to think, the better it is for socialism.

Heym also spoke about the changes which were needed to make literature serve a creative purpose:

They cannot be made in outright opposition to the leadership of the Party or to the Soviet Union. They will come about because socialism is developing. And we must be active in helping these changes to come about. That is, or should be, the position of responsible writers in the socialist world. I am trying to act along those lines.

Unlike many of his colleagues, Heym stayed in East Germany. He is still living in East Berlin and remains in touch with Western friends.

But however rationally the independent writers tried to explain their position, there was more than enough in their work to revive the fears of the 'hardliners' in the East German Communist Party. What they dreaded above all was a repetition of the 'Prague Spring' in Czechoslovakia in 1968, when many writers in the country supported the Dubcek reforms which ended in the Soviet invasion. They were also worried by the rapid expansion of contacts with West Germany which followed a Four-Power Agreement on Berlin in September 1971 and the treaty between East and West Germany signed in December 1972. Under that treaty, the restrictions on travel from West Germany to the GDR were greatly relaxed. The two governments set up diplomatic missions in Bonn and East Berlin. West German correspondents and television reporters started working in East Berlin and sent back recorded interviews with nonconformist writers like Heym and Kunze which were published and broadcast in the West. The West German broadcasts were heard by millions of East Germans who could receive them in their own homes quite legally, and indeed on radio and television sets equipped to receive West German programmes and sold in East German shops.

Honecker reverted to a tougher line in May 1973 at a Congress of the Party's Central Committee, when he criticised writers whose characters 'imposed their own private sufferings on society'. He spoke of 'various films and plays which portray lonely and isolated human beings, living in a vacuum, bereft of social relationships. These characteristics show that the basic attitudes of such works do not match up to, indeed are opposed to, the claim made by socialism on art and literature.' Honecker was saying, in effect, that Communist dogma insists on maintaining an outward picture of collective joy, manifested in organised processions of banner-waving, cheering citizens counting their blessings. The harsh reality of life under a Communist regime must at all costs be concealed.

At this same meeting Honecker also showed annoyance over a remark in a play by Volker Braun then running in East Berlin that 'the GDR is the most boring country in the world'. In 1965, in an essay called *The Boredom of Minsk* on the role of the writer in a Communist society, Stefan Heym had already repeated a remark made by the famous Communist playwright, Bertolt Brecht at a Soviet Writers' Congress in 1955, when he said:

I'll tell you when the Soviet Union has a real literature again – when a novel appears there which begins something like this: 'Minsk is one of the most boring towns in the world.'

Nevertheless, the cultural thaw still held in 1975, when Reiner Kunze, the poet already mentioned, was allowed to travel in the West and to give a public reading of his poetry in East Berlin for the first time since 1968. A volume of his poems entitled *Letter with a Blue Seal* was published containing many references to the pressures of life in East Germany which drove some people even to suicide. Honecker may have hoped to persuade Kunze to return to the fold by lenient treatment, or perhaps he thought it best to avoid giving the West any more ammunition on human rights until the Helsinki Conference was over. But in November 1976 his patience gave out and the regime clearly decided to make an example. The victim they chose was Wolf Biermann, a popular writer and singer of satirical ballads to his own guitar accompaniment, a kind of strolling minstrel who had become almost a folk hero in East Germany.

Biermann, born in Hamburg in 1936, was the son of a Communist dockworker who took part in anti-Nazi activities during the war and died in the concentration camp at Auschwitz. The young Biermann left West Germany in 1953, aged 17, and settled in East Berlin, where he joined Bertolt Brecht's group, the 'Berliner Ensemble'. In 1963, he was expelled from the Communist Party because of his seditious songs, and in 1965 he was banned from publishing or performing in East Germany. He continued to write books and make records which were produced in West Germany where he was equally popular, although he constantly reaffirmed his position as a loyal Communist, his dislike of the capitalist system, and his refusal to emigrate.

In November 1976 Biermann was allowed to make a concert tour in West Germany for the first time since 1964, a surprising move by the East German regime which was widely assumed to be a sort of peace offering. While he was still in West Germany, however, he was deprived of his GDR citizenship for 'grossly insulting the state' and forbidden to return home. It certainly looked as if the permission given for his tour had simply been a device to get rid of him. But the effect was quite the reverse of what the Communist government must have hoped and expected. Far from silencing the dissenters, it evoked a show of unity among them which had previously been lacking.

A letter of protest calling on the Party leadership to reconsider its treatment of Biermann was signed by twelve East German writers and artists, and other names were soon added bringing the number up to about a hundred. The original signatories included Ulrich Plenzdorf, Stefan Heym and Volker Braun, already mentioned, and four other well-known writers: Christa Wolf and Gunther Kunert, both poets, Jurek Becker and Stephan Hermlin. Among those who added their names were another writer, Jurgen Fuchs, two 'rock' musicians, Gerulf Pannach and Christian Kunert, and members of a 'rock' group disbanded in 1976 for performing dissident songs; also Sarah Kirsch, a prizewinning lyrical poet and two more poets, Kurt Bartsch and Bernd Jentzsch.

A separate protest was made by Professor Robert Havemann, a friend of Biermann and one of the earliest critics of the regime, a man of exceptional distinction. He was sent to a Nazi concentration camp during the war for his Communist beliefs, where Erich Honecker, the East German leader, was also imprisoned. After the war, Havemann moved to East Germany and was appointed Professor of Chemistry in the Humboldt University in East Berlin. In 1968 he condemned the occupation of Czechoslovakia by the Warsaw Pact forces and in the winter of 1973-74, he gave a series of lectures on socialist democracy calling for an amnesty for political prisoners, a socialist opposition party, a free press and free trade unions. For this he was expelled from the Communist Party and dismissed from his posts in the University and the Academy of Sciences. He then devoted himself to the study of philosophy and politics, but he continued to express his views in terms which made him an unofficial spokesman for the dissenters.

After his protest against Biermann's treatment, Professor Havemann was arrested, but then released and kept under house arrest, with his telephone cut off and a police picket stationed outside. He was not allowed to have visits from Western journalists, but could still travel occasionally inside East Germany subject to official permission and police escort. In December 1976 his daughter Sybille was expelled from the Humboldt University where she was a student. His son, however, had already left for the West and Biermann had deplored this flight in one of his songs. Indeed, it was probably Biermann's own fixed determination to stay in East Germany which decided the authorities to banish him while he was out of the country.

The better-known dissenters were treated less severely by the Communist regime than the lesser lights who had no Western contacts. This supports the belief that Western publicity does not increase the danger of reprisals against dissenters, as is sometimes assumed in the West, but may actually reduce it. Some signatories of the letter defending Biermann were arrested, among them Jurgen Fuchs, Pannach, and Christian Kunert (not to be confused with Gunther Kunert) and about forty students in Jena University who also protested in favour of Biermann. Others lost their jobs in universities, the theatre, or factories. But none of the twelve original signatories was arrested. Four of them, Gunther Kunert, Gerhard Wolf, Jurek Becker, and Sarah Kirsch, were expelled from the Party and six others were officially reprimanded. Two of them had second thoughts and recanted, one being Stephan Hermlin, a friend of Honecker. No action was taken against Stefan Heym, perhaps the most formidable of the rebels.

At a meeting of Party members belonging to the East Berlin branch of the Writers' Union, a resolution supporting the judgment passed on Biermann, and condemning those who defended him, was passed by 110 votes to 6, with 4 abstentions.

Biermann received strong support from Communist Parties in Western Europe. The Italian Communist paper, *L'Unita*, commented:

Our position on the Biermann case is extremely clear. We are supporters of the freedom to express opinions, in newspapers and books,
in political speeches and through works of art – drawings and paintings,
poetry and songs. We stand for the freedom to approve and to dissent.
We are in favour of freedom of expression for everyone, including
those with whom we disagree. We believe not only in the right, but
the duty to discuss and have the truth emerge from the confrontation
of even opposing ideas. We are against consensus imposed through
coercion . . . Biermann's right to express his political thought in
poetic form, by singing, is therefore beyond discussion for us. The
punitive measure by which the authorities of the GDR decided to
prevent his return to the country, and thus to silence him in his own
country, is unacceptable.

Whether any West European Communist Party would act differ-
ently, if and when it gained power, still remains an open question.

The removal of Biermann was a clear sign that Honecker's
cultural 'thaw' was over, and this was welcomed, not only by
the Party cavemen, but also by many East German writers who
earned a good living by toeing the Communist Party line. But the
Party leadership showed a preference for disposing of their more
troublesome critics by getting them to leave East Germany
'voluntarily', after threats of more drastic treatment if they refused to go.

In December 1976 the authorities gave immediate exit visas
to Nina Hagen, a friend of Biermann; Katharina Thalbach, a
young actress; and Thomas Brasch, a writer and son of a former
Communist Deputy Minister for Culture. As a university student
in 1968 Brasch was arrested for taking part in student demonstrations against the Soviet invasion of Czechoslovakia and his
father was sacked. In April 1977 Reiner Kunze emigrated with
his family to West Germany. He was in poor health, his daughter
had been forced to leave school, and his wife had been harassed
in her work as a doctor.

K.D.   177   M

In June 1977 a leading singer and actor, Manfred Krug, was also allowed to emigrate. He held an East German national prize for his art, but he had signed the letter supporting Biermann and been punished by having his state contracts cancelled, his new films blacklisted, his concerts broken up by hooligans and his telephone cut off. On his arrival in West Berlin, Krug said he had found it almost impossible to continue his career, but that leaving East Germany felt like 'an amputation'. Commenting on the exodus of writers to the West, Krug said: 'The last man out will turn off the lights.' He could think himself fortunate, however, in being allowed to take with him not only his family, but a housekeeper and two cars.

Tilo Medek, a composer and a Biermann supporter, also left for the West at this time, after writing to Honecker to protest against a ban on his music. What finally decided him to get out was a new law imposing prison sentences of up to two years for 'public defamation of state organs'. More names were added to the list in August and September when exit visas were given to Jurgen Fuchs, Gerulf Pannach and Christian Kunert, who had been in prison for nine months awaiting trial; Sarah Kirsch, the lyrical poet already mentioned, and two other writers, Wolfgang Hinckeldey and Michael Sallman, who had signed the Biermann protest; Karl-Heinz Nitschke, a doctor, held in prison since September 1976 after drawing up a petition to the United Nations demanding full human rights in East Germany which was signed by about a hundred people; and Professor Hellmuth Nitsche, a German-language scholar, not to be confused with Nitschke, who was arrested with his wife in April 1977 for writing to President Carter about East German violations of human rights, but was now allowed to leave with his family.

In a television interview in West Berlin given by Fuchs, Pannach, and Kunert, they stressed that they had not emigrated of their own free will, but only after being threatened with a ten-year prison sentence if they refused to renounce their critical views and denounce their friends. Professor Nitsche said at a press conference that the struggle in East Germany must go on until all political prisoners were freed. He attributed his release to a combination of President Carter's stand on human rights, publicity for his case by friends in the West, and diplomatic negotiations then in progress between East and West Germany.

In December 1977 the writer Jurek Becker decided to emigrate after putting up a stiff resistance. Becker was a prominent Jewish author born in Poland in 1937 and brought up in the ghetto of Lodz, followed by confinement in Nazi concentration camps. He was no longer regarded as a pillar of the East German literary establishment, but he was one of the original signatories of the Biermann protest in November 1976. He was then dismissed from the executive committee of the Writers' Union, expelled from the Communist Party, and forbidden to give public readings of his work or lectures for eight months. Like Biermann and many others, he did not want to leave East Germany, but he refused to hold his tongue. While still in East Germany, he gave an interview to a West German magazine in which he said he believed he must now openly criticise the regime, and he added: 'If it is a question of keeping my mouth shut, then I would rather keep it shut in the Bahamas.'

The East German leaders may have felt that their technique of exporting dissenters was working well, but a bombshell exploded on their own doorstep in August 1977, when a Communist Party member and economic official called Rudolf Bahro gave interviews to West German journalists at his flat in East Berlin. He told them that he had written a book called *The Alternative: A Critique of Socialism as it really Exists*, which would be published in Cologne in the Federal German Republic on 31 August. Anticipating arrest, Bahro also smuggled out to his publishers a tape recording in which he explained the purpose of his book. This was played at a press conference in Cologne on the day his book came out, by which time Bahro had duly been arrested.

Bahro was a highly unusual kind of dissenter. He was neither a professional writer, nor an intellectual like Havemann, nor an actor or singer, but a candidate-member of the Party at sixteen and a full member at eighteen. True, he had misbehaved at the time of the Hungarian rising in 1956, when he was a student at the Humboldt University and put up a notice on the board demanding an explanation from the Party leadership about the events in Hungary. But he was let off lightly and sent to the provinces as editor of a local Party paper in a small town manu-facturing agricultural machinery and tractors. A year later, he was promoted to editing the Party paper in Greifswald University and then transferred to East Berlin as a Party reporter on scientific matters. In 1965 he got a plum job as deputy editor of the Young Communist League paper *Forum*, but lost it soon after when he published a story by Volker Braun about the workers which offended the Party chiefs. He then found himself a job in a Berlin rubber factory as adviser on industrial problems, which he still held when he was arrested.

For ten years or more, Bahro used his spare time to gather information and make notes for his book. In his interview with West German journalists in East Berlin, and in the tape recording he sent to his publishers in Cologne, he talked at some length about his aims and ideas. His book is not intended to be a programme for overthrowing Communist rule, but a theoretical basis for attacking and demolishing its present bureaucratic structure so as to replace it by a more democratic and enlightened system which will provide genuine consultation and participation at all levels from the lowest upwards. Bahro stressed the influence on his thinking of Dubcek's reformist plans in Czechoslovakia and the Soviet invasion, which he described as a 'drastic, decisive political experience'. He calls his book a weapon that 'stabs the Party apparatus in the heart' and says that the political police will be helpless against it because it is addressed to loyal Party members in their capacity as thinking men. It would take far too long to repeat his comments in full, but a few extracts will bring out some of the main points. He sums up his central purpose in these words:

What I would like to achieve is a Communist opposition. I do not want to found a Party tomorrow. That is not the way history or politics works. But the true purpose of my book is to provide a theoretical basis for this Communist opposition, for which a potential exists in all the true Socialist countries. In these countries there is now a mass of surplus awareness, meaning intellectual energy and ability which is no longer tied down in daily work, in the daily functioning of the apparatus. The Party organisation is conditioned like a Pavlovian dog, needing a long time before it can abandon a trained reaction to a given signal, if and when the meaning of the signal changes.

Bahro sees a close connection between religious reformation through the ages and the regeneration of the Communist Parties today in Eastern Europe. As he puts it:

It is an invariable feature of all church organisations that their reformation derives from their most devout heretics; those who destroy the temple to rebuild it more beautifully, who drive out the moneychangers in order to make room for the believers. There is no doubt that this pattern plays a part in the present situation, namely the rapid ideological decay of our 'Catholic' Party. Just as church reformations presuppose Christian beliefs, so must Party reformations presuppose Communist ones . . . But one thing must be clear; that the new Communist Party must differ more from the inherited type of Party, including the Bolshevik one, than any reformed church does from its predecessor.

Bahro leaves any number of pertinent questions unanswered. He does not ask how any Communist Party could accept an opposition in its own ranks and still retain its monopoly of power; or whether there is any possibility that the Communist rulers in Moscow would allow such a thing to happen, either in the Soviet Union or in the satellite states. But none of this changes the impact of Bahro's book as an act of unprecedented sacrilege and blasphemy in the Communist temple. He told foreign correspondents that two or three hundred copies would probably find their way into East Germany and circulate underground, but he is clearly not looking for a mass audience. His target is the upper echelon of the Communist Party and he is convinced that many Party members will look for a chance to read his book, either as official watchdogs or from sheer curiosity. There is a striking similarity between Bahro's ideas and those expressed by Roy Medvedev, the Soviet dissenter, in his book *On Socialist Democracy* which came out in English translation in 1975.

Bahro himself is still in prison at the time of writing and some of the emigrants fear for his life. The restrictions on Professor Havemann's movements have been redoubled. A West German television correspondent, Lothar Loewe, was declared *persona non grata* on 22 December 1977, and ordered to leave the country within forty-eight hours. He had said in a broadcast that East German frontier guards had orders 'to shoot at people like rabbits', and this was described as a scandalous slander. But there were all too many tragedies to prove it true. In August 1976, to recall an unfortunate example, East German frontier guards shot and killed an unarmed Italian truck driver, Benito Corghi, at the Hirschberg customs post on the East German side of the Bavarian frontier. He was walking back to collect some papers which he had left by mistake on the Western side and nobody knew why they shot him. He was a Communist, and as a token of official regret, the East German chargé d'affaires in Rome attended the funeral in Corghi's home town. The widow had this to say to him:

We hope that the price we have paid will be of some use if it will help you to understand that you cannot defend socialism by killing people. I have in mind Benito's comrades and the state of mind they must be in at this moment. What is your government doing to ensure their safety at work? I speak to you as a Communist and as the widow of a friend of East Germany. (The *Guardian*, 12 August 1976)

Whether the East German envoy made any reply, or whether he even reported this incident, is not recorded.

The East German authorities have had other problems with religious dissenters as well as critical writers. Most practising Christians in East Germany are Protestants and nearly all of them are members of either the German Evangelical or Lutheran Church. Its leaders have settled their relations with the Communist state on a submissive basis of peaceful co-existence, but in August 1976 Pastor Oskar Brusewitz burned himself to death on the steps of his church in Zeitz, near Leipzig, in protest against the harsh treatment of young Christians by the regime. His superiors did not approve of this act, but they admitted that it was evidence of a deep division between the bishops and their congregations. They issued a letter which was read from the pulpits of all the Protestant churches, pointing out the social tensions which underlay the pastor's suicide. The Church Synod called on the government to join in a discussion of official discrimination against Christian youth, but there has been no improvement.

In September that year, a Protestant church in Prenzlau openly defied the regime by providing the hall for a concert by the controversial ballad singer, Wolf Biermann, his first in East Germany since 1965. It was an unwelcome portent to the East German authorities of religious protest. Up to that point, they

183

had reason to feel satisfied with the results of their drive against religion. They had introduced a form of secular confirmation for young people, the *Jugendweihe*, to compete with the Christian service, and this was taken by a large majority of boys and girls, mainly as a kind of personal insurance, but also by some who received Christian confirmation. On the other hand, the problems and frustrations of life in a Communist society made more and more people who were not Christians turn to the Protestant pastors for help and advice. The Brusewitz suicide also contributed to a revival of Christian belief among East German youth.

Young people were involved in a clash with police on the Alexanderplatz in East Berlin on 7 October 1977. This occurred during a 'People's Festival' to celebrate the 28th anniversary of the East German Communist state. Eyewitness reports said that more than a thousand people were drawn into what became the biggest anti-Soviet and anti-government demonstration since the riots of 1953. Apparently the trouble started when two youths saw two Russian officers and shouted 'Russians out'. The riot police quickly intervened, but this attracted a large crowd of sympathisers with the young men, who were throwing paving stones at the police. They were only dispersed by the use of truncheons, tear gas and water cannon. The official explanation was that youths at a jazz concert had 'interfered' with police taking away other youths after they fell from a wall and were injured.

The biggest sign of rising popular discontent is the flood of applications for permission to emigrate, chiefly inspired by the clauses on human rights in the 1975 Helsinki agreements. In 1976 about 10,000 East Germans were allowed to leave the country, most of them being elderly people who were regarded as a burden on the East German economy, but the number of applications for emigration permits soared to a figure approaching

300,000. This was clearly a direct result of the hopes aroused among East Germans by the humanitarian clauses of the Helsinki Final Act. Most of the applicants produced copies of the Communist Party paper *Neues Deutschland* in which the full text of the Helsinki agreements had been published in accordance with the undertaking given by all the participants. The East German authorities responded by announcing that in future permission to emigrate would be granted only in genuine cases of family reunification. In January 1977 they posted guards outside the West German diplomatic office in East Berlin to block the entry of East Germans seeking advice on emigration, but withdrew them after strong Western protests.

The mere act of applying for an exit permit is often severely punished in East Germany, especially when previous applications have been refused already. In June 1974, for example, a Leipzig surgeon, Dr Werner Schalike, was arrested for preparing and circulating leaflets protesting against the refusal of the East German authorities to let him go to West Germany for a serious operation. In April 1975 he was sentenced to six years in prison on a charge of 'incitement against the state'. Despite his weak condition, he was refused permission to see the prison doctor and forced to do heavy manual labour.

Late in 1976 a group of seventy people in the small Saxon town of Riesa applied to renounce their German citizenship as they were entitled to do under the East German constitution. They were all forced to withdraw their applications and seven of them were imprisoned. The right to emigrate is also granted in the Constitution, but it was superseded by a passport law in 1954 which provided for prison sentences of up to three years or a heavy fine for leaving East Germany 'without the necessary authorisation'. This offence has since been incorporated in the East German penal code, Paragraph 213, which provides for imprisonment up to two years, and in so-called 'serious' cases up to five years, for 'illegally crossing the border'. Aiding and abetting escape from East Germany is called 'subversive traffic in human beings' and is punishable under Paragraph 105 of the penal code, as amended in April 1977, by imprisonment for not less than two years and by life imprisonment in 'particularly serious cases'.

The East German frontier barriers include metal fencing, minefields, spring-guns discharging sharp-edged iron fragments when set off, and constant armed patrols with guard-dogs. Under East German border regulations issued in June 1972 the frontier guards have orders to shoot, if necessary, to prevent unauthorised crossings. During the fifteen years from 1963 to 1977 inclusive, 171 people were killed while trying to escape, 70 of them at the Berlin Wall. (This information is taken from the December 1977 issue of *The Review* published by the International Commission of Jurists in Geneva.)

The East German controls over travel from West Germany to East Germany were greatly relaxed by the treaty between the two governments in 1972. Prior to the treaty, people living in West Berlin were allowed to visit East Berlin in large numbers, but travel from West Germany to the GDR was strictly controlled and on a small scale. Since 1972, however, about six million West Germans have been visiting East Germany or East Berlin every year. Conversely, travel by East Germans to countries out-side the Soviet bloc was on a much smaller scale, though still surprisingly large under a Communist regime with a harsh reputation. The number of such journeys showed a slight decline from 1,360,571 in 1973 to 1,292,577 in 1975. These figures in-clude East German travel to Yugoslavia, a popular holiday resort for visitors from Eastern Europe. Over the same period, however, visits by East Germans to West Berlin increased by nearly half a million, from 891,589 in 1973 to 1,350,938 in 1975. (Source: *Statistical Yearbook of the GDR* 1976.)

In the Amnesty International Annual Report for 1977, the

number of political prisoners in East Germany was estimated as 'several thousand'. Most of them are people who tried to escape illegally over the frontiers, often after their applications for exit visas had been refused. Political prisoners and their families are frequently subjected to further persecution by preventing them from resuming professional work and forcing them to do poorly paid manual labour; by excluding their children from higher education; and by restricting their place of residence. They receive no compensation for property confiscated when they are arrested.

Under a general amnesty in 1972-73, about 4,000 political prisoners were released but soon replaced by others. The East German government has conducted a trade in human bodies by deporting political prisoners to West Germany in exchange for hard currency and scarce commodities which the German Democratic Republic badly needs. In 1977 a total of 1,000 such releases was agreed with the Federal German government at a price of 40 million West German marks or about £10 million, a human exchange rate of about £10,000 per head.

In October 1977 a young journalist in Leipzig, Rolf Mainz, was sentenced to four and a half years in prison after writing an article for the West German weekly *Die Zeit* on the way the East German government punished dissenters by denying them the right to work in their professions. In January 1978 he was condemned to a further term of five years because of his 'unyielding conduct' in prison. In other words, he had held out against the process of 're-education' which is applied to political prisoners to make them submit. An appeal for Western support on his behalf was made by an international 'Committee for the Protection of Freedom and Socialism' in West Berlin. He was released in December 1978 and deported to West Germany.

A year earlier, in January 1978, the West German news magazine *Der Spiegel* caused a sensation by publishing what it described as a manifesto drawn up in East Germany by a Federation of Democratic Communists of Germany formed by Party officials working under cover in small groups. The contents of this manifesto were highly dramatic. It opposed the Soviet system in East Germany, as reflected in the Communist dictatorship, and demanded a choice of political parties; an independent parliament and judiciary; the elimination of the Communist Party bureaucracy; the reunification of a Germany governed by Social Democrats, Socialists and democratic Communists; and the withdrawal of all foreign troops in order to make Germany a bridge for peace between East and West. The manifesto is a long indictment of Communist rule in East Germany which is unsigned and appears to be the work of several contributors. Their aims are described as follows:

It is our objective to work in all of Germany towards a democratic-communist order in which all human rights are fully implemented according to the Marxist statement that it is necessary to destroy all circumstances under which man is an oppressed, contemptible, enslaved being. We do not believe in God Marx, Jesus Engels, or even Holy Ghost Lenin or in the fatalistic inevitability of history, but we value the 'classical interpreters of Marxism-Leninism' as significant members of a long chain of thought from Thomas More and Campanella through the French, English and German utopians, the enlightenment, the classical period, up to Bebel, Rosa Luxemburg and Liebknecht . . . up to Bloch, Harich, Havemann and Bahro.

The authors were under no illusion about Soviet motives for seeking detente with the West. As they put it:

It was out of economic-technical backwardness that the USSR approved the detente policy. At the same time, it is doing everything to make its military machinery superior through co-operative agreements, scientific-technical co-operation, and war. Hence there is no alternative to detente. Detente alone creates the possibility of a peaceful, fundamental reform within the Soviet power sphere, a transition from the Asian production method of bureaucratic state capitalism to the socialist national economy and society.

The authors of the manifesto summed up their proposals by saying that they were in favour of 'totally reformed Communism theoretically and politically; party pluralism and an independent parliament emerging from free elections; and an independent Court where every citizen could protest about the misuse of power'. They also denounced the privileges of the Communist ruling classes:

No ruling class of Germany has ever sponged so much and secured itself against the people as those two dozen families who run the country like a self-service store. None has ever had such excessively golden ghettos built in the forests which are guarded like fortresses. None has so shamelessly corrupted and enriched itself in special stores and private imports from the West, through decorations, bonuses, and special clinics, pensions and presents, as has this caste. Look closely at them. Did even one of these self-appointed leaders ever come up with an idea, write a book or at least an article in any specialised field or at least in the sphere of politics? No. They employ personal aides and institutions to fabricate their leaden rubbish called speeches.

It is hard to judge whether this was the genuine product of an opposition group or a cleverly drafted hoax. The echoes in the manifesto of Bahro's ideas and those expressed by some Western Communist Parties give it some credibility, but not enough to support the belief that an organised conspiracy exists in East Germany which the security police have failed to discover. Moreover, *Der Spiegel* has since modified its original attribution of the document to 'medium and high-level functionaries' and has called it a 'discussion paper'. On the whole, there is enough evidence in the manifesto to suggest that it is indeed the authentic work of dissenters in East Germany. But they are probably ordinary Communist Party members holding no positions of power or influence.

The East German authorities certainly helped to give the document wide publicity by their hasty and violent reactions. They accused the Federal German intelligence service of inventing the whole story and *Der Spiegel* of aiding and abetting. Its office in East Berlin was closed down and one of its correspondents sent from Hamburg was refused entry into East Berlin. Protests and counter-protests were exchanged between East Berlin and Bonn, but *Der Spiegel* maintained that its source of information had been carefully checked and was genuine.

There are other and more concrete reasons for Honecker and his colleagues to feel worried. They have managed to get rid of some active dissenters by turning them out of the country, and more of them have taken this way of escape than in Poland or Czechoslovakia, where organised groups maintain their open defence of human rights. But the East German exiles have not been silenced. On the contrary, their views are transmitted across the frontier by West German radio and television broadcasts to a far larger audience in East Germany than they had before.

Another, and more serious, problem for the East German regime is the widespread anger and resentment caused by the special privileges of the Communist ruling class. The crux of the matter here is the greatly superior purchasing power of the West German Deutschmark as compared with its East German equivalent. The prices of many basic foodstuffs and consumer goods are held down in East Germany by massive government subsidies which in themselves impose a mounting strain in economic and financial terms, but the 'luxury' articles, which in East Germany include cars, television sets, good-quality clothes, furniture and many other goods plentiful in the West, are so scarce and expensive in East German currency that they can only be obtained in the black-market by cashing West German marks. And these are even harder to obtain for most East Germans.

East German workers have gone on strike with demands for part of their wages to be paid in West-marks, as in the case of those working on the repair of motorways leading to the West, who argue that the costs were borne by the West German, and not the East German, government. Women workers at the Narva electric lamp factory in East Berlin went on strike in December 1977 demanding that they should be partly paid in West-marks because the lamps they made were being sold to West Germany. Even the normal household services like plumbing and repairs, usually have to be paid for in 'illegal' West-marks.

The East German authorities have made matters worse by setting up exclusive shops where Western imported goods can be bought for payment in West German currency. This limits the customers to a small minority of high-ranking Communist officials and a few other people with ways and means of evading the strict exchange controls. There was an immediate outcry from the large majority of East Germans who are not in this favoured position. The Communist regime then allowed the consumer goods in the special shops to be bought with East German money, but they fixed these prices at almost the same rate of exchange as the black-market rate of five East-marks to one West. This again put the special shops out of reach for most East Germans and caused a fresh outburst.

This surging tide of popular discontent strongly reinforces the opposition to the regime by writers and intellectuals, religious dissenters, and young people chafing under the drab conformity and frustrations of Communist rule. It is much more difficult for the regime to crush widespread protests of this kind than those of individuals. When the Communist measures against emigration are also taken into account, directed against the whole people, there is abundant proof that the government has totally failed to inspire any loyalty among its subjects or to provide them with a tolerable substitute for the political, economic and social advantage enjoyed by the people in West Germany. That failure is not only the biggest defeat suffered by the East German Communist regime, but also it greatest continuing danger.

CHAPTER 7

MOSCOW RULES
IN BULGARIA

The influences of national traditions and European civilisation,
which play such a dominant part in the struggle for human
rights in other Soviet satellites, have had a much less stimulating
effect in Bulgaria under Communist rule. The medieval kingdom
of Bulgaria was destroyed by the Ottoman Turks in the fifteenth
century and only reborn in 1878, after four hundred years of
Turkish occupation which sealed the country off from Western
Europe. The lines of communication with the West were then
reopened, but again cut off, after less than seventy years, by the
arrival of Soviet forces in 1944 and the installation of a Communist dictatorship which has proved to be more fanatically
devoted to Soviet interests than any of its fellows. In this respect,
the Bulgarian Communists resemble the Bosnian feudal chief-
tains who adopted the Moslem religion after the Turkish conquest and treated their people more cruelly than the Sultan's
own officials.

The Communist seizure of power in Bulgaria was achieved
by tactics similar to those used in other East European countries.
The Bulgarian Communist Party, which in 1944 numbered only
about 25,000 members, was too weak and isolated to form a
government by itself immediately after the war, even with the
support of the Red Army. It therefore began by setting up the

Fatherland Front in which other parties were associated, including the Agrarian Party and its peasant leader Nikola Petkov, who had fought bravely with the Communists in wartime resistance against the Bulgarian government under King Boris which was an ally of Nazi Germany.

A coalition government was formed in which the Communist Party held the key Ministries of the Interior and Justice, and in November 1945 Georgi Dimitrov arrived from Moscow to take over as the Communist leader. He had been arrested and tried in 1933 by the Nazi German government for alleged complicity in the Reichstag fire, but was freed by Soviet intervention and went to Moscow. On returning to Bulgaria after the war, he took his orders directly from Andrei Vishinsky, the notorious Soviet public prosecutor.

Dimitrov carried out wholesale executions and purges to wipe out all opposition, exceeding in ferocity and scale even the Communist butchery in other Soviet satellites. A general election was staged in October 1946 in what was described by the British government as 'an atmosphere of terror'. Nevertheless, the Agrarian Party led by Petkov polled 1,300,000 votes. Petkov was elected leader of the Opposition in the National Assembly and fearlessly denounced Communist crimes both in the Assembly and outside it, knowing that his life was at stake. In his last article, published in April 1947, he wrote:

Never before have the ghastly results of the enslavement of independent thought by totalitarian government so appalled the freedom-loving peoples of the world. Today more than ever, it has been proved that if men in power destroy the liberty of speech and Press, all excesses soon become permissible. Such men proclaim themselves infallible and decide the fate of peoples arbitrarily, without any control on their activities whatever. The citizens of such a state cease to be a society of thinking men and women and become a flock of sheep, with no opinions or ideas of their own. Once freedom is destroyed, all other foundations of human society crumble into ruins. A flock of two-legged sheep, even if they have a human appearance and are well fed and well shod, is not a society of human beings. States under such a regime can be saved only when liberty is restored. Otherwise they are bound to collapse.

Petkov was arrested in the Assembly chamber in June 1947 by armed militiamen who had to force a passage through Opposition deputies who surrounded him and tried to protect him with their bare hands. After a mock trial, he was tortured and hanged in Sofia on 23 September 1947. His last request for the services of a priest was ignored, but his political testament endures. A small group of nine brave Social Democrats somehow maintained their opposition in the Assembly until 1948, when they all received prison sentences of ten to fifteen years.

When Khrushchev succeeded Stalin, he rewarded his Bulgarian lackeys by announcing that their country would be a 'show case' for Communist rule in the Balkans. Soviet subsidies were poured into Bulgaria on a lavish scale which enabled the regime to provide an artificially high standard of living, when measured by conditions in a poor and backward country, but at a heavy cost to its economic development. The Russian bounty was mostly spent by the Communist leaders on providing themselves with the spoils of power in houses, servants, cars and high living, and on building up their support by means of the Party bureaucracy, a large army, and an even larger force of security police.

A Bulgarian exile told us that the number of Communist policemen in Bulgaria equals the combined police force in Britain, and this in a Bulgarian population of only about eight million. He also said that prohibited literature was secretly duplicated and circulated in Bulgaria, similar to the Russian *samizdat*, and that he himself had taken a hand in it. He was convinced that the Pan-Slav ties which formerly made Bulgarians look to Imperial

Russia as their protector had long turned to a hatred of Soviet domination.

The vacuum in Bulgarian relations with Western Europe has now been filled by the Soviet Union and cemented by an ignorant and brutish regime which deals harshly with all potential seeds of opposition. Against this background of post-war history, it is hardly surprising that the outward and visible signs of dissent in Bulgaria are few. This does not mean that individual voices of protest have ceased to exist, but only that they are isolated and seldom heard in the West. There are no Western correspondents resident in Sofia, and visits by Western reporters are discouraged and strictly controlled.

Occasionally, however, there are echoes which reach the outside world. Amnesty International, in its Report for 1977, mentions several Bulgarian cases in which it is interested. One of them concerns Asen Andonov, who was sent to a psychiatric clinic in 1968, after making several attempts to leave the country without official permission. Such attempts are punishable under the penal code, *Article 279*, by prison sentences of up to five years, or banishment to a remote part of Bulgaria. Andonov was banished in 1971 with his family to a village where he worked as a stonemason.

A similar case is that of Stefan Marinov, a physicist who worked in the Bulgarian Academy of Science. He applied for a passport several times, starting as early as 1960, but it was always refused. In 1965 he was arrested after distributing leaflets about his case to foreign delegates attending an international youth conference in Sofia. Like Andonov, he was given psychiatric treatment and drugs, but was released after a year and resumed work at the Academy. After making further applications for a passport, which were again rejected, Marinov went to the American Embassy in Sofia and applied for political asylum, but this was also refused. On leaving the Embassy, he was arrested and badly beaten up by the police, and was then confined in a psychiatric hospital where he remained for over a year. Shortly after being released he was summarily dismissed from his job, but in April 1977 he was again arrested and taken to a mental institution in Sofia after trying to organise an unofficial international symposium on physics. The authorities declared this meeting illegal, but some foreign scientists arrived for it and Marinov was allowed to meet them.

Amnesty International says that it does not have consistent or detailed evidence that psychiatric methods are being used in Bulgaria as an instrument of political repression, but adds that the Marinov case gives renewed grounds for concern. It is also disturbed by a number of cases in which Bulgarians with foreign business or professional connections have been convicted of 'espionage' and sentenced to death. Three such cases were reported in 1974 and 1975, involving Solomon Ben Joseph, Heinrich Spetter and Nicholas Chamurlisky. In 1976 another case came to light, that of Dr Peter Kondofersky, who was arrested in June 1971, charged with espionage, and sentenced to twelve years in prison with confiscation of his property. He was a graduate of the Montpellier and Toulon Universities in France, and said to be acquainted with some French officials. After returning to Bulgaria, he worked as a gynaecologist near Sofia and maintained contacts with his daughter, living in France, and former French colleagues. Since his confinement in Stara Zagora prison, he is reported to have had several heart attacks. His case is under investigation by Amnesty International.

This organisation has also adopted as a 'Prisoner of Conscience' Ljuben Hadji-Dimitrov, an architect in Vinica, who was arrested with his wife in September 1976, after their three children failed to return from a visit to Switzerland, where they had been granted political asylum. The parents were accused of planning to cross the Bulgarian border illegally, and they were also charged with possession of 'propaganda hostile to the regime'. Apparently this consisted of letters from their children which were found during a police search of the parents' flat carried out during their absence. The Hadji-Dimitrovs were sentenced to four years' imprisonment, but the wife was released after a few months because of bad health.

Bulgarian citizens who publicly express critical views of the regime are subject to charges under *Article 108* of the penal code, which authorises prison sentences of up to five years for 'anti-state propaganda'; or *Article 109*, which prescribes sentences of three to twelve years for membership of any organisation whose activities are 'aimed at the destruction of the people's democracy'. In March 1977 a scientist, Alexander Strezov, was tried in Sofia under *Article 108* after publicly expressing support for human rights and sympathy with the Charter 77 movement in Czechoslovakia.

Stefan Gusenko, an electrician with a wife and two children, was arrested in December 1976 and arbitrarily sentenced to three years in prison on charges of 'inciting mistrust among the people' and 'disseminating derogatory statements that harm the social order'. These charges were based on the fact that he was in possession of Western literature which he distributed among his friends and which was described by the Bulgarian authorities as 'anti-Communist'. While awaiting trial, Gusenko was kept in solitary confinement and his family were not allowed to see him. After his arrest, his wife and relatives were kept under constant watch and harassed by the police.

It is difficult to obtain information about the treatment of Bulgarian political prisoners. Amnesty International has had reports that some are detained in prison in Sofia, including Stara Zagora, and some condemned to forced labour in the mines of Bobov and Kremikov. Sentences of internal exile are applied in some other cases instead of, or added to, imprisonment. Former political prisoners have supplied reports about the island prison of Belena, where they estimate the number of prisoners, some political, as between four and six thousand. Political prisoners in other prisons are said to be held in overcrowded conditions and only allowed very restricted exercise and visits. Former inmates of the Stara Zagora, Belena, and Sofia Central prisons, where political prisoners are held while awaiting trial, say that they are kept incommunicado for months on end, sometimes in cells without daylight. An amnesty was announced by the government in October 1974 for people who had left Bulgaria without permission, or who left legally but failed to return. There seem to have been few, if any, who took this opportunity to go back.

Some further pieces of information are available from other sources. In March 1973 the United Press Agency reported that Dimitar Chavdarov, a satirical writer using the pen-name of Chelkash, had died in a psychiatric hospital, aged sixty-one, after bitterly denouncing his fellow-members of the Writers' Union, the Bulgarian Communist regime and the Soviet Union. *The Times* reported in September 1973 that Vladimir Makarov, a retired chemistry researcher, had been arrested and sentenced to five years in prison on a charge of 'ideological subversion'. Two friends were arrested with him, one being Catherine Lvoff, a French researcher doing a course in Sofia. She was sentenced to four years, but released after French diplomatic intervention. She said she intended to marry Makarov.

Most Bulgarian writers have come to terms with the Communist regime and publish work approved by the authorities for which they are well rewarded. There are some exceptions, however, to this rule. At the time of the Soviet invasion of Czechoslovakia in 1968, the government tried to get statements from leading intellectuals supporting the invasion, but a number of them refused. Similarly, when Solzhenitsyn was exiled from the

Soviet Union in 1974, the authorities called in leading writers to denounce him, but some of them refused, including several literary prize-winners in the Stalin era.

In August 1975 a well-informed report by the research section of Radio Free Europe stated that four journalists working for the leading Bulgarian literary monthly *Septemvri*, including its chief editor, Kamen Kalchev, had been dismissed, and two others demoted. This followed the publication in *Septemvri* of a story by Georgi Bozhinov entitled *Green Woods, Cool Water*, describing the Soviet prison camps in the Gulag Archipelago through the eyes of five Bulgarians living and working in the Soviet Union who were arrested during the Stalin reign of terror and spent some twenty years in these camps. Bozhinov was clearly influenced by Solzhenitsyn and other Russian authors who wrote about the Stalin period, but his story seems to have been a powerful and moving contribution in its own right to the international literature of dissent.

In February 1977 three reports of dissent symptoms in Bulgaria were published in the West. The Vienna newspaper *Die Presse* said that forty Bulgarian intellectuals had been interrogated by the security police, and four of them detained, following the circulation in Sofia of the text of the Charter 77 manifesto on human rights, copied and translated from the French paper *Le Monde*. The Bulgarian government news agency, BTA, denied this report and issued statements allegedly made by the four writers said to have been detained, in which they described the report as a slanderous fabrication. One of them was Kamen Kalchev, whose dismissal from *Septemvri* has already been mentioned, but who had since been appointed deputy chairman of the Writers' Union. The other three were Valeri Petrov, a poet, Gocho Gochev, a theatre critic, and Hristo Ganev, a writer of film scripts. They all declared that they were working freely and normally. Kalchev said that his new novel would be published shortly, and that he had just heard that new translations of his work had appeared abroad. How far these statements were purely voluntary, or made under pressure, is not known.

The second report came from a press conference in Vienna given in February 1977 by six Bulgarian exiles who had formed a civil rights group. They included the leader of the Bulgarian Social Democratic Party in exile, Stefan Tabakoff, and Alexander Skartatov, who got out of Bulgaria in 1976. The group announced that it had made an appeal for support, written by Skartatov, to the Italian, French, and Spanish Communist Parties. They also claimed that it had been sent to Bulgaria, and that intellectual dissidents there were in agreement with it.

The third report, also in February, said that the Bulgarian authorities had confiscated part of an issue of the Communist Youth newspaper *Narodna Mladezh* in January and sacked six of its staff, including the editor, Gencho Arabdzhiev. This was because the paper had published some remarks made by a satirical poet, Radoi Ralin, and a cartoonist, Boris Dimouski, at a youth club meeting in Sofia, when they sharply criticised the luxurious living of high Party officials, and also the educational system. Both men had been in trouble before, in 1968, when they published a cartoon of a pig whose curly tail exactly matched the signature of the Party leader, Todor Zhivkov. They were apparently not arrested for it, but Ralin was banned from publishing his work and Dimouski lost his staff jobs on several journals. After the second incident, a government spokesman denied that Arabdzhiev had been dismissed from his editorial post and said that he had been simply transferred to other duties as executive secretary of the Bulgarian Journalists' Union.

A much more serious source of danger for the Bulgarian Communist leadership is to be found in its own internal jealousies and ambitions. In all political parties, including those in the West, such rivalries are common, but in Communist parties the struggle for personal power is waged with a venom all the stronger for being concealed. The Bulgarian Communist Party is particularly susceptible to this secret warfare. Its total subservience to Moscow compels the contenders for seats in the Politbureau, and for the leadership itself, to watch every passing twist and turn in the Kremlin with anxious care. The winners are those who read the signals correctly, the losers those whose political radar is off beam.

In 1949 for example, when the Bulgarian Communist leader, Georgi Dimitrov, died, the man most likely to succeed him was thought to be Traicho Kostov. He was defeated, however, by his chief rival, Vulko Chervenko, who gained control of the Party. Kostov was hanged on a trumped-up charge of wanting to pursue Tito's independent Yugoslav line in Bulgaria. Chervenko followed this up by a drastic purge of Communist Party members, only to fall in his turn after the death of Stalin in 1953. Like Ulbricht in East Germany, he wanted to carry on with Stalin's methods, but Khrushchev switched to a milder line which favoured Chervenko's opponents in his Party. Chervenko was replaced by Zhivkov in 1954 and his life was spared. He was deprived of his Party posts, but not finally disgraced until 1962. He had his Party membership card restored in 1969.

In April 1965 a plot to get rid of Zhivkov was revealed, involving ten men, one of whom committed suicide while the others received prison sentences. Some members of this group were former officers who had fought as guerrillas in Bulgaria during the war, when Bulgaria sided with Hitler. They may have acted against Zhivkov from nationalist feelings and a desire to make Bulgaria less dependent on Moscow, as Professor Richard Staar suggests in his book, *Communist Regimes in Eastern Europe*. There was further trouble in May 1977 when a curt statement was issued in Sofia announcing that the deputy Party leader, Boris Velchev, had been dismissed from the Politbureau and all his other Party posts 'for reasons of expedience'. Velchev had been in charge of the Party apparatus since 1959 and his removal was a clear indication of divisions at the highest level. Since then, Zhivkov seems to have consolidated his power, but he is getting old like many other Communist leaders. He was sixty-eight in 1979 and his successors may be content to bide their time.

Like other Communist regimes, the Bulgarian rulers take a hard line, not only against intellectual dissenters, but also against religious freedom and the rights of national minorities. The Bulgarian Orthodox Church is by far the largest, claiming a membership of six million, or three-quarters of the population. It took the leading part in sustaining the Bulgarian national consciousness and its traditions during the four centuries of Turkish rule, but since 1949 its leaders have followed a policy of submission and obedience to Communist government, and have shown it in words and deeds. They supported the Communist policy of collective farming and called for special services in honour of Stalin's 70th birthday, a demand refused by some priests who were arrested and sent to prison or labour camps. The Synod authorised the clergy to join pro-Communist organisations, and it ratified the government decision to end religious education in schools. The Bulgarian Orthodox Church has adopted much the same conformist line as the Russian Orthodox Church, with which it maintains close relations.

A Communist law passed in 1949 acknowledged that the Orthodox Church was 'the traditional religion of the Bulgarian people' and offered state subsidies if they were required. But under this law all church activities and appointments were brought under state control. The social work of the Church and its activities among young people were taken over by the Communist Party. A number of churches were closed and several monasteries were turned into tourist hotels. The theological faculty was separated from the Sofia University and compelled to add Marxism to its teaching. This information is taken from Trevor Beeson's book *Discretion and Valour*. He maintains that, despite its restrictions, the Bulgarian Orthodox Church today enjoys far greater freedom than could have been imagined in Stalin's time. He remarks that, although organised church work among young people is forbidden, the clergy are free to order their parishes on traditional lines, with regular celebrations of the liturgy and as much pastoral work as they can undertake.

Next to the Orthodox Christians, the Moslems are by far the largest religious group, and in 1966 they numbered 650,000, or about one in twelve of the population. The great majority are Turks, but there are also some Bulgarian Moslems called Pomaks. The Roman Catholic and Protestant Churches are small and have been much more harshly treated than the Orthodox. The Roman Catholic Bishop of Nikopolis, Bishop Bossilkov, was arrested and executed in 1952, together with the head of the Catholic seminary in Plovdiv and two other priests. In February 1949 fifteen prominent Protestant ministers, including Evangelical, Baptist, Congregational, and Pentecostal leaders, were tried in Sofia on charges of 'high treason, espionage and illegal foreign currency transactions', and sentenced to prison terms ranging from one year to life. All churches with headquarters outside Bulgaria were ordered to close, but since Stalin's death in 1953, and Zhivkov's appointment as Party leader, there has been some limited relaxation. Before the last war, there were 50,000 Jews in Bulgaria, but most of them were saved from Nazi extermination by King Boris, who dispersed them in remote villages. About 40,000 emigrated to Israel between 1948 and 1955.

As one of its weapons against all forms of religion, the Communist regime has introduced secular substitutes for religious ceremonies, similar to the *Jugendweihe*, or Communist confirmation, in East Germany, but on a much wider scale. In November 1975 the Communist paper *Kooperativno Selo* referred to civil ritual celebrations of many traditional religious festivals, including Shepherds' Day and Vine Growers' Day. The same paper described a village ceremony of the Communist kind in memory of local people who had died during the year:

Soft music fills the hearts of those present with sorrow. Three sacrificial urns raise fiery tongues to the sky. On a pedestal covered with a black cloth is the text 'Man is mortal, mankind is immortal'. The chairman of the municipal committee of the Fatherland Front, Velichka Boneva, delivers a speech filled with emotion in which she mentions the names and merits of all the inhabitants of the village who died during the year. Then she lights a torch from the flames of the sacrificial urn and hands 'the fire of life' to a Pioneer and a Komsomol member. There are tears in the eyes of those present.

But the same article also gave a warning about the danger of familiarity breeding contempt. If the same songs were sung year after year, the paper said, and the same speech made, and the same torch lit, the tears of the mourners might give way to irony. Repetition must therefore be avoided and variations introduced. The authorities tried to solve this problem by training 'well-qualified people' to organise and conduct these ceremonies, but obviously had difficulty in finding them. An atheist official, Magdalina Georgieva, said that there were 164 'civil ritual inspectors', but only 24 of them had received any higher education. Doubts must also persist about the extent to which the new Communist ceremonies can compete with the solemn and splendid chanting of the Orthodox liturgy which they seek to replace.

There is a large Turkish minority in Bulgaria which in 1945 numbered about 800,000. Between 1949 and 1951, more than 150,000 were allowed to emigrate to Turkey, but the process was then halted. In March 1968, however, an agreement was reached between Bulgaria and Turkey for the repatriation of Turks with close relatives in Turkey who had emigrated before 1952. It was estimated that only about 30,000 would qualify under these terms for further emigration, but nearly 40,000 actually left between 1969 and 1973, when this new exodus also seems to have stopped. Bulgarian and Turkish officials met in Ankara in November 1977 and agreed on measures to assist further emigration. The Bulgarian Deputy Minister for Foreign Affairs, Nikolay Minchev, revealed that more than 80,000 Turks had applied for, and received, Bulgarian exit permits, but that, since 1973, the Turkish authorities had slowed down the issue of entry visas. It should be added that the Turkish economy was in poor shape and the government was having difficulty in coping with the very large number of Turks who had gone to work in foreign countries and were now coming home.

Communist policy in Bulgaria, as in the other Communist states, seeks to destroy the separate identities of national minorities and assimilate them in a uniform Communist pattern. The Bulgarian authorities have made this very clear in their own statements. A Communist official of Turkish origin, Nayde Ferhadova, wrote an article in *Nov Zhivot* in October 1977 in which she said that 'the struggle against Turkish bourgeois nationalism' was one of the foremost tasks of the Bulgarian Communist Party. She revealed that special operational groups of Party officials were working in Turkish villages. Their tasks were to 'neutralise rumours spread among the population'; to visit houses 'where the radio sets are tuned around the clock to Istanbul and Ankara stations'; and to 'discourage' Moslem religious practices, especially those in which children and young people took part. She blamed 'Turkish bourgeois nationalism' for confusing basic religious rites with nationalism. The ultimate goal in the struggle, she wrote, was 'to make the Turkish population part of the Bulgarian nation'.

On her own admission, however, this was clearly proving to be a difficult task:

A considerable part of the Turkish population in our villages cannot tell the difference between socialism and capitalism, and are unable to find the correct landmark in the sea of facts and phenomena. It is clear that the mass political initiatives carried out by us do not always open everyone's eyes to the truth.

The Yugoslav Communist paper *Nova Makedonija* put it more bluntly. It said that the reasons for Turkish emigration from Bulgaria should be sought in the massive campaign to force assimilation; in the obligation to learn Bulgarian as the mother tongue; and in 'recently issued documents which have made it virtually impossible for minority groups in Bulgaria to declare their nationality officially'. Amnesty International says in its Report for 1977 that it has received information that an undisclosed number of dissidents belonging to the Turkish or Bulgarian Moslem groups are being detained in prison or restricted to officially designated places of residence.

The reactions of the Bulgarian government to the Helsinki agreements strictly adhered to the Soviet line laid down in Moscow. In December 1975 the Bulgarian Ministry of Education issued instructions to all primary and secondary schools for the inclusion in their programmes of a carefully edited version of the Helsinki Final Act and listed the ideological aspects which should be stressed. The teachers were told to point out 'the importance of the conference as a victory for Soviet foreign policy', and to describe the recognition of the post-war frontiers in Europe as 'a triumph for the realistic policies of the Soviet Union'. The role of the Soviet and Bulgarian Communist Parties, and the personal contributions of Brezhnev and Zhivkov, must be thoroughly studied, and the text of the Final Act, and the speeches of all Communist leaders, should be discussed. The pupils should be taught 'to grasp the essence of peaceful coexistence as a form of class struggle at the present stage', and told to participate in 'a large-scale offensive against anti-Communism and anti-Sovietism, and against imperialist reactionaries who are taking an active part in the ideological struggle'.

In August 1977 the Communist Youth paper *Narodna Mladezh* marked the second anniversary of the Helsinki conference by devoting three articles in one issue to aspects of the 'Basket Three' proposals on cultural exchanges and tourism. Their general purpose was to claim that Bulgaria had done far more than the West to implement these clauses. One article attacked the abuse of tourism by Western tourists who brought in undesirable material, and said:

Attempts have been made to import great quantities of pornographic literature – 680 magazines and 49 novels – religious books (24 Bibles and 3 New Testaments) . . . and several magazines full of vulgar slanders and attacks on our country.

The import of Bibles and other religious literature is forbidden in Bulgaria, but the author of this article seemed to realise that the equation of pornography with the Bible was going a bit far, even for atheist Communists. He added that the Bulgarian Constitution guaranteed religious freedom, and that nobody was ever persecuted for his religious beliefs, statements which ignored the fact that the constitutional provisions on religious freedom and other human rights are consistently violated in practice.

Another article in the same issue also complained of tourist offences:

Tourist exchange is used by certain capitalist countries to fan the flames of an ideological campaign against the socialist camp as a whole . . . Many foreigners admit that they came to this country with erroneous conceptions, owing to lack of information or even the dissemination of slanders, lies, and fabrications on the part of Western mass information media.

In a third article, the head of the Directorate of Cultural Contacts Abroad, Emil Alexandrov, maintained that Bulgaria had done infinitely more to publicise Western literature and arts than the West had done for Bulgaria, but some of his arguments were contradictory. Thus, while alleging that Western interest in Bulgarian culture was lacking, he pointed out that Bulgarian art exhibitions had been staged with great success in many cities of Western Europe and North America. He also admitted that a large number of Western art exhibitions had been given in Bulgaria, but complained that the West restricted Bulgarian access to Western cultural achievements.

Alexandrov accused the West of interfering in Bulgarian domestic affairs by 'propagandising the art of so-called dissidents'. Bulgaria, he added, did not allow on its territory 'Western pseudo-art that praises human degradation, pornography and horror'. But like all Communist spokesmen on cultural exchanges, he ignored the fact that their regimes only permit the publication and export of books and papers which follow the Party line. These arouse little interest in countries where people are free to buy them, or not, as they please.

In March 1977 the Bulgarian Communist paper *Rabotnichesko Delo* reported that the import of some Western newspapers and magazines would be increased, and also the export of Bulgarian papers and periodicals to the West. In June that year, reports from Sofia said that Western papers had appeared for sale on some newspaper stands and in large hotels, but it is not clear whether this has become a regular practice, or whether it is a seasonal concession in aid of Bulgarian efforts to attract Western tourists and their hard currency.

Also in March 1977 the US State Department announced that since the Helsinki Final Act the Bulgarian authorities had settled 24 claims for family reunification by allowing people living in Bulgaria to join their kinsfolk in the West. This was described as 'a significant improvement' over the year before Helsinki, but the number of such cases still outstanding was not given.

In cases where parents have emigrated 'illegally' leaving their children behind them, the Bulgarian Communist regime does not allow the children to join them and deprives the father and mother of their parental rights. In September 1967, for example, Spas Marev and his wife, Ivanka, left Bulgaria on a tourist visit to Turkey without their two small daughters and sought asylum there. They moved on to the USA and became American citizens. The children had a grandmother living in Bulgaria, but they were put into an orphanage and only allowed to stay with their grand-mother during the summer. The parents made repeated appeals to the Bulgarian authorities for their children to be permitted to join them, and the US State Department took up their case, but all in vain.

Article 60 of the Bulgarian Family Code published in 1968 says that children who have not come of age are obliged to live with their parents, but *Article 63* authorises district prosecutors to 'place children under appropriate care' and allows Bulgarian courts to deprive parents of their rights if their behaviour is 'in-appropriate'. This can clearly be used to cover anything from parental neglect to emigrating without permission. In March 1977 the Communist district prosecutor in Varna took legal action to deprive the Marevs of their parental rights.

Until quite recently, it was widely assumed in the West that no organised form of support for human rights existed in Bul-garia, but in April 1978 the Vienna paper *Die Presse* published a statement by Bulgarian dissenters entitled 'Declaration 78' which protested against the suppression of human rights by the Communist regime and called for action under six heads. These were:

1. An end to the violations. Non-intervention in private life, free-dom of the press and cultural expression. Free elections and free criticism. Freedom of religion and the abolition of censor-ship.

2. Free exchange of information and personal contacts. The right to emigrate, the opening of the frontiers, and passports for foreign travel by all Bulgarians. The abolition of Paragraphs 280 and 281 of the Penal Code whereby people going abroad and not returning to Bulgaria are liable to imprisonment should they come back.
3. The improvement of social insurance benefits. Higher pensions. The creation of a realistic relationship between prices, wages and salaries to provide a genuine rise in living standards.
4. Independent trade unions to defend the true interests of the workers.
5. Abolition of privileges in all spheres of public life.
6. Publication of this Declaration in all daily papers.

The authors did not give their names, but only the group initials of 'ABD'. *Die Presse* said that observers of the Bulgarian scene regarded the Declaration as genuine and thought it was the work of nonconformist intellectuals in Sofia. If so, it suggests that the human rights campaigners in Bulgaria are more active than had previously seemed possible in one of the toughest Soviet satellites.

Some indication of this had already been given late in 1977 when a French journalist, Annie Daubenton, visited Bulgaria and talked to a leading poet, Blaga Dimitrova. An account of these talks was published by the French journal *Les Nouvelles Littéraires* and it provided some interesting information about the attitude of Dimitrova and some other Bulgarian dissenters to the Communist regime.

Annie Daubenton asked Dimitrova whether dissidence could be said to exist in Bulgaria and she replied:

What is terrible here is the lack of information, which makes us live in the ebb and flow of rumours and counter-rumours. In such a situation, it is difficult to find one's own way and to preserve one's equilibrium. There are, however, in this country intellectuals who work away quietly, but are unknown to the rest of the world.

The French journalist pressed her point by asking whether there were actual cases of internal dissidence in Bulgaria, and referred to Dimitrova's own protest against a television serial which gave a distorted picture of a national hero, Vasil Levski, who resisted Turkish domination late in the nineteenth century. Dimitrova replied that this 'latent revolt' had been provoked by the distortion, which was interpreted by the public as a personal insult. The television film had been condemned in public discussion. She added:

I do still hope that we will be able, with the help of youth and the people, to impose a more humane freedom, as well as our unrestricted right to have our works published.

Questioned about the role of the poets in Bulgarian society, Dimitrova replied:

The poets are the ones who react most rapidly to events. For instance, Radoi Ralin has become almost a myth, a legendary image . . . He had his books published, but they were very much criticised. Even when his corrosive epigrams are not published, one has the feeling that they are in the air.

As noted earlier, Ralin's satirical comments on conditions in Bulgaria had already incurred official anger and reprisals, and it was risky even to mention his name. But Dimitrova also associated four other writers with him, naming Yordan Radichkov, Marko Ganchev, Stanislav Stratiev and Valeri Petrov among those whose work she admired. And she commented: 'Strangely enough, in periods of oppression, humour, as a means of reaction, is twice as merry.'

Dimitrova was equally frank on the subject of emigration by writers. She would have none of it and gave her reasons:

Emigration is not a solution. To me personally, the idea of leaving my country does not even occur. Even if you face prison, you have to stay in your country . . . We must constantly measure a writer's resistance when facing new difficulties. We must daily ask ourselves the question: Is it more important to speak out or to remain silent? And every day we must fight for freedom.

As a result of her talks with Annie Daubenton, and their publication in the French literary journal, Blaga Dimitrova was subjected to a hostile interrogation by the official Bulgarian news agency, BTA, which was clearly intended to make her retract her views. She was not helped by the fact that the French account of the conversations had been edited in a condensed form which omitted some of her remarks and quoted others out of context. But she stood firm on the basic issues and even managed to add some further evidence. For example, she was asked by the official interviewer the loaded question of whether it was true that she had spoken of 'subversive public opinion'. She replied:

I pointed out that, in this country, there is a public opinion on which creative artists, and I personally, rely. I gave two examples of expressed, but not subversive, public opinion; the TV serial about Levski and the recent, still more striking case of the film, *Return from Rome*. The second example, one doesn't know why, was dropped from the interview, but it was essential, since the film-maker is the son of a formerly prominent Party leader. By the way, the very fact that I have enumerated so many names of satirists whose books are being read and sell out immediately, and for whose plays it is impossible to find a ticket, speaks for itself.

The 'son of a formerly prominent Party leader' was, in fact, Ilya Velchev, whose father, Boris Velchev, was the former Politbureau member and deputy Party leader dismissed from all his posts in May 1977.

In the official interview, Dimitrova also spoke of her wish to rectify mistaken ideas in the West about Bulgarian intellectuals:

In my endeavour to break the deep-rooted Western notion about Bulgarian intellectuals, I have demonstrated that I am not afraid to say what I think . . . In this way, I contribute a little to the reputation of Bulgaria, to which some Europeans respond with a bored grimace, as if they were dealing with a country of drabness, fear and silence.

At the same time, with some justification, Dimitrova criticised the French version of her talks with Annie Daubenton as inaccurate, adding that a half-truth could easily become a lie. There is no reason to doubt, however, that she did make the remarks attributed to her, both in her talks with Daubenton and in the official interview later. Despite the pressure she was under, she defended her basic position and even reaffirmed it. She was asked by the Bulgarian news agency inquisitor whether the other writers she had named, and she herself, could be considered as 'dissidents'. She replied that the word 'dissident' was a borrowed one which sounded unpleasant and denied that it applied to her. All that she and the others hoped to do was to emphasise that there were different points of view in Bulgaria. She had simply tried, she said, to have her own opinion and defend it in her writing.

And therein, of course, lay her sin. Bulgarian Communist rule does not recognise any distinction between a 'dissident' and a writer expressing his or her own views, but treats them as one and the same thing. The post-war Communist leader, Georgi Dimitrov, was Secretary-General of the Cominform in Moscow from 1935 to 1943 and a Soviet citizen when Stalin sent him to Bulgaria to wipe out all opposition. Dimitrov's successors in Sofia today are merely Soviet agents dressed up in native clothing. The ghost of Stalin is alive and well and living in Bulgaria.

CHAPTER 8

MORALITY AND
REALITY

The states represented at the 1975 Helsinki Conference on
Security and Co-operation in Europe met again in Belgrade from
October 1977 to March 1978 to review developments since Helsinki and consider further measures for improving their relations.
After six months of barren talks, the Belgrade Conference ended in
a stalemate. This failure was acknowledged in a concluding document which amounted only to an agreement to disagree. The
signatories decided to meet again in Madrid in November 1980,
after preparatory talks in September. Before the Madrid conference, three meetings of experts were to take place; the first to consider a Swiss proposal for the peaceful settlement of disputes;
the second to discuss the establishment of a 'Scientific Forum';
and the third to examine ways of promoting co-operation between the CSCE states in the Mediterranean area.

The Belgrade closing statement made no mention of human
rights, an omission forced on the conference by the attitude of
the Soviet Union. The Western governments and some of the
neutral and non-aligned countries drew attention to the failure
of the Communist countries to fulfil the humanitarian provisions
of the Helsinki Final Act and offered to submit to cross-examina-
tion on their own performance. The Western allies showed a
united front, with the United States giving a strong lead on

human rights and the West European partners in the European Economic Community, particularly Britain, expressing their support in less forceful terms.

The Western participants also made new proposals for increasing human contacts and exchanges of information between East and West; for relaxing travel restrictions on people seeking to be reunited with their families in the West or to visit relatives; and for improving the working conditions of journalists and the exchange of newspapers, other publications and broadcasts. None of these proposals came up for consideration.

The chief Soviet delegate, Yuri Vorontsov, flatly refused to take part in any discussion on the treatment of human rights in Russia, maintaining that Western concern with this issue was an unwarranted interference in Soviet domestic affairs. He also refused to discuss the Western proposals, and his attitude was faithfully echoed by the satellite spokesmen. This arrogant dismissal of the humanitarian elements in detente was in itself a flagrant breach of the Helsinki Final Act, which established the treatment of human rights on an equal footing with the military and economic aspects of East-West relations and fully justified their review at Belgrade. But under the CSCE rules all conference decisions require unanimous approval and this enabled Vorontsov to impose a veto, as the Soviet Union has done so often in the United Nations.

The Soviet delegation came to Belgrade with a bulky file of charges against the West of violating human rights, ranging from British actions in Ulster to the treatment of Negroes in the United States. The Western democracies have not denied their blemishes and they have done much to remove them, but the Soviet government, with far worse crimes against human rights on its record, dare not face any publicity or discussion.

The British Foreign and Commonwealth Office issued a White Paper in March 1978 (Cmnd. 7126) which tried to make the best of a bad business. It pointed out that the Helsinki Final Act was 'a charter and code of behaviour' for a long-term process of achieving a more normal and open relationship between governments and peoples in Eastern and Western Europe. The White Paper saw hope for the future in the fact that despite the Soviet refusal to discuss human rights, the principle had now been established that all CSCE states have the right to comment on the way other signatory states are carrying out their obligations under the Helsinki Final Act. It described this as an important new event in East-West relations, and added:

The Soviet Union and its allies frequently invoked the principle of non-intervention in the internal affairs of other states in order to claim that the criticism directed at them was impermissible. But the firm insistence of Western countries on the right to criticise won the day, as the continued presence of the Soviet delegation tacitly confirmed. It may in time be possible to develop this into the dialogue which was missing on this occasion.

This seems to us a somewhat slender thread on which to hang hopes of improvement in the treatment of human rights in Eastern Europe. It could more cogently be argued that the Soviet government served notice at Belgrade that it excluded any further discussion of human rights in the future. It now looks as if the Kremlin only accepted the inclusion of human rights in the Helsinki agenda because it never thought that they were meant to be taken seriously, and because it seemed a small price to pay in return for Western recognition of the post-war frontiers in Europe and Western economic support. The Soviet leaders were shocked and angered by the encouragement which the humanitarian clauses in the Helsinki Final Act gave to the human rights campaigners in Russia and elsewhere in Eastern Europe, and at Belgrade they decided to stop the rot.

The small crumbs of comfort which the British government

professed to find in the failure of the Belgrade meeting were in marked contrast with the kind of language British Ministers were using before it began. In March 1977 both the Prime Minister, Mr Callaghan, and the Foreign Secretary, Dr David Owen, publicly expressed their support for President Carter's firm stand on human rights worldwide. Dr Owen said in London that the Communist countries 'must recognise that concern for human rights is not a diversionary tactic but an integral part of foreign policy in the Western democracies'. He indicated, however, that the British approach would be more cautious and pragmatic than the American when he added: 'We have to balance morality with reality. The art lies in striking the right balance.'

The Minister of State for Foreign Affairs, Lord Goronwy-Roberts, answering questions in the House of Lords on 1 February 1978 about British aims in Belgrade, said: 'We shall not accept a purely cosmetic document. We shall insist on there being a substantive concluding document and we are working on that now.' Brave words, but the final statement at Belgrade was a 'cosmetic document' if ever there was one.

The Kremlin's tougher line was put into action as soon as the Belgrade Conference ended, as if to add injury to insult. Two members of the Ukrainian monitoring group on violations of human rights, Miroslav Marinovich and Mykola Matusevich, were sentenced to seven years in a labour camp followed by five years' exile in a remote part of Russia, the maximum sentence for first offenders. A former Red Army General, Pyotr Grigorenko, a founding member of the Moscow group monitoring human rights, was deprived of his citizenship while visiting the United States for medical treatment, and thus exiled. Grigorenko, who fought with distinction against Nazi Germany and held many Soviet decorations, was a leading campaigner for human rights. He is best known for his defence of the Crimean Tartars, a whole people numbering 200,000 to 250,000 who were deported to

Central Asia by Stalin at the end of the war against Hitler and still forbidden to return home. He had already been reduced to the ranks, expelled from the Communist Party, twice declared insane and confined in psychiatric hospitals for long periods when he continued to speak out for human rights. Upon losing his citizenship he applied for political asylum in the United States but said he was willing to face an open trial in Russia.

At the same time the world-famous Russian cellist, Mstislav Rostropovich, and his wife, Galina Vishnevskaya, the well-known Bolshoi soprano, were also deprived of Soviet citizenship. They were allowed to leave Russia in 1974 and were living in the United States where Rostropovich accepted the post of principal director of the National Symphony Orchestra. He was accused of 'committing acts harmful to Soviet prestige'. Rostropovich replied that he and his wife did not accept the legality of the charges against him, and like Grigorenko he demanded a public trial in his own country. He could only appeal to the United Nations to intercede for the return of his Soviet citizenship which under the Soviet constitution can be revoked by decree without right of appeal.

The distinguished Russian novelist, Vladimir Voinovich, announced that the loss of citizenship suffered by Grigorenko and Rostropovich and his wife had made him decide not to apply for permission to visit the West. Voinovich, who was expelled from the Soviet Writers' Union in 1974, had received invitations to lecture in the United States, France and West Germany, but in a statement shown to Western journalists he said that any trip he made abroad would now be the same as voluntary exile. He also issued a copy of a letter he had written to the Soviet Minister of the Interior and police chief, Nikolai Shchelokov, protesting that the police in the Ukraine had told his parents that he was missing and believed dead, knowing him to be alive and living in Moscow.

The best-known Soviet dissenter, Andrei Sakharov, was summoned to an interview with the Deputy City Prosecutor of Moscow after leading a demonstration against Kremlin support for the Palestine Liberation Organisation. He was told that he had broken the law by actions 'bordering on hooliganism' and warned that any repetition would have serious consequences. He has received many similar warnings before, but his international reputation as a physicist has so far helped to shield him from prosecution. This immunity may not last much longer.

In May 1978 the founder of the Moscow monitoring group on human rights, Dr Yuri Orlov, was put on trial after he had been held in custody for fifteen months. He was charged with 'anti-Soviet agitation and propaganda'. Like all Soviet procedure in political cases, the Orlov trial was a mockery of justice. The court refused to let him call any defence witnesses and Western correspondents were barred from entry. The American Embassy in Moscow sent an observer, the only Western Embassy to do so, but he too was refused admission. A small group of Orlov's friends stood outside the court, watched and photographed by secret police and jeered at by Russian onlookers.

Orlov received a maximum sentence of seven years in a prison camp of the 'strict' category, followed by five years' banishment in Russia. The Soviet authorities clearly intend to break him morally and physically, and for an eminent scientist like Orlov, aged fifty-three in 1978, the sentence also meant the end of his career. Western reactions were strongly expressed. The US State Department described the verdict on Orlov as 'a gross distortion of internationally accepted standards of human rights'. The British Foreign Secretary, Dr Owen, said that Soviet action against dissenters was 'endangering detente'. An official British delegation which was in Moscow to sign an agreement on sports exchanges was instructed to cancel the ceremony and return home. A member of the Swedish Parliament, Olle Waestberg, nominated Orlov as a candidate for the Nobel Peace Prize.

The day after Orlov's trial ended, a Soviet court in Tbilisi, capital of Soviet Georgia, passed sentences of three years in a labour camp followed by two years of banishment on two members of a Georgian group monitoring the observance of human rights, Zviad Gamsakhurdia and Mirab Kostava. Both men had been in prison for over a year awaiting trial. They received lighter sentences than Orlov because they pleaded guilty, no doubt after being subjected to severe pressure. Gamsakhurdia admitted on Soviet television that he had prepared and distributed literature slandering the Soviet state and its social system.

Two American correspondents, Craig Whitney and Harold Piper, visited Tbilisi and reported to their papers that they had talked to relatives and friends of Gamsakhurdia who claimed that his television statement had been fabricated by the Soviet authorities. An action for 'slander' was then brought against these journalists in a Moscow court, and Gamsakhurdia himself was marched in under guard to testify that his admission of guilt was genuine. The two journalists did not attend the proceedings and left for a holiday in the USA, after protesting that their reports were accurate and objective. They also thought that their appearance in court might be used to make them disclose their sources and thus lead to reprisals against their informants.

The Soviet court ordered the correspondents to publish retractions of their reports within five days in Russia and the United States, and to pay legal costs equivalent to £800. The two journalists refused to withdraw their reports and were supported by their editors, who agreed to pay legal costs. The court verdict took no notice of a demand by the Soviet prosecutor for a review of the accreditation of the journalists, who announced that they had made arrangements to return to Moscow.

The Soviet authorities had put themselves in a difficult position. They had committed an obvious breach of the provisions in the Helsinki Final Act safeguarding the free exercise of their duties by foreign correspondents and had advertised to the whole world the Kremlin's fear of Western reporting on events in Russia. It remained to be seen whether they would strain detente still further by refusing to allow the two American correspondents to return to Moscow, a step which was not only certain to provoke restrictions on Soviet correspondents in the USA, but would also be a threat to all Western reporting from the Soviet Union.

The Kremlin's determination to stamp out all manifestations of dissent in the Soviet Union was brutally reaffirmed in July 1978, when several other leading spokesmen for human rights were brought to trial. Alexander Ginzburg, already twice imprisoned for his defence of freedom, was charged with 'anti-Soviet agitation and propaganda' and sentenced to eight years in a hard labour camp on a severely limited diet. As a founder member of the Helsinki monitoring group in Moscow and the administrator of the Solzhenitsyn fund for the relief of political prisoners and their families, he was a prime target for Soviet reprisals.

Anatoly Shcharansky, a computer engineer and a leading campaigner for the right of Jewish emigration from Russia, was sentenced to three years in prison and ten more in a hard labour camp. He was accused of high treason and espionage for the USA, although President Carter himself had informed Mr Brezhnev that Shcharansky had never worked for American intelligence. Another leading dissenter, Viktoras Petkus, member of a human rights monitoring group in Lithuania, was sentenced to three years in prison and seven in a hard labour camp, followed by five of internal exile.

The Soviet rulers seem to be living in a dream world of obsolete Marxist-Leninist dogma and shutting their eyes to the lessons of change which even a superpower like the Soviet Union cannot safely ignore. They were certainly well aware of the outcry which these trials and sentences would cause in Western countries and they must have weighed very carefully the risks of Western reactions damaging to Soviet interests. They apparently assumed that these responses would again be limited to verbal protests which, though sharper than before, would only demonstrate the incapacity or unwillingness of Western governments and diplomats to take any effective action. And indeed, at first sight, this calculation seemed well-founded. President Carter and his Administration understandably resisted demands in Congress for a suspension of the SALT talks on nuclear arms limitation. The British Prime Minister, Mr Callaghan, and his Foreign Secretary, Dr David Owen, deplored the sentences on the human rights campaigners, but made only the token gesture of cancelling a visit to Britain by the Soviet Minister for Coal, Bratchenko. At the same time, they appealed to the Soviet government to take up the largely unused balance of British trade credits offered to Russia by Mr Harold Wilson in 1975. However, Dr Owen announced in the House of Commons that British Embassies in the Soviet Union and Eastern Europe had been instructed to report regularly on the Communist treatment of human rights, and that these reports would be made available to Members of Parliament half-yearly. We welcome this as a step in the right direction.

The Kremlin had far more reason to fear American reactions. President Carter cancelled the sale of an advanced American computer system to the Soviet news agency, TASS, and appealed successfully to Britain, France, West Germany and Japan not to fill the gap. He also announced that sales of oil-drilling equipment to Russia would be carefully scrutinised and subject to export licences, thus warning that badly needed American technological aid should no longer be taken for granted while Soviet violations of their human rights promises continued.

The Soviet leaders may have decided to go ahead with the

223

trials of dissenters regardless of consequences, whatever they might be, but they have created new tensions in East-West relations and revealed a fear of contagion in Russia from the small band of human rights defenders which is a sign of weakness, not of strength. And even inside the Kremlin itself, there may be growing doubt and disagreements over the choice between political and economic priorities.

Further evidence has appeared of brutal psychiatric methods used by the Soviet authorities against dissenters. An Amnesty International Report issued in April 1977 noted that the confinement of political prisoners in Soviet psychiatric hospitals was continuing 'at a disturbing rate'. In August 1977 a report by the United States Commission dealing with the implementation of the Helsinki Final Act quoted testimony from Russian sources suggesting that psychiatric abuses may even be increasing. For example, Peter Starchik was held for two months in a lunatic asylum outside Moscow after the Soviet signing of the Helsinki Final Act for writing 'anti-Soviet' songs and singing them to his friends. Aleksandr Voloschuk, a Baptist living in Gorky, decided that religious persecution compelled him to apply for permission to emigrate with his wife and children, and visited Moscow for that purpose in March 1977. He was arrested and taken, bound and gagged, to a mental hospital in Moscow, where he was said to be suffering from 'schizophrenia with religious delusions'. His wife organised a campaign on his behalf and he was released a month later.

There have been other cases where Russians who went to Moscow to appeal against unjust dismissal from work or on similar grounds of ill-treatment have been subjected to psychiatric punishment. For example, Nadezhda Gaidar went from Kiev to the capital to make a complaint to Communist Party officials and was sent to a psychiatric hospital where the doctor who treated her was told that 'she is suffering from nervous exhaustion due to her search for justice'.

In March 1978 Amnesty International published a Report issued by a group calling itself The Association of Free Trade Unions of Workers in the Soviet Union, together with an open letter signed by forty-three workers. These documents protested against the confinement in psychiatric hospitals of Soviet workers who defended their rights, and quoted many individual cases. Among them was that of Vladimir Klebanov, foreman in a coal-mine and spokesman for a group of miners. He was given psychiatric treatment and told that he was suffering from 'paranoid development of the personality' and 'a mania for struggling for justice'. Dr Stanislav Korolev, working in the special (KGB) psychiatric hospital in Kazan, was quoted as saying that anti-Soviet beliefs were a 'natural impossibility' and must be the result of either 'mental illness, cynicism or ignorance'. According to these reports seven doctors in Moscow had refused to take part in the abuse of psychiatric methods against political prisoners. They were all dismissed and two were sent to prison. It is impossible to judge the size and significance of this Association of Free Trade Unions, but Amnesty International thinks it may have had its origins in talks between people who tried in vain to get a hearing for their grievances from Communist officials in Moscow. An Amnesty appeal on behalf of Soviet workers is being made to trade unions throughout the world, but if past experience is any guide it will fall mostly on deaf ears.

The International Labour Organisation in Geneva has refused for many years to discuss Soviet violations of labour rights, much less to condemn them. Western efforts to raise the issue have been blocked by Soviet opposition backed by neutral and pro-Soviet countries. At the ILO conference in June 1977, a report was submitted by an international committee pointing out that Soviet law was preventing the implementation of ILO covenants which gave Soviet workers the right to form independent trade unions free from Communist State or Party control. When this report came up for discussion, the conference failed to produce the necessary quorum of members present and it was shelved, this being the first time such a thing had happened. This blatant exhibition of double standards in favour of the Soviet Union led to the withdrawal of the United States from the ILO.

Psychiatric 'treatment' for prisoners apart, the punishments meted out to political offenders continue unabated. In Kiev, Pyotr Vins, a member of the Helsinki monitoring group, was accused of 'parasitism' and sent to a labour camp for a year. Balis Gayauskas, a Lithuanian who helped to distribute money raised by the Solzhenitsyn fund for gaoled Soviet dissidents, was sentenced to ten years in a labour camp for 'anti-Soviet agitation'. As we write, the agony of a woman refused permission to join her husband abroad was dramatically underlined by Antonina Agapov, who tried to commit suicide by drinking poison outside the Moscow emigration office after four unsuccessful attempts to escape by light plane had failed. Nureyev's mother has been waiting for twenty-one years for a visa to join her son. It is not only intellectuals who are made to suffer, or who refuse to suffer in silence.

In the Soviet Union, concern for human rights is still treated as a 'disease' and dissenters are suffering worse punishment than they did before the Helsinki Final Act. But among the satellite regimes there are marked differences in the strength and organisation of the human rights campaigners and the reactions of the Communist rulers. In one or two satellites, moreover, there is evidence of economic reforms which could indirectly make some contribution to personal freedom. Contrasts in national character, past history, and varying scales of living standards combine to make each of the satellites a special case.

Thus, in Poland, the spokesmen for human rights are active and gaining in strength, supported as they are by a Roman

Catholic Church which has great national influence and the power to act as a mediator between the Communist state and its people. The Polish dissenters are now producing underground literature, issuing public statements, and holding private meetings and seminars for students which the security police either cannot prevent or are ordered to handle with care. In April 1978, when Nicholas Carroll visited Warsaw for the *Sunday Times*, he was told by Adam Michnik, a leading dissenter, that the two human rights movements in Poland known as KOR and ROPCO were publishing between them more than a dozen unauthorised journals as well as information bulletins and even books. Another prominent dissenter and friend of Michnik, Jacek Kuron, told Carroll that the output of clandestine publications was running at about 15,000 copies monthly and they were read by an estimated 150,000 people.

Still more significant, it was revealed in January 1978 that a group of Communist Party members, including some formerly in high positions such as the former Party leader, Edward Ochab, had sent a letter three months earlier to the present leader, Gierek, in which they called for more democracy in the Party and an 'open dialogue' with the nation to solve Poland's economic problems. Poland is the only country in Eastern Europe where such differences of opinion at a high Party level have been openly revealed.

In Hungary, on the other hand, there is no organised body of dissent and the Communist leader, Janos Kadar, has taken much of the steam out of the human rights issue by allowing a certain amount of harmless grousing about the government, and by adopting economic measures which have given the Hungarian people better living standards. The Hungarians also have more freedom to travel abroad and to the West than exists in the other satellites, except perhaps in Poland. The main questions are how far Kadar can go without causing a breach with Moscow;

and who will succeed him if and when he retires at the end of his present term of office in 1980, when he will be sixty-eight. The most likely candidate seems to be Karoly Nemeth, whose promotion in April 1978 as Secretary in charge of administration, cadres and mass organisations marked him out as Kadar's heir, and who is still relatively young.

In Czechoslovakia, the Charter 77 movement for human rights has been badly mauled by the harsh repression of the Husak regime and weakened by the exile of some of its leading members.

The resignation of Dr Jiri Hajek in April 1978 not only deprived Charter 77 of the last of its original spokesmen, but also revealed disagreements within its own ranks. It is by no means a spent force, but its position is far more isolated from public support than that of the dissenters in Poland. This is partly due to the relatively high living standards in Czechoslovakia, where industry is more advanced than in most other satellites, and also to fears of reprisals against any open criticism of the regime. The divisions between Czechs and Slovaks also present a striking contrast with national unity in Poland, stiffened by a powerful and ably led Roman Catholic Church.

The East German Communist regime, which under Ulbricht's leadership was generally regarded as Moscow's most humble servant and one of the toughest satellites in its domestic rule, is showing signs of strain under Ulbricht's successor, Erich Honecker. The flood of applications for emigration to West Germany after the Helsinki Final Act was signed revealed, more than anything else, the failure of Communist rule to compete with the magnetic attractions of freedom and prosperity so near at hand. The post-war recovery in East Germany, though impressive, does not begin to match the performance of West Germany. Honecker has got rid of his most troublesome dissidents by giving them one-way visas, but he cannot stop millions of East Germans from listening avidly to West German radio and television programmes which rub home daily the fact that they are the poor relations. Worse still for Honecker, there seem to be stirrings of revolt within his own Communist Party, though it is difficult to measure their importance.

Bottom place in the satellite order of human rights is shared by Rumania and Bulgaria. The Rumanians suffer the worst of both worlds, political and economic. Their Communist leader, Nicolae Ceausescu, takes an independent line in foreign policy which flatters Rumanian national pride and jars on Moscow, but he maintains a harsh internal regime as the price for renewing his driving licence in Moscow. His ruthless pursuit of industrial development at the expense of better living standards has turned Rumania into a huge labour camp and imposes great sacrifices and hardship on his people. The strike by Rumanian miners in August 1977 was a warning which he seems to have brushed aside. Among Rumanian writers and intellectuals there are few manifestations of open support for human rights, and the most active dissenter, Paul Goma, was surprisingly given leave of absence to visit the West with his family. He may not be allowed to return home.

In Bulgaria, the Communist regime is totally subservient to Moscow and large Soviet subsidies have enabled it to improve living standards. The security police are omnipotent and more numerous in proportion to the population than in any other satellite. But this has not stopped a few courageous individuals from protesting openly against violations of human rights. The appearance in April 1978 of an anonymous group calling itself 'Declaration 78', and demanding major reforms in Communist rule, showed that the human rights campaigners in Bulgaria were more active than Western opinion had previously assumed. Fundamentally, however, Communist rule in Bulgaria remains what it has been from the start; the seizure of power by a band of brigands from the mountains who have taken over the big city in Sofia and brook no opposition to their enjoyment of the spoils.

The question now is what follow-up there will be to the challenge on human rights thrown down by the Soviet rulers in Belgrade. The British White Paper defined Western reactions as follows:

The British Government, together with the other Governments of Western Europe and North America, will continue to monitor carefully the way in which the (Helsinki) Final Act is implemented everywhere in Europe. They will be guided by its provisions in all their bilateral and multilateral contacts with other signatory states between now and the Madrid meeting. The Government will continue to promote the ideas for improving implementation which they put forward and supported during the Belgrade meeting. In particular, they will continue to insist that the provisions of the Final Act which relate to the rights of the individual and human contacts should be finally implemented in all participating countries. Without this, detente cannot command popular support.

The only conclusion which emerges from this statement is that the British government will continue to make verbal protests through diplomatic channels to the Soviet Union and its satellites about their violations of human rights, as they have been doing ever since the Yalta agreement with Stalin, but with no real hope of gaining satisfaction except in a few individual cases. The Kremlin will continue to treat such protests as an intolerable intrusion into its internal affairs and everything will go on as before. And indeed it may seem that Western governments have no other option short of an open breach with the Soviet Union and an end to hopes of improving relations between the Western and the Communist camps.

We do not share this negative view, which begs the question of how the Western countries 'insist' on the implementation of human rights. Believing as we do that the Communist suppression of freedom and independence in Eastern Europe is the greatest danger to the future peace and stability of Europe, we think it is as much in Soviet as Western interest to reduce the threat by allowing a gradual process of change and reform. The difficulty, of course, is to persuade the Soviet rulers to see matters in that light. The essence of the Kremlin's dilemma is that it must choose between a policy of continuing to suppress human rights and national aspirations in the satellite states and risk an explosion; or allow some degree of relaxation which might get out of hand and even put in peril the Communist monopoly of power and satellite loyalty to Moscow.

When Brezhnev visited Prague in May 1978 he was clearly in no mood to tolerate any repetition of the Dubcek reform programme. His talks with the Czechoslovak leader, Husak, reaffirmed the Soviet right to intervene in any satellite country where 'socialism' was threatened and sanctified it under the name of 'fraternal international assistance'. Some leading members of Charter 77 were detained by the secret police before Brezhnev arrived. His visit was clearly a mark of approval for Husak's hard line on human rights and a warning to other satellite leaders to watch their step.

Passive Western attitudes limited only to words have merely encouraged the Kremlin to maintain and even reinforce a policy of repression. An effective method of bringing Western influence to bear is needed, and in our view it can be found by using Western economic leverage to link Communist concessions on human rights with their benefits from Western technology, grain supplies and trade credits. But before discussing this further, it is necessary to stress the importance of well-informed Western public opinion, both in acting as a spur to Western governments and in supporting those who defend human rights in Russia and Eastern Europe.

In Britain, newspapers and broadcasting services provide

numerous and accurate reports of violations of human rights both in Russia and in the Soviet empire. There are, however, some people in this country who doubt quite sincerely whether it serves any useful purpose for Britain to become involved in defending human rights in Eastern Europe. Yet some of them see no inconsistency in passionately demanding British action against Chile or South Africa.

Somebody may say: 'What the Communist governments do to their people is no concern of ours. There's nothing we can do about it. These dissenters know the risks they take. If they choose to break the rules, they must be prepared to pay for it. Anyway, it's none of our business.'

Others think that the dissenters in Communist countries are so few and so isolated from the rest of the population that their cause is hopeless. They ask how Communist dissenters can demand liberal reforms and still call themselves Communists. They point out that none of the Communist states, except Czechoslovakia, have ever been democracies in the Western sense, so why worry about them now? There are also fears of giving the Soviet government a platform for attacking our own performance on human rights and 'reviving the cold war'.

Such fears need to be answered. As we see it, no country in the modern world can be insulated from the explosive effect of cruelty and oppression in any other. The suppression of human rights in Eastern Europe is not an academic question but a threat to the West, since it endangers peace. It could lead to a new confrontation between the Soviet Union and the NATO allies starting, perhaps, with another crisis over the status of West Berlin.

The defenders of human rights in Communist countries may be relatively few in number, but so they have always been in history from the early Christians to the crusaders against the slave trade. In any generation, few people have the moral and physical courage required to face torture and execution. The astonishing thing about the dissenters today in Eastern Europe is not that there are so few, but that there are so many.

It is true that some who now stand up for human rights and still call themselves Communists are so warped by dogma and habit, and so reluctant to admit that they have spent the best part of their lives worshipping false gods, that they cling to the illusion of Communist reformation in a 'socialist' guise. Some of them are former Communist politicians who may still hope to return to power one day dressed in that new clothing. But whatever their motives may be, they represent an element of revolt within the Communist system which must worry the Kremlin.

As for comparisons between the Communist and Western records on human rights, they should be welcomed. Our own government has offered to submit its performance to Communist scrutiny in open and reciprocal debate. It has accepted the jurisdiction of the European Court of Human Rights and pointed out that there is no conflict between any of the provisions in the European Convention and the law in Britain and its administrative practice. In the case which the Irish government brought against us in the European Court over the treatment of terrorist suspects in Ulster, the final verdict was that the methods used did not amount to torture but were inhuman and degrading. The British government had already put a stop to them in 1971. On the other hand, the Soviet Union and its satellites refuse to accept any international judgment of their own far more evil practices from fear of exposure.

The monitoring of the Helsinki Final Act in all its aspects is the task undertaken by an unofficial group in Britain set up in March 1977 under the chairmanship of Lord Thomson of Monifieth, succeeded by Lord Caccia, and under the auspices of the David Davies Memorial Institute for International Studies. The group membership represents a wide range of political experience and expert knowledge of foreign affairs. Its objectives are as follows:

To attempt to remedy the lack of attention paid by the public in the United Kingdom to the (Helsinki) Conference on Security and Co-operation in Europe and its Final Act by stressing their importance in the long drawn-out attempt to improve East-West relations in Europe; to monitor the implementation of the Final Act in order to provide an independent source of information both for the general public and those engaged in the negotiations at the Belgrade follow-up meeting; and, where appropriate, to suggest further steps which could usefully be considered at Belgrade as a means of improving and deepening East-West relations.

It will be noted that this statement does not mention human rights specifically. The group has issued a report prepared for it by the David Davies Institute and summing up developments since Helsinki in the military, economic, cultural and humanitarian aspects of East-West relations before the Belgrade meeting. It has also issued a further report on the results of that conference. The Institute is keeping members informed about developments after the Belgrade talks and is to decide whether they should meet again before the next CSCE conference in Madrid in November 1980. While paying tribute to the work done by the Institute, we regret that the group would appear so far to have made little impact on public opinion.

In its report on the Belgrade conference, the group pointed out that the British government has undertaken to monitor the implementation of the Helsinki Final Act. It suggested that a Parliamentary Select Committee should be set up for that purpose and that its findings should be made available to the public at regular intervals. We warmly welcome this proposal, on which no action has yet been taken.

In the United States, a Commission on Security and Co-operation in Europe was established by Congress in June 1976,

consisting of six members from the Senate, six from the House
of Representatives, and one each from the Departments of State,
Defence and Commerce. The Commission was instructed to
monitor the actions of the Helsinki Final Act signatories 'which
reflect compliance with, or violation of, the Final Act of the
Conference on Security and Co-operation in Europe *with particular regard to the provisions relating to Co-operation in
Humanitarian Fields*' (our italics). This mandate was later extended to include 'the expansion of East-West economic co-
operation and a greater interchange of ideas between East and
West'. The Commission is serviced by State Department officials
who maintain close contact with many private experts and organisations working on East-West relations.

In November 1976 five members of the Commission carried
out a study mission in Europe and had meetings with officials,
institutions and private citizens in eighteen West European
countries. The Commission has also produced a valuable survey of conditions in the Soviet Union affecting Jewish emigration,
based on interviews with recent Jewish *émigrés* in Israel, Italy
and the USA. The results are given in a Commission Report
submitted to Congress on 1 August 1977. This Report also in-
cludes a preliminary survey of religion in the Soviet Union.

Beginning in January 1977, the Commission had by August
that year held fourteen public hearings in Washington at which
fifty-six witnesses gave evidence on the interpretation and implementation of the Helsinki Final Act, with special reference to
its provisions on human rights.

This official American body is matched by the Committee on
the Present Danger which was formed in 1976 by nearly 150
eminent private citizens, many of whose names are household
words. The Chairman of the Executive Committee is Eugene
Rostow, and founder members include ex-Ambassadors, three
former Secretaries of the Treasury, and retired servicemen (three

of them former NATO chiefs) as well as leading academics, lawyers, bankers, industrialists and trade unionists. Their object is to alert the nation, in a period of increasing danger, to the need to change the course of United States' policy. The country's economic and military strategy, through concerted alliance diplomacy and peaceful deterrence, must assure peace with security rather than accepting an illusory detente. In the course of some excellent publications, they draw special attention to the way in which the ruling élite in the Soviet Union has deprived the Soviet people of basic human liberties while taking maximum advantage of 'capitalist' credit and know-how to strengthen the Soviet economy and its growing military capacity. We think there is just as much need for such a private committee in Western Europe to inform and educate public opinion and bring pressure to bear on governments, and hope that one will be formed to work closely with this influential body in the USA.

Even allowing for national differences in political organisation and general outlook, the American monitoring of the Helsinki Final Act is clearly far more comprehensive and more closely in touch with public opinion than its counterpart in Britain. We would like to see Parliament involved in the monitoring process, perhaps in the form of a Joint Select Committee of both Houses, as suggested by the UK monitoring group, with powers to call witnesses, hold public sessions and publish reports. But we would add to this a special requirement for the Committee to report on violations of human rights and their damaging effects on detente in Europe.

Western foreign-language broadcasts to Eastern Europe countries supply listeners there with reliable news and comments which the Communist regimes prefer to hide, and here the BBC European Service makes an important contribution. It works in close co-operation with the Foreign and Commonwealth Office and receives financial support from the government, but it has almost complete editorial freedom. The sad fact is that the BBC broadcasts are not getting through to many listeners in Eastern Europe because the technical equipment is obsolete. The main transmitter in Yorkshire dates back to the last war. It would cost only between £10 million and £12 million, spread over five years or so, to overcome this problem and this seems well worth paying to make Britain's voice heard loud and clear in the Soviet domain. All the more so because Communist jamming of BBC broadcasts stopped just before the Helsinki Conference in 1975 and has not so far been resumed.

The leading place in Western broadcasts to Eastern Europe is held by Radio Free Europe, the American station in Munich founded in 1950. It does not cover East Germany, which is well served by West German stations, nor the Soviet Union, which is covered by another American station, Radio Liberty. The RFE network broadcasts to five satellite countries; Czechoslovakia, Poland, Hungary, Rumania and Bulgaria. RFE and RL were amalgamated into one corporation in 1976.

Both services were originally financed by US government grants paid through the Central Intelligence Agency, with some private contributions, but their connections with the CIA were completely severed in 1971. Direct Congressional grants were made through the State Department until 1973, when Congress passed an Act setting up an independent Board for International Broadcasting which manages both stations and administers funds voted by Congress for their support. They both have editorial freedom.

The Radio Free Europe research and analysis department in Munich is the largest private source of information on conditions in the Communist satellites and its material is used and valued by other broadcasting services, foreign affairs specialists and journalists in Western countries. It makes a close study of listening in Eastern Europe to Western broadcasts by means of interviews with people from the satellite countries visiting the West for holidays or to see relations. The field work is carried out by independent public opinion research institutes and the people interviewed are not told that this is for RFE. The samples are rigorously checked to ensure as far as possible that they represent a fair cross-section of the home populations.

A survey made by RFE of listening to Western broadcasts in 1976-77 in Poland, Czechoslovakia, Hungary and Rumania showed that RFE was easily the most popular Western station with average audiences as large as listeners to all other Western broadcasts put together. The BBC and the Voice of America each counted about one listener in five. Of those interviewed, only between a quarter and a third did not listen to any Western station.

The main reason for the success of Radio Free Europe is its concentration on providing accurate news and comments on events in Eastern European countries which the listeners cannot get from Communist broadcasts. Put in another way, RFE supplies the information that a responsible, uncensored newspaper or radio station would give if they were allowed to exist under Communist rule. RFE is equipped with powerful modern transmitters and also broadcasts on medium wavelengths which are those most easily received in Eastern Europe, despite intermittent Communist jamming of RFE in Czechoslovakia, Bulgaria and, to a lesser extent, Poland. Radio Liberty broadcasts to the Soviet Union are also jammed. RFE maintains its own correspondents in a few Western cities chosen for their sources of information about developments in Communist countries and Western reactions to them.

The BBC European Service, on the other hand, suffers badly from financial limitations. It cannot afford to have its own correspondents abroad and finds it difficult to pay the programme staffs in London the high salaries and fees offered by other

Western broadcasting services for programme organisers and speakers with the necessary command of East European languages and background.

Priority has rightly been given to maintaining the essential foreign-language programme staffs, but this has only been rendered possible by making economies in the administrative services. It has imposed a much heavier burden of work on senior management which is willingly accepted, but which inevitably makes demands on time and energy which reduce the capacity of people in the most responsible positions to concentrate on their proper job. It might be called a system of 'planned obsolescence', like savings on the maintenance and repair of a house which end in a slow decay of the whole structure. Additional government help would be a more sensible and effective remedy and the sums involved are relatively quite small.

One of the proposals agreed to in the Helsinki Final Act was an expansion of East-West contacts. In this field the British Council makes an outstanding and invaluable contribution. The Council has had a representative in Poland since 1948. Its work in the Soviet Union, Rumania, Hungary, Czechoslovakia and Bulgaria is handled by Cultural Attachés in the British Embassies and a similar arrangement in East Germany was under negotiation in March 1978. The Soviet Union and most of its satellites insist on dealing with cultural affairs through government channels.

The wide range of British Council activities is best illustrated by the example of Poland where there is a great demand for British help in English language teaching, both in general classes and in special courses for scientists and technologists. The Council is at present subsidising ten lectureships in English at the universities of Warsaw, Bydgoszcz, Cracow, Lublin, Poznan, Sosnowiec and Wroclaw. It supplies tutors and materials for a large number of English language courses organised by Polish universities and research institutes for students and scientists and for teacher-training courses in English. The Council also arranges exchange visits between Poland and Britain by medical specialists, scientists, postgraduate students, librarians and youth groups. In 1976-77 about 400 Poles visited Britain with British Council help, and about 100 British visitors went to Poland under the Council's auspices. Continuity has been one of the keys to success, and this has too often been interrupted by financial stringency. Here again, more government support would allow the Council to do an even more effective job. The scale of its effort in Eastern Europe is a lot smaller, for instance, than that of France, although British scholarship and culture are at least as much in demand.

The Central Policy Review Staff, the so-called 'Think Tank' which recently examined British diplomatic performance, recommended the abolition of the British Council or alternatively its preservation as an operational base in London but stripped of its overseas staff. The Berrill Report also took the cynical and short-sighted view that 'educational aid should not be provided unless there is a good chance that we can land profitable educational contracts'. This, among many of the recommendations and indeed the tenor of the whole Report, has been severely criticised by press and Parliament, notably by the all-Party Defence and External Affairs Sub-Committee of the Expenditure Committee in their Report of 7 March 1978. For our part we strongly disagree with such callow proposals and regard government financial support for the British Council as a first-rate national investment. The Council already earns a substantial revenue from its foreign educational programmes, and this was expected to be about £17 million in 1978-79.

The Great Britain-East Europe Centre in London, founded in 1967, also makes a valuable contribution to better understanding between East and West in Europe. It arranges 'Colloquia' or discussion meetings between people in Britain and their East European colleagues who share professional interests in economic, scientific, agricultural, educational and environmental problems. The Centre has sponsored four such meetings with participants from Bulgaria, four with Rumania, four with Hungary and three with Czechoslovakia. The Centre also arranges individual visits to Britain by professional people from these East European countries which enable them to meet British specialists in their subjects.

The Royal Institute for International Affairs (Chatham House) organises 'Round Table' discussions between British and Russian participants which provide for a frank and well-informed exchange of views on Anglo-Soviet relations. 'Round Table' unofficial conferences are also held between British representatives and others from Poland and Hungary. Political and ideological differences are not disguised, but these meetings help to remove misunderstanding on practical problems of mutual interest.

Other countries in Western Europe, and of course the United States, carry on similar activities and we see great merit here in diversity. In November 1977 the Venice Biennale festival chose as its subject 'cultural and political dissent in the Soviet Union and Eastern Europe and the suppression of personal and moral freedom'. Invitations were sent to leading spokesmen for human rights in Communist countries and most of them accepted, but their applications for exit permits were all refused. The Biennale Director, Carlo Ripa di Meana, went to the Belgrade Conference to protest against this manifest breach of the Helsinki pledge to allow 'free circulation of people and ideas', but to no avail. Some well-known political exiles took part in the Biennale, including the Soviet scientist Zhores Medvedev, the Polish philosopher Leszek Kolakowski, the Soviet writers Amalrik and Turchin, and Jiri Pelikan, a Czech journalist in exile. The meeting opened with a message from Dr Sakharov sent from Moscow.

K.D.   241   Q

The Council of Europe formed a special committee in 1950 to watch the interests of European nations which were not represented in the Council, with special reference to violations of human rights. This was intended to show the concern felt by parliamentarians in Western Europe over the suppression of freedom in the Soviet bloc, but it has remained little more than a token gesture. The Committee was reduced to a lower status in 1967, thus making it even more ineffective. We consider that its original watchdog function should be restored with terms of reference expressing the determination of the Council of Europe to seek the restoration of freedom and self-determination to the captive peoples of Eastern Europe by peaceful means.

In the European Economic Community, the Political Committee of the European Parliament expressed its 'deep concern' that the Belgrade concluding document made no reference at all to human rights and fundamental freedoms, a feature of the Helsinki Accord regarded by the Committee as 'particularly important'. We would like to see the European Parliament, through the Political Committee, receiving an annual report on detente and human rights from the President of the Council of Ministers and the Commission and debating it in plenary session. The founding fathers of the European Community never doubted that European unity must embrace the whole of Europe. The importance attached to human rights in Western Europe by the EEC is shown by its approach to Spain and Portugal after the end of their dictatorships and the deferment of an Association agreement with Greece while the 'Colonels' were in power. The lack of a common EEC foreign policy prevents the application of the same criterion to Community relations with the Communist countries in Eastern Europe.

We have so far been summing up the general background to the abuses of human rights in Eastern Europe, but we now return to our earlier suggestion that Western trade and co-operation agreements with the Soviet bloc countries should be linked with the implementation of Communist undertakings on human rights in the Final Act of the Helsinki Conference.

As matters stand, our Communist trading partners are getting much the best of the bargain. Despite a marked increase in the value of East-West trade since 1970, the COMECON countries still account for less than 5% of the total trade turnover of the Western countries in the Organisation for Economic Co-operation and Development (OECD), while about 25% of Soviet bloc trade is with the West. American deliveries of grain, which that country alone can provide on a sufficient scale, have regularly enabled the Soviet government to overcome its serious shortages. Western exports of sophisticated industrial machinery, technology and know-how provide substantial benefits for many sectors of the Soviet economy and for the satellite states, notably in energy, chemicals, metallurgy, machine tools, scientific instruments, aircraft and transport equipment of various kinds, textiles and shipbuilding. Purchases of Western plant and technical processes have allowed new Soviet industries to be created, as for example in the field of synthetic fibres and the fertiliser sections of the chemical industry, and in steel. Imports of Western industrial equipment (including drill bits, compressors, large diameter pipes and refining equipment for oil and natural gas exploration and development) have also enabled Soviet industry to use more of its own resources to meet other demands.

In some sectors of the Soviet economy, too, imported Western machinery and highly specialised components have made an essential contribution to the quality of production. Over and above the economic value of these imports from the West, the savings on research and development costs represent a substantial gain to the Soviet and satellite economies.

Soviet military power also derives valuable advantages from

Western technological aid which contributes indirectly to military production. Western exports of strategic materials and components serving this purpose are controlled by a Co-ordinating Committee (COCOM) which does not have treaty status, comprising all the NATO allies except Iceland, and including Japan. In many cases it is hard to distinguish between Western industrial exports which can serve a military purpose, and those which cannot. There are differences of opinion on this subject between the Western allies. Constant vigilance is needed to prevent exports of industrial goods and technology, which can sometimes arrive by way of third countries, from helping to increase the Soviets' already formidable military strength. Defence expenditure has for many years absorbed between 11% and 12% of the Soviet gross national product.

The COCOM lists of goods subject to strategic embargo obviously require full Western agreement and strict enforcement to work effectively, and in our view they should be reviewed more often and more thoroughly. But we do not see a direct link between Western 'strategic' limitations on trade and the human rights question. Trade between Western and COMECON countries is conducted under bilateral trade co-operation agreements and some very large deals are involved. For example, after the Foreign Secretary visited Moscow in 1977, there was talk of Russian orders for exports of British machinery worth several hundred million pounds to expand Soviet offshore oil exploration. A United States-Japanese consortium is said to be near to agreement in a multi-billion dollar deal to develop Soviet natural gas reserves with the help of Western technology. In the spring of 1978, on the eve of a visit by Brezhnev to West Germany, the Soviet Union's biggest Western trade partner, the Krupp firm, announced the signing of three large contracts for supplying polyester fibre plants to the Soviet Union. These and other West German contracts signed a little earlier were worth

DM 3 billion and were largely financed by a West German banking consortium.

British trade with the Soviet bloc is heavily subsidised. In 1975 a British Labour government made available to the Soviet Union cheap credits amounting to £950 million over five years. Under half the credit has been taken up and the volume of British goods sold to Russia remains small; less than half our exports to Norway and about the same as to Finland. Our trade balance with the Soviet Union has for many years been greatly in Soviet favour and in 1977 it showed an accumulated British deficit of £6,000 million. Moreover, the Wilson credits are lent to the Soviet Union at an interest rate of 7% to 7½%, far less than it costs the British government to raise the money. Cheap credits and narrow margins may even combine to make this trade unprofitable.

According to the United Nations Economic Commission for Europe, the debt of the Soviet Union and East European countries to the West rose from £17,000 million in 1976 to £20,000 million in 1977. There is no agreement between Western governments as to the amount of credits which can be granted to Soviet bloc countries and the interest charged, although a 'gentleman's agreement' was reached in 1977 to avoid competition in export credit rates. This should be urgently reviewed.

Western trade with Communist countries often takes the form of 'compensation' or 'buy-back' agreements; a form of barter providing for part payment in goods produced by the Communist plant concerned. This is particularly so in the chemical and petrochemical industries and the result may be a flood of politically priced Communist exports to the West which undercut Western producers. As a veteran expert on trade with Communist countries, Mr Harry Neustein, has put it: 'Eastern Europe is never going to be able to absorb all that ammonia and all that methanol capacity it is building. These countries are going to have to export it and someone's going to get indigestion. The West has sold this technology and it is going to come back and bite it.'

A complete ban has had to be put recently on dumped Soviet steel exports to Britain, and the European Community is considering proposals to counter the 'aggressive' behaviour of Communist shipping lines, especially the Soviet merchant fleet, which has been charging freight rates generally 15% to 20% below competitive commercial rates and sometimes as much as 40% less. At the same time, Western shipping has been effectively barred from seeking trade in the Soviet Union.

There is a striking contrast between Western support for trade with the Soviet bloc and trade discriminations against South Africa coupled with the threat of United Nations sanctions. Expediency, not morality, seems to be the watchword. Much as we dislike apartheid, South Africa at least does not seek to export its social system as the Soviet Union does. Moreover, South Africa is a valuable trading partner of the West and not least of Britain, whose exports to South Africa were valued at £581 million in 1977 compared with £347 million to the Soviet Union. We depend significantly on South Africa for some essential raw materials, among them manganese, vanadium, chromium and platinum, but not on the Soviet Union. Above all, the Cape route is generally acknowledged to be vital to the West's defences in time of war. Yet British governments have no hesitation in linking human rights with South African trade, while refusing let such a connection influence our trade with the Soviet bloc.

Even large private banks such as our own Midland and America's second largest, Citicorp, have agreed under pressure not to make loans to the South African government or its departments. In the USA, the House banking committee has voted, subject to Congress approval, to stop the United States Export-Import Bank from supporting any American business activity in South Africa in order not to 'finance apartheid'. In the same week, the General Assembly of the United Nations approved by a majority of eighty-eight a proposal to impose sanctions against South Africa. The South African government had just accepted a proposal by eighteen Western countries for free elections in Namibia under UN supervision and those countries merely abstained in the vote for sanctions.

We are not suggesting that Western trade with the Soviet bloc should be curtailed or used to put pressure on Communist governments to make major changes in their internal political systems to conform with Western democratic practice. That would be futile and even counter-productive. It would stand no chance of acceptance and might only draw the satellites closer to Moscow, whereas the main Western purpose should be to reduce that dependence.

We do feel, however, that the Soviet Union in particular, and the satellite regimes to a lesser extent, are sufficiently dependent on Western economic assistance for this to be used selectively as a means of inducing them to fulfil their pledges on human rights at Helsinki. Admittedly, such a policy calls for a co-ordination of Western attitudes which is not easily achieved, but it might be applied bilaterally and such action by the United States would certainly carry great weight. In return for the benefits they derive from Western trade and credits, the Communist countries might be asked to honour their commitments at Helsinki by removing controls on emigration, relaxing censorship, lifting restrictions on Western journalists, and ceasing to interfere with communications between Helsinki monitoring groups and the West by post and telephone.

Successive British governments have argued that the paramount need for a country like ours, whose prosperity depends on a free flow of world trade, is to expand our exports to the Communist countries regardless of political differences; and that this trade helps to create new jobs in Britain and relieve unemployment, which is a high priority for any British government. There are also fears that economic pressure on the Soviet Union and its allies will only harden their attitude on human rights still further and perhaps make the Soviet leaders break off the SALT talks with the USA on the limitation of strategic nuclear weapons. There are similar fears of a total breakdown in the talks on mutual and balanced reduction of conventional forces (MBFR) which have been deadlocked since they began in October 1973.

In our view, these arguments are highly misleading and largely unfounded. Fears that Western economic pressure might cause the Soviet Union to break off talks in nuclear and conventional arms limitation show a complete misunderstanding of Soviet negotiating aims and tactics. The main Soviet purpose in these talks is to neutralise the American nuclear deterrent, thus knocking out the linch-pin of Western defence, and to consolidate Soviet superiority in conventional forces. Some Western experts believe that the talks have already put Western Europe at greater risk, not less. The Soviet rulers are not going to allow what they regard as a storm in a teacup over human rights to interfere with their strategic objectives. They are much too hard-headed and realistic to indulge in such hysterical reactions.

In any event, it is too late to lock the stable door separating economic policy from human rights, because that horse has already bolted. The EEC Commissioner for Relations with Developing Countries, M. Claude Cheysson, said in January 1978 that the treatment of human rights by countries receiving EEC aid under the Lomé Convention would have to be considered in the present negotiations on its renewal. This proposal had a mixed reception, but was strongly supported by the British government. The EEC countries had already agreed in 1977 to take full account of violations of human rights in Uganda in their future consideration of aid for a cruel regime. The difficulty of distinguishing between aid for a cruel regime and relief for its suffering people may inhibit EEC action, but the fact remains that the British government has accepted a connection between human rights and economic policy.

The United States Trade Act of 1974 laid down under Section 402 that no country would be eligible to receive most-favoured-nation tariff treatment (MFN) or US government credits, credit guarantees or investment guarantees if it denied its citizens the right or opportunity of emigration or imposed more than nominal charges for issuing the necessary exit visas and other travel documents. Poland and Yugoslavia were already receiving MFN treatment under those terms and it was granted to Rumania in 1975. It has since been offered to Hungary as well. Other political concessions have been made by Communist regimes in return for economic rewards, as in the East German release of political prisoners to West Germany for hard cash, and the Polish agreement with the Federal German Republic allowing a greatly increased rate of emigration by Germans living in former German territory acquired by Poland after the Second World War.

There are also signs of a growing divergence between the economic interests of the Soviet Union and those of the satellites which may provide opportunities for exerting Western economic influence. The East German leader, Erich Honecker, talking to Party officials in February 1978, protested strongly against the policy of industrial specialisation imposed by COMECON, with which his country had a favourable trade balance until 1972. He complained that this policy had narrowed the range of products made in East Germany. 'Nobody', said Honecker, 'has the right to halt production of GDR goods until the products we have to import (from COMECON members) have been tried and tested in our own country, and as long as commercial import agreements and planned deliveries have not been guaranteed'. He also pointed out that the COMECON measures 'caused gaps in supplies to the population as well as a loss of lucrative export goods'.

Coming from an East German regime with a reputation for obedience to Moscow, these remarks were doubly significant. The East European countries would certainly prefer to import their raw materials, especially oil, from Western countries if this could be done on more favourable terms, but Soviet control in COMECON usually prevents it.

Rumania has been a member of the International Monetary Fund since 1973. Now Poland, Hungary and Czechoslovakia, all barred by the Kremlin from a share of American Marshall Plan aid after the Second World War, have indicated that they may be interested in joining the IMF. Presumably this has tacit approval in Moscow, since it would help satellite regimes with their foreign exchange problems. On the other hand, IMF rules would require the release of more economic and commercial information and thus help to reduce barriers between East and West.

But if Britain and other Western European countries hope to create a sound basis for their relations with the Soviet bloc, a psychological change of attitude on their part is essential. They were unable to prevent Stalin from breaking his promises of non-interference and free elections in Eastern Europe and thus had to swallow the installation of Communist puppet regimes. They have since remained on the defensive and the initiative has been kept in Soviet hands. Until President Carter took his firm stand on human rights, successive British governments have avoided the issue of Communist violations apart from formal protests. This passive attitude is virtually the same as saying that the continued suppression of human rights in Eastern Europe is a safer way of keeping the peace than pressing for relaxations. We think the reverse is true and that it is the failure by Communist regimes to make such concessions which sows the seeds of war.

In the balance sheet of detente so far, the West has gained

very little and lost a lot. The Soviet Union still has an army of twenty divisions in East Germany and eleven more in Czechoslovakia, Hungary and Poland, totalling close on 400,000 men, which represents a standing menace to NATO. Their equipment with modern tanks, artillery and aircraft matches that of the West in design and far exceeds it in numbers and offensive capability. Soviet naval expansion has nearly achieved parity with the United States, and the Russians have built a powerful submarine fleet well capable of cutting Western sea communications and supplies. Soviet warships now patrol every ocean and support Soviet military intervention using Cuban mercenaries.

The root of the trouble is that the Soviet and Western concepts of detente are totally different. The Western negotiating position is based on a genuine will for agreement expressed by mutual compromise and concessions. The Soviet leaders, from Lenin to Brezhnev, have made it clear that any truce with the 'bourgeois imperialists' is merely another step towards their destruction. They are now exploiting Western economic assistance in the spirit of Lenin's dictum that the capitalist countries would make the rope to hang themselves, brought up to date by *Pravda*'s comment at the time of Helsinki that 'the struggle will continue between world socialism and the bourgeoisie up to the complete and final victory of Communism on a world-wide scale'. The Kremlin's success in lulling so many in the West into a false sense of security has perhaps surprised even the Soviet rulers themselves.

And yet there are some serious flaws behind the daunting façade of Soviet might. For a start, there must be a question mark over the loyalty of some of the satellite armed forces and their readiness even to protect the Red Army lines of communications in wartime. Next, Soviet relations with Communist China have long been strained and their deep-seated ideological and territorial differences force Moscow to keep an army of well over half a million men on the Chinese border. Chinese influence is already competing with that of the Soviet Union in many parts of the world and is likely to grow as China gains in strength and confidence. Soviet intervention in the Middle East has suffered serious reverses, the Egyptian case being an outstanding example. The Kremlin has played its hand clumsily, forgetting that nationalism and the desire to be master in one's own house are stronger than Communist doctrine and likely to remain so.

In 1977 the Soviet economy had its worst year since 1945. The growth in the national income was the lowest for more than thirty years. Several vital targets, including plans for raising industrial efficiency, were not met and agricultural output fell short of expectations by at least 15%.

Moscow's claim to leadership of world revolution has been finally demolished by declarations of independence from Communist countries in Western Europe and even in Communist Rumania. The 'Euro-Communist' deviations of Berlinguer in Italy and Carrillo in Spain have shocked Moscow by their support for human rights in Eastern Europe. A typical example was a front-page article published on 24 May 1978 by the Italian Communist Party paper L'Unita which strongly condemned the sentences passed on Dr Orlov and other Russian spokesmen for human rights. The article said that the repetition of these acts of persecution raised problems of a political nature going beyond their juridical and legal aspects and could harm the process of international detente. The policy of peaceful co-existence must not be limited to its diplomatic and military aspects, but must extend to a confrontation of politics and ideas. It was necessary to defend and reinforce the values of democracy and the rights of man everywhere.

It is not the behaviour of Western Communist Parties in their own countries which is likely to cause alarm in the Kremlin.

Their conversion to democracy is still highly doubtful and their participation in Western governments, if and when it should come, would actually serve Soviet purposes by creating divisions be-between Western Europe and the United States, thus weakening NATO.

What the Soviet rulers must fear above all is the infection of 'Euro-Communist' ideas among Communist Parties in the Soviet empire. That would cut to the bone in Moscow by reviving the concept of 'socialism with a human face' which Dubcek tried to introduce in Czechoslovakia and challenging the Soviet right of intervention under the 'Brezhnev doctrine'. And indeed the first signs of internal Party dissension have already appeared in Eastern Europe. One of them is the manifesto issued in East Germany by Communist disciples of Rudolf Bahro and calling for radical changes in Communist rule. Another and more formidable example was the open letter sent to the Polish leader, Gierek, by prominent Party members, including Ochab, a former Party leader, in which they called for a 'dialogue' between government and people. Even in Russia itself, can the ageing men in the Kremlin feel quite sure that these new ideas will make no impression on younger and ambitious aspirants for power?

Some of the satellite regimes are already trying to win over their unruly subjects by making concessions to the Churches, hoping to enlist their influence for political ends. In Poland, Gierek is bargaining with the Roman Catholic Primate, Cardinal Wyszynski, along those lines. In East Germany, Honecker has offered the Protestant Churches religious programmes on radio and television, pensions for the clergy, and financial support for the celebrations in 1983 of the 500th anniversary of Martin Luther's birth. In Hungary, where Kadar seldom misses a chance of gaining public approval, the Communist authorities have dealt severely with hooligans who broke up a Roman Catholic church service and their punishment was given full publicity in the Communist papers and broadcasts.

After so many years of incessant Communist propaganda about the alleged evils of Western democracy, the Helsinki Final Act has given the West a golden opportunity to challenge the Kremlin squarely on the issue of human rights. That chance must not be allowed to go by default. In our view, the Western governments can effectively translate verbal protests into action by linking their economic assistance to the Communist states with the fulfilment on their part of the modest commitments on human rights laid down in the Helsinki agreements. And we have quoted evidence to show that some hesitant movement in this direction has already started.

The British Foreign Secretary, Dr David Owen, was right when he said that British policy has to draw a fine line on human rights between measures that stand a chance of being effective and those which could be counter-productive. But he added: 'We have to balance morality with reality. The art lies in striking the right balance.' Leaving aside the Soviet Union, where conditions are so different, we see no such conflict in dealing with the Communist suppression of human rights in the formerly independent states of Eastern Europe. In their case, surely morality and reality are one and the same thing.

ACKNOWLEDGMENTS

This book could not have been written without generous help from a great many people too numerous for us to mention all by name. Mr Jim Brown, Deputy Director of Radio Free Europe in Munich, and the RFE Research and Analysis Department, have taken immense time and trouble to keep us up to date about developments in Eastern Europe. We are grateful to Mr Alexander Lieven, Controller of the BBC European Service, and his East European language sections for their unfailing co-operation and for the help we received from Mr Janis Sapiets. We are also much indebted to Sir John Llewellyn and his staff in the British Council; Mr Niall MacDermot, Secretary-General of the International Commission of Jurists; Mr Richard Davey, special correspondent of *The Times*; Mr Matthew Parris; Mr Paul Sieghart of Amnesty International; Miss Mary Sibthorp, Director of the David Davies Memorial Institute for International Studies; and Mr Mark Bonham Carter, Chairman of the Outer Circle Policy Unit.

Our thanks are also due to the Foreign and Commonwealth Office for so readily providing us with facts and figures whenever we sought their aid, to the American Embassy in London, and to the staff of the House of Lords' Library. We have had invaluable advice from Mr Max Hayward of St Antony's College, Oxford, who is our publisher's Adviser in Russian Literature; and from Mrs Marjorie Villiers, Editor of the Harvill Press, and her fellow director, Mr Robert Knittel. They and many of their staff have done much to smooth our path. And to our wives we would like to express our warm appreciation of their patience and support through many months of domestic dislocation.

MAIN SOURCES

International Covenants on Economic, Social and Cultural Rights; and on Civil and Political Rights with Optional Protocal (United Nations). HM Stationery Office, London. Cmnd. 3200 1966/67 and Cmnd. 6702 1977.

Helsinki Conference on Security and Co-operation in Europe. Final Act. HM Stationery Office, London. Cmnd. 6198. August 1975.

Belgrade Meeting to follow up the Helsinki Conference. HM Stationery Office, London. Cmnd. 7126. March 1978.

US Commission on Security and Co-operation in Europe: Reports. Washington, DC.

Amnesty International: Reports. Tower House, 8-14 Southampton Street, London WC2.

Association of Polish Students and Graduates in Exile. *Dissent in Poland.* 42 Emperor's Gate, London SW7.

BEESON, TREVOR, *Discretion and Valour: Religious Conditions in Russia and Eastern Europe.* British Council of Churches. Collins, Fontana Books, London 1975.

BLAKER, PETER, MP, JULIAN CRITCHLEY, MP, MATTHEW PARRIS, *Coping with the Soviet Union.* Conservative Political Centre, 32 Smith Square, London SW1, 1977.

BOURDEAUX, MICHAEL, HANS HEBLY, EUGENE VOSS. Editors. *Religious Liberty in the Soviet Union.* Keston College, Keston, England, 1976.

CRANSTON, MAURICE, *What Are Human Rights?* The Bodley Head, London 1973.

Free Central European News Agency (FCI): Reports. 43 Tregunter Road, London SW10.

Index on Censorship. Journal published by Writers and Scholars International Ltd, 21 Russell Street, London WC2.

International Commission of Jurists. *The Review.* PO Box 120, 1224 Chêne-Bougeries, Geneva.

JONES, BILL TREHARNE, 'East German Cultural Scene'. Article in *Survey (East-West Affairs)* London, October 1975.

Keston College. *Religion in Communist Lands*. Journal. Keston, near London.

LUCE, RICHARD, MP, JOHN RANELAGH. *Human Rights and Foreign Policy*. Conservative Political Centre, 32 Smith Square, London SW1.

PELIKAN, JIRI and others. *Civil and Academic Freedom in the USSR and Eastern Europe*. Spokesman Books, Nottingham 1975.

REDDAWAY, PETER, SIDNEY BLOCH. *Russia's Political Hospitals: The Abuse of Psychiatry in the Soviet Union*. Gollancz, London 1977.

SMITH, HEDRICK, *The Russians*. Sphere Books, London 1977.

STAAR, RICHARD. F., *Communist Regimes in Eastern Europe*. Hoover Institution Press, Stanford University, USA. 3rd edition 1977.

UK Helsinki Review Group Reports. *From Helsinki to Belgrade.* September 1977. *Belgrade and After.* Spring 1978. Published by David Davies Memorial Institute for International Studies, 34 Smith Square, London SW1.

United Nations Special Commission on Hungary. *The Hungarian Uprising.* HM Stationery Office, London 1957.

URBAN, GEORGE, *Detente: Interviews on East-West Relations.* Maurice Temple Smith Ltd, 37 Great Russell Street, London WC1, 1976.

APPENDIX I

HELSINKI CONFERENCE: FINAL ACT

Extracts relating to Human Rights and Self-Determination

I (a) Declaration on Principles Guiding Relations between Participating States

I. Sovereign equality, respect for the rights inherent in sovereignty
The participating States will respect each other's sovereign equality
and individuality as well as all the rights inherent in and encompassed
by its sovereignty, including in particular the right of every State to
juridical equality, to territorial integrity and to freedom and political
independence. They will also respect each other's right freely to choose
and develop its political, social, economic and cultural systems as well
as its right to determine its laws and regulations.

Within the framework of international law, all the participating
States have equal rights and duties. They will respect each other's
right to define and conduct as it wishes its relations with other States
in accordance with international law and in the spirit of the present
Declaration. They consider that their frontiers can be changed, in
accordance with international law, by peaceful means and by agreement. They also have the right to belong or not to belong to international organisations, to be or not to be a party to bilateral or
multilateral treaties including the right to be or not to be a party
to treaties of alliance; they also have the right to neutrality.

II. Refraining from the threat or use of force
The participating States will refrain in their mutual relations, as
well as in their international relations in general, from the threat
or use of force against the territorial integrity or political independence

of any State, or in any other manner inconsistent with the purposes of the United Nations and with the present Declaration. No consideration may be invoked to serve to warrant resort to the threat or use of force in contravention of this principle.

Accordingly, the participating States will refrain from any acts constituting a threat of force or direct or indirect use of force against another participating State. Likewise they will refrain from any manifestation of force for the purpose of inducing another participating State to renounce the full exercise of its sovereign rights. Likewise they will also refrain in their mutual relations from any act of reprisal by force.

No such threat or use of force will be employed as a means of settling disputes, or questions likely to give rise to disputes, between them.

III. Inviolability of frontiers

The participating States regard as inviolable all one another's frontiers as well as the frontiers of all States in Europe and therefore they will refrain now and in the future from assaulting these frontiers.

Accordingly, they will also refrain from any demand for, or act of, seizure and usurpation of part or all of the territory of any participating State.

IV. Territorial integrity of States

The participating States will respect the territorial integrity of each of the participating States.

Accordingly, they will refrain from any action inconsistent with the purposes and principles of the Charter of the United Nations against the territorial integrity, political independence or the unity of any participating State, and in particular from any such action constituting a threat or use of force.

The participating States will likewise refrain from making each other's territory the object of military occupation or other direct or indirect measures of force in contravention of international law, or the object of acquisition by means of such measures or the threat of them. No such occupation or acquisition will be recognised as legal.

VI. Non-intervention in internal affairs

The participating States will refrain from any intervention, direct or indirect, individual or collective, in the internal or external affairs falling within the domestic jurisdiction of another participating State, regardless of their mutual relations.

They will accordingly refrain from any form of armed intervention or threat of such intervention against another participating State.

They will likewise in all circumstances refrain from any other act of military, or of political, economic or other coercion designed to subordinate to their own interest the exercise by another participating State of the rights inherent in its sovereignty and thus to secure advantages of any kind.

Accordingly, they will, *inter alia*, refrain from direct or indirect assistance to terrorist activities, or to subversive or other activities directed towards the violent overthrow of the regime of another participating State.

VII. Respect for human rights and fundamental freedoms, including the freedom of thought, conscience, religion or belief

The participating States will respect human rights and fundamental freedoms, including the freedom of thought, conscience, religion or belief, for all without distinction as to race, sex, language or religion.

They will promote and encourage the effective exercise of civil, political, economic, social, cultural and other rights and freedoms all of which derive from the inherent dignity of the human person and are essential for his free and full development.

Within this framework the participating States will recognise and respect the freedom of the individual to profess and practise, alone or in community with others, religion or belief acting in accordance with the dictates of his own conscience.

The participating States on whose territory national minorities exist will respect the right of persons belonging to such minorities to equality before the law, will afford them the full opportunity for the actual enjoyment of human rights and fundamental freedoms and will, in this manner, protect their legitimate interests in this sphere.

The participating States recognise the universal significance of human rights and fundamental freedoms, respect for which is an essential factor for the peace, justice and well-being necessary to ensure the development of friendly relations and co-operation among themselves as among all States.

They will constantly respect these rights and freedoms in their mutual relations and will endeavour jointly and separately, including in co-operation with the United Nations, to promote universal and effective respect for them.

They confirm the right of the individual to know and act upon his rights and duties in this field.

In the field of human rights and fundamental freedoms, the participating States will act in conformity with the purposes and principles of the Charter of the United Nations and with the Universal Declaration of Human Rights. They will also fulfil their obligations as set forth in the international declarations and agreements in this field, including *inter alia* the International Covenants on Human Rights, by which they may be bound.

VIII. *Equal rights and self-determination of peoples*

The participating States will respect the equal rights of peoples and their right to self-determination, acting at all times in conformity with the purposes and principles of the Charter of the United Nations and with the relevant norms of international law, including those relating to territorial integrity of States.

By virtue of the principle of equal rights and self-determination of peoples, all peoples always have the right, in full freedom, to determine, when and as they wish, their internal and external political status, without external interference, and to pursue as they wish their political, economic, social and cultural development.

The participating States reaffirm the universal significance of respect for and effective exercise of equal rights and self-determination of peoples for the development of friendly relations among themselves as among all States; they also recall the importance of the elimination of any form of violation of this principle.

IX. *Co-operation among States*

The participating States will develop their co-operation with one another and with all States in all fields in accordance with the purposes and principles of the Charter of the United Nations. In developing their co-operation the participating States will place special emphasis on the fields as set forth within the framework of the Conference on Security and Co-operation in Europe, with each of them making its contribution in conditions of full equality.

They will endeavour, in developing their co-operation as equals, to promote mutual understanding and confidence, friendly and good-neighbourly relations among themselves, international peace, security and justice. They will equally endeavour, in developing their co-operation, to improve the well-being of peoples and contribute to the fulfilment of their aspirations through, *inter alia*, the benefits resulting from increased mutual knowledge and from progress and achievement in the economic, scientific, technological, social, cultural and humanitarian fields. They will take steps to promote conditions favourable to making these benefits available to all; they will take into account the interest of all in the narrowing of differences in the levels of economic development, and in particular the interest of developing countries throughout the world.

They confirm that governments, institutions, organisations and persons have a relevant and positive role to play in contributing toward the achievement of these aims of their co-operation.

Co-operation in Humanitarian and other Fields

1. Human Contacts
(a) Contacts and Regular Meetings on the Basis of Family Ties
In order to promote further development of contacts on the basis of family ties the participating States will favourably consider applications for travel with the purpose of allowing persons to enter or leave their territory temporarily, and on a regular basis if desired, in order to visit members of their families.

Applications for temporary visits to meet members of their families will be dealt with without distinction as to the country of origin or destination: existing requirements for travel documents and visas will be applied in this spirit. The preparation and issue of such documents and visas will be effected within reasonable time limits; cases of urgent necessity – such as serious illness or death – will be given priority treatment. They will take such steps as may be necessary to ensure that the fees for official travel documents and visas are acceptable.

They confirm that the presentation of an application concerning contacts on the basis of family ties will not modify the rights and obligations of the applicant or of members of his family.

(b) *Reunification of Families*

The participating States will deal in a positive and humanitarian spirit with the applications of persons who wish to be reunited with members of their family, with special attention being given to requests of an urgent character – such as requests submitted by persons who are ill or old.

They will deal with applications in this field as expeditiously as possible.

They will lower where necessary the fees charged in connection with these applications to ensure that they are at a moderate level.

Applications for the purpose of family reunification which are not granted may me renewed at the appropriate level and will be reconsidered at reasonably short intervals by the authorities of the country of residence or destination, whichever is concerned; under such circumstances fees will be charged only when applications are granted.

Persons whose applications for family reunification are granted may bring with them or ship their household and personal effects; to this end the participating States will use all possibilities provided by existing regulations.

Until members of the same family are reunited meetings and contacts between them may take place in accordance with the modalities for contacts on the basis of family ties.

The participating States will support the efforts of Red Cross and Red Crescent Societies concerned with the problems of family reunification.

They confirm that the presentation of an application concerning family reunification will not modify the rights and obligations of the applicant or of members of his family.

The receiving participating State will take appropriate care with regard to employment for persons from other participating States who take up permanent residence in that State in connection with family reunification with its citizens and see that they are afforded opportunities equal to those enjoyed by its own citizens for education, medical assistance and social security.

(c) *Marriage between Citizens of Different States*

The participating States will examine favourably and on the basis of humanitarian considerations requests for exit or entry permits from persons who have decided to marry a citizen from another participating State.

The processing and issuing of the documents required for the above purposes and for the marriage will be in accordance with the provisions accepted for family reunification.

In dealing with requests from couples from different participating States, once married, to enable them and the minor children of their marriage to transfer their permanent residence to a State in which either one is normally a resident, the participating States will also apply the provisions accepted for family reunification.

(d) Travel for Personal or Professional Reasons

The participating States intend to facilitate wider travel by their citizens for personal or professional reasons and to this end they intend in particular:

gradually to simplify and to administer flexibly the procedures for exit and entry;

to ease regulations concerning movement of citizens from the other participating States in their territory, with due regard to security requirements.

They will endeavour gradually to lower, where necessary, the fees for visas and official travel documents.

They intend to consider, as necessary, means – including, insofar as appropriate, the conclusion of multilateral or bilateral consular conventions or other relevant agreements or understandings – for the improvement of arrangements to provide consular services, including legal and consular assistance.

* * *

They confirm that religious faiths, institutions and organisations, practising within the constitutional framework of the participating States, and their representatives can, in the field of their activities, have contacts and meetings among themselves and exchange information.

2. Information
The participating States,
Express their intention in particular:

(a) (i) *Oral Information*
To facilitate the dissemination of oral information through the encouragement of lectures and lecture tours by personalities and specialists from the other participating States, as well as exchanges of opinions at round table meetings, seminars, symposia, summer schools, congresses and other bilateral and multilateral meetings.

(ii) *Printed Information*
To facilitate the improvement of the dissemination, on their territory, of newspapers and printed publications, periodical and non-periodical, from the other participating States.

To contribute to the improvement of access by the public to periodical and non-periodical printed publications imported on the bases indicated above.

They intend to improve the possibilities for acquaintance with bulletins of official information issued by diplomatic missions and distributed by those missions on the basis of arrangements acceptable to the interested parties.

(iii) *Filmed and Broadcast Information*
To promote the improvement of the dissemination of filmed and broadcast information.

(c) *Improvement of Working Conditions for Journalists*
The participating States, desiring to improve the conditions under which journalists from one participating State exercise their profession in another participating State, intend in particular to:

examine in a favourable spirit and within a suitable and reasonable time scale requests from journalists for visas;

grant to permanently accredited journalists of the participating States, on the basis of arrangements, multiple entry and exit visas for specified periods;

facilitate the issue to accredited journalists of the participating States of permits for stay in their country of temporary residence and, if and when these are necessary, of other official papers which it is appropriate for them to have;

ease, on a basis of reciprocity, procedures for arranging travel by journalists of the participating States in the country where they are exercising their profession, and to provide progressively greater opportunities for such travel, subject to the observance of regulations relating to the existence of areas closed for security reasons;

ensure that requests by such journalists for such travel receive, in so far as possible, an expeditious response, taking into account the time scale of the request;

increase the opportunities for journalists of the participating States to communicate personally with their sources, including organisations and official institutions;

grant to journalists of the participating States the right to import, subject only to its being taken out again, the technical equipment (photographic, cinematographic, tape recorder, radio and television) necessary for the exercise of their profession;*

enable journalists of the other participating States, whether permanently or temporarily accredited, to transmit completely, normally and rapidly by means recognised by the participating States to the information organs which they represent, the results of their professional activity, including tape recordings and undeveloped film, for the purpose of publication or of broadcasting on the radio or television.

The participating States reaffirm that the legitimate pursuit of their professional activity will neither render journalists liable to expulsion nor otherwise penalise them. If an accredited journalist is expelled, he will be informed of the reasons for this act and may submit an application for re-examination of his case.

* While recognising that appropriate local personnel are employed by foreign journalists in many instances, the participating States note that the above provisions would be applied, subject to the observance of the appropriate rules, to persons from the other participating States, who are regularly and professionally engaged as technicians, photographers or cameramen of the press, radio, television or cinema.

266

3. Co-operation and Exchanges in the Field of Culture

The participating States jointly set themselves the following objectives:

- (a) to develop the mutual exchange of information with a view to a better knowledge of respective cultural achievements.
- (b) to improve the facilities for the exchange and for the dissemination of cultural property,
- (c) to promote access by all to respective cultural achievements,
- (d) to develop contacts and co-operation among persons active in the field of culture,
- (e) to seek new fields and forms of cultural co-operation.

4. Co-operation and Exchanges in Education and Science

(a) Extension of Relations

They also express their intention to expand and improve co-operation and links in the fields of education and science, in particular by:

concluding, where appropriate, bilateral or multilateral agreements providing for co-operation and exchanges among State institutions, non-governmental bodies and persons engaged in activities in education and science, bearing in mind the need both for flexibility and the fuller use of existing agreements and arrangements;

promoting the conclusion of direct arrangements between universities and other institutions of higher education and research, in the framework of agreements between governments where appropriate;

encouraging among persons engaged in education and science direct contacts and communications, including those based on special agreements or arrangements where these are appropriate.

National minorities or regional cultures. The participating States, recognising the contribution that national minorities or regional cultures can make to co-operation among them in various fields of culture, intend, when such minorities or cultures exist within their territory, to facilitate this contribution, taking into account the legitimate interests of their members. (A further clause recognises the contribution that national minorities or regional cultures can

267

make to co-operation in education and calls on the participating States to facilitate this contribution.)

Follow-up to the Conference

2. The participating States declare furthermore their resolve to continue the multilateral process initiated by the Conference:

    (a) by proceeding to a thorough exchange of views both on the implementation of the provisions of the Final Act and of the tasks defined by the Conference, as well as, in the context of the questions dealt with by the latter, on the deepening of their mutual relations, the improvement of security and the development of co-operation in Europe, and the development of the process of detente in the future;

    (b) by organising to these ends meetings among their representatives, beginning with a meeting at the level of representatives appointed by the Ministers of Foreign Affairs. This meeting will define the appropriate modalities for the holding of other meetings which could include further similar meetings and the possibility of a new Conference.

3. The first of the meetings indicated above will be held at Belgrade in 1977.

APPENDIX II

Text of Charter 77

Translated from the German text, dated 1 January 1977, as published in *Czechoslovakia: From 1968 to Charter 77* by Josef Josten.

(Institute for the Study of Conflict. No. 86)

The International Covenant on Civil and Political Rights and the International Covenant on Economic, Social and Cultural Rights – both signed in 1968 in the name of our Republic, confirmed in Helsinki in 1975 and put into effect in our country on 23 March 1976 – were published under No. 120 in the collection of *Laws of Czechoslovakia* on 13 October 1976. Since then it has been both the right of our citizens and the duty of our State to abide by them. Human freedoms and rights guaranteed by these two covenants are important values of civilisation; their achievement has been sought by numerous progressive forces in history; and their enactment can make a significant contribution to further the humane development of our society. We therefore welcome the fact that the Czechoslovak Socialist Republic (CSSR) has acceded to these covenants.

At the same time their publication urgently reminds us that in our country many fundamental civil rights – regrettably – exist only on paper. The right of free expression of opinion, as guaranteed by Article 19 of the first covenant, for instance, is quite illusory. Tens of thousands of citizens are prevented from working in their professions merely because they hold views at variance with the official ones. Moreover, they often become the targets of all kinds of discrimination and chicanery by the authorities and social organisations; being deprived of any possibility of defending themselves, they become in effect victims of *apartheid*. Hundreds of thousands of other citizens are deprived of 'freedom from fear' (see the preamble of the first covenant) because they are forced to live in constant danger of losing their jobs or other facilities should they express their opinion.

Contrary to Article 13 of the second covenant which guarantees the right to education for everybody, innumerable young people are refused admission to higher education merely because of their views or even the views of their parents. Countless citizens have to live in fear that, if they express themselves in accordance with their convictions, they themselves or their children may be deprived of the right to education.

Criticism suppressed
Insistence on the right 'to seek, receive and impart information and ideas of all kinds, regardless of frontiers, either orally, in writing or in print (or) in the form of art' (paragraph 2, Article 19, of the first covenant) is persecuted not only outside the courts but also by the courts themselves, often under the pretext of criminal indictment (as evidenced, *inter alia*, by the trials of young musicians).

The freedom of public expression of opinions is suppressed as a result of the central administration of all media and of the publishing and cultural institutions. Neither any political, philosophical or scientific view nor any artistic expression can be published if it deviates in the slightest degree from the narrow framework of official ideology or aesthetics; public criticism of manifestations of social crises is made impossible; it is out of the question to conduct a public defence against untrue and defamatory assertions in official propaganda organs (there is in practice no legal protection against 'attacks on honour and reputation' as explicitly guaranteed in Article 17 of the first covenant); false accusations cannot be refuted, and any attempt to obtain a remedy or rectification from the courts is futile; and in the field of intellectual or cultural work no open discussion is possible. Many who are active in academic and cultural affairs, and other citizens, are being discriminated against merely because years ago they published or openly expressed views which are condemned by the existing political power.

Freedom of conscience, expressly guaranteed in Article 18 of the first covenant, is systematically limited by arbitrary acts of those in power – by curtailing the activities of the clergy who are constantly threatened by withdrawal or loss of the State's permission enabling them to exercise their functions; by reprisals affecting, in respect of their livelihood or otherwise, persons who express their religious convictions in word or deed; and by the suppression of religious instruction, etc.

The limitation, and often the complete suppression, of a series of civil rights is effected by a system of *de facto* subordination of all institutions and organisations in the State to the political directives of the ruling party's apparatus and the decisions of despotically influential individuals. The constitution of Czechoslovakia, other laws and legal norms regulate neither the contents, the form nor the application of such decisions; they are mainly taken behind closed doors, often merely verbally; they are unknown to citizens in general and cannot be checked by them; their authors are responsible to no one except themselves and their own hierarchy; but they exert a decisive influence on the activities of legislative and executive organs in the administration of the State, the courts, trade unions, professional and all other social organisations, other political parties, enterprises, works, institutions, authorities, schools and other establishments – their orders taking precedence even before the law.

If, in the interpretation of their rights and duties, organisations or citizens come into conflict with the directives, they cannot appeal to any impartial arbitrator because there is none. All these facts seriously limit the rights resulting from Articles 21 and 22 of the first covenant (on freedom of assembly and the prohibition of any restriction of exercising this freedom), as well as from Article 25 (equality before the law). This state of affairs prevents workers and other employees from establishing trade unions and other organisations and freely to apply the right to strike (paragraph 1, Article 8, of the second covenant) in order to protect their economic and social interests without any restriction.

Official surveillance
Further civil rights, including the express prohibition of 'arbitrary interference with privacy, family, home or correspondence' (Article 17 of the first covenant), are also gravely violated by the fact that the Ministry of the Interior controls the lives of citizens in various ways, e.g. by telephone tapping, observation of homes, control of mail, personal surveillance, searches of homes, and the establishment of a network of informers from among the population (often recruited by means of unlawful threats or by promises), etc. In such cases the Ministry often interferes with employers' decisions, inspires discriminatory acts by authorities and organisations, exerts influence on the organs of justice and also directs propaganda campaigns

through the media. These activities are not regulated by laws, they are secret and the citizen has no defence against them.

In cases of politically motivated prosecutions the investigative and court organs violate the rights of the defendants and their defence, as guaranteed by Article 14 of the first covenant and also by Czechoslovak laws. In our prisons persons thus convicted are treated in a manner which violates their human dignity, endangers their health and aims at breaking them morally.

Generally, violations are also carried out in respect of paragraph 2, Article 12, of the first covenant, which guarantees a citizen's right freely to leave his country; under the pretext of 'protecting national security' (paragraph 3) this right is tied to various unlawful conditions. There is arbitrary procedure also in the granting of entry visas to nationals of foreign states, many of whom cannot visit Czechoslovakia because, for instance, they have had professional or friendly contacts with persons discriminated against in our country.

Many citizens draw attention – either privately, at their place of work, or in public (which in practice is possible only in foreign media) – to the systematic violation of human rights and democratic freedoms and demand remedies in concrete cases; in most instances, however, their voice finds no echo or they become targets of official investigations.

The responsibility for maintaining civil rights in the country lies, of course, above all with the political power and the State – but not exclusively. Every person has his share of responsibility for the general conditions and thus for the observance of the codified covenants, which is obligatory not only for governments but also for all citizens. The feeling of such co-responsibility, the belief in the meaningfulness of civil commitments and the will to carry them out, as well as the general need to find new and more effective expressions for them, has given us the idea of forming Charter 77, the establishment of which is announced today.

Charter 77 defined

Charter 77 is a free, informal and open community of persons of varying convictions, religions and professions, joined together by the will to work individually and collectively for respect for civil and human rights in our country and in the world – those rights which are granted to man by the two codified international covenants, by the Final Act of the Helsinki conference, by numerous other documents opposing war, the use of force and social and intellectual oppression, and which have been expressed succinctly in the UN Universal Declaration of Human Rights.

Charter 77 is based on the solidarity and friendship of people who are motivated by a common concern for the fate of the ideals to which they have attached, and are still attaching, their lives and their work.

Charter 77 is no organisation, has no statutes, no permanent organs and no organised membership. Everyone belongs to it who agrees with its idea, takes part in its work and supports it.

Charter 77 is no base for oppositional political activity. It wishes to serve the common interest, as do many similar civic initiatives in various countries of the West and the East. It therefore does not intend to draw up its own programmes for political or social reforms or changes but wants to conduct, within its sphere of activity, a constructive dialogue with the political and State authorities, in particular by drawing attention to various concrete cases in which human and civil rights are infringed, by preparing their documentation, proposing solutions, submitting various general suggestions aimed at strengthening these rights and their guarantees, and acting as a mediator in situations of conflict which may be caused by the unlawful measures.

Charter 77 emphasises, by its symbolic name, that it is created at the beginning of the year which has been declared the Year of the Rights of Political Prisoners, and in the course of which the Belgrade conference is to review the fulfilment of the Helsinki obligations.

As signatories of this manifesto we entrust Professor Jiri Hajek, Dr Vaclav Havel and Professor Jan Patocka with the task of acting as spokesmen for Charter 77. These spokesmen are empowered to represent Charter 77 before State and other organisations, before the public in our country and in the world, and by their signature they guarantee the authenticity of Charter 77 documents. They will find in us, and in other citizens who will join us, collaborators who, together with them, will support the necessary actions, undertake specific tasks and share all responsibility with them.

We believe that Charter 77 will contribute to enabling all citizens of Czechoslovakia to work and live as free human beings.

INDEX

INDEX

277